The
Family

The
Family

At home in a heartless world

Meditations
and prayers
for those
who live
with others

Rowland Croucher

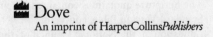
Dove
An imprint of HarperCollins*Publishers*

To Sarah and Reg; Jan; Paul, Karen, Amanda, and Lindy; Lai Kiong and Ross; Abbie, Coralie and Jay

wonderful parents, wife, children, daughter-in-law, son-in-law, and grandchildren

with love and deep appreciation

A Dove publication
An imprint of HarperCollins*Religious*
A member of the HarperCollins*Publishers* (Australia) Pty Ltd group
(ACN 008 431 730)
22–24 Joseph Street
North Blackburn, Victoria 3130, Australia

First published 1995
Designed by William Hung
Cover design by William Hung
Cover photographs by Jacqueline Mitelman, Bill Thomas and Rowland Croucher

Typeset in Janson by Emtype Desktop Publishing
Printed in Australia by Griffin Paperbacks

National Library of Australia Cataloguing-in-Publication data:

Croucher, Rowland.
    The family: at home in a heartless world: meditations and prayers for those who live with others.
    ISBN 1 86371 389 1.

    1. Family—Biblical teaching. 2. Family—Prayer-books and devotions. 3. Family—Religious life. I. Title

Contents

Foreword

Family is the place where, when you get there, they have to take you in. Family is where you argue and disagree with the rules, but when you haven't got it, you miss it.

There is a universal mystery here. Every ethnic group, every national people, every hilltribe in the world, has a larger or smaller family/kinship system which is essential to their social stability and provides a grid of meaning for individuals.

Why should we be surprised at such anthropological insights? They match nicely the biblical teaching on the creation of man and woman, the distinctive desire of humans for intimacy, and their capacity for spiritual satisfaction.

Rowland Croucher brings together insights from sociology, counseling, biblical perspectives, and life experience into a devotional tapestry around the theme of family. *The Family* will encourage parents to think all is not lost, and maybe even teenagers to think that God is still interested in them and that Jesus could be a role model.

Family is one theme that Christians must not abandon in the market place of ideas. All families need nurture and support from relatives, neighbors and governments, for they form the basis of daily living of ninety per cent of Australians. The ideal is so strong in people's minds that when one family breaks down, the individuals start searching for another family unit.

How to bring the world of social reality together with Christian faith is an extremely important quest. This book, read on a daily or weekly basis, will enable readers to unite the two worlds and make sense of their own experience.

Alan Nichols
Alan Nichols is an Anglican minister currently working for World Vision Australia

Preface

My three happiest hours last week stand out very clearly. Our youngest daughter Lindy lounged in a chair in my study one night and we talked Big Theological Questions for an hour. Two days later our soon-to-be-married daughter Amanda said, "Dad, let's go for a walk!" and then took four kilometres to put the perfect marriage together! Then yesterday, en route to the airport, Jan and I did again what we are now doing regularly – a mini marriage check-up.

There is no greater happiness than to be a child, or a parent, in a happy home. In happy families we are loved unconditionally, enjoy a deep sense of belonging, and develop "competencies." It's only in family, community, that we become "fully human, fully alive."

But not all families or communities are happy. A friend who is a clinical psychologist says marriage is "an impossible arrangement between two imperfect people."

I am not so pessimistic. Happy families, communities, marriages are possible. My prayer is that this book, with wisdom compiled from many sources, will help enhance your intimate relationships.

I am deeply grateful to have had two faithful parents. My father died "full of years" while this book was being edited. After thirty-five years of happy marriage, I am still amazed that I should be privileged to have the best woman I've ever known for a wife, and mother of our four great children.

Shalom!
Rowland Croucher

John Mark Ministries
7 Bangor Court
Heathmont
Victoria 3135
Australia

1

No one is an island: you can't be "fully human, fully alive" alone

We do not live to ourselves, and we do not die to ourselves (Romans 14:7).

The Lord God took the man and put him in the garden of Eden to till it and to keep it ... Then the Lord God said, "It is not good that the man should be alone; I will make him a helper as his partner"... So the Lord God caused a deep sleep to fall upon the man, and he slept; then he took one of his ribs and closed up its place with flesh. And the rib that the Lord God had taken from the man he made into a woman and brought her to the man. Then the man said,

"This at last is bone of my bones
and flesh of my flesh;
this one shall be called Woman,
for out of Man this one was taken."

Therefore a man leaves his father and his mother and clings to his wife, and they become one flesh (Genesis 2:15–24).

But it is you, my equal,
my companion, my familiar friend,
with whom I kept pleasant company;
we walked in the house of God ... (Psalm 55:13–14)

How very good and pleasant it is when kindred live together in unity! (Psalm 133:1). This is my commandment, that you love one another as I have loved you (John 15:12). I am the vine, you are the branches. Those who abide in me and I in them bear much fruit, because apart from me you can do nothing (John 15:5).

Paul Simon sang of the self as a "rock" and an "island." But that's all wrong. "Truth is found less *in* human beings than *between* them."

No one is an island, wrote John Donne. We are fulfilled only through meaningful contact with others. Friendless people are never truly themselves. We need deep friendships with those who will love us anyway. Man Friday helps Robinson Crusoe find himself. The prisoner in solitary confinement seeks the friendship of a rat. (The agony of his punishment is isolation, being "an island.")

We need one another. When spiders weave webs together, says an African proverb, they can tie up a lion. In the movie *Crocodile Dundee*, the Aussie bushman, during his first visit from the wilds of Australia to New York City, is amazed by all the people who are seeing psychiatrists. New York City, he had thought, would be a friendly place. When told that most New Yorkers are in therapy, he cannot comprehend why anyone would need to pay someone to sit and listen. In shock he exclaims, "Don't they have any mates?"

Life for most of us is complicated, but it becomes intolerably so if we're chronically lonely. "I watch others with loved ones laughing together – in public places or on TV – and I feel so painfully jealous and angry," said an unmarried forty-year-old woman to me. The ultimate question "Who am I?" is only ever satisfactorily answered in honest community with loving, significant others. This idea will reverberate throughout the present book: God is still in the business of incarnation – coming to us in the real flesh-and-blood love of another. We will only become whole people that way.

At weddings I give a little homily to the bride and groom. "Jack, Jill your bride is a gorgeous creature, and you'd better not think you can change her. You'll want to, but don't. Just love her unconditionally ... Jill, this handsome man will have habits and attitudes that will bug you. Love and accept him anyway. People change and grow when they're loved in spite of their weaknesses and faults. Every culture has a proverb which says something like 'The sun does not command the bud to become a flower. It provides a climate of warmth, and a beautiful flower emerges.' God's love for us is love-before-worth, not love-responding-to-worth. He loves us while we are yet sinners, not after we've stopped being sinners. He creates worth in us, so in the climate of that warm love we grow and change into the beautiful people he intends us to be. Go into your marriage and do likewise!"

Jean Vanier, from his experience in communities with handi-capped people, argues that "to accept our weaknesses and those of others is the very opposite of sloppy complacency ... It is essentially a concern for truth so that we do not live in illusion and can grow from where we are and not where we want to be, or where others want us to be" (Jean Vanier, *Community and Growth*, Sydney: St Paul, 1979, p. 18).

The "Genesis" of love-before-worth goes back to a God who creates man/woman, and takes delight in what he has made. These humans are formed "in his image," like himself – but each is unique.

He walks – shares fellowship – with Adam, as good friends do. In this heart-to-heart dialogue, both find great joy. God desires his friend to have a partner and so creates Eve. But these humans break off dialogue with God and the result is disharmony, conflict, death. When we distance ourselves from God, all other relationships are affected. We compete with others instead of empowering them. We are jealous instead of enjoying their success. We think and say and do violent things against others when they invade our space.

But God is actually still near to us: closer to us than we are to ourselves. He desires to be "in relationship" with us. He is more than an artist or architect designing beautiful creatures in a beautiful world. He is also a loving parent, a devoted lover, longing for us to return from the far country. Although we are damaged by our fallen-ness, as Artist-Redeemer he is touching us up all the time. Each of us becomes a "cathedral" in which God dwells, a sanctuary for his peaceful presence. He is the divine physician who heals our self-despisings and our alienation. The images of his concern for us are legion.

But we are only re-created through dialogue – with God and with others and with oneself. Jesus is God's "Word" to us, reminding us that we do not struggle alone. He is our friend, caring for us, and we are transformed by the grace involved in this encounter. But he is also our Lord, demanding our unconditional allegiance (which is the only way to be "in the kingdom" – to be whole). We say "Yes, I will" to whatever God invites us to do. Then we begin to be transformed.

Paul's letter to the Ephesians (4:32) offers three simple rules for relating to others: "be kind to one another, tenderhearted, forgiving one another." Kindness, according to my dictionary, is showing a generous, sympathetic, gracious and considerate attitude towards others. It is more than deeds, says Albert Schweitzer: "As the sun makes ice melt, *kindness* causes misunderstanding, mistrust, and hostility to evaporate." To be *tenderhearted* is the opposite of being hardhearted. And *forgiveness* is something we do for others, not out of a sense of paternalistic pride (you've done wrong so I'm going to be big enough to forgive you), but as a fellow-sinner (I too need God's forgiveness always and your forgiveness sometimes).

A guard beat a Christian prisoner until he was half-conscious, and while kicking him demanded, "What can your Christ do for you now?" The Christian quietly replied, "He can give me strength to forgive you."

Selected Quotations

Everybody needs somebody. God has not only made us "for himself" but also for one another. Jesus needed his friends: we too are not "islands." We are never whole unless we are in community: the Christian group is far more than the sum of so many individuals. As Goethe put it, "All true life is in meeting."

To be complete I need you and you need me. I need you to help me understand who I am. Unless I am a contortionist, I can't see more than seventy per cent of my body without the aid of a mirror: so too I can't see my *self* without the aid of the mirror you hold up to me. I am incomplete psychologically or emotionally without your love. I have practical needs where you can help. If I am sick, pray for me. If I am lonely, be with me. If I am troubled, listen to me. If I am discouraged, give me fresh hope ...

Chuck Colson, who became a Christian before being jailed for his alleged involvement in the Watergate conspiracy, offered some advice for new Christians: "Surround yourself with people who care about you, who will help you, who will encourage you when you need it, and knock you down when you need that. The only way you can have spiritual power is through a fellowship of others who will really help you and guide you and be as one with you."

"Community: Spiritual Gifts Meeting Human Needs," *The Best of GRID*,
World Vision of Australia, 1993, p. 141.

It is a serious thing to live in a society of possible gods and goddesses, to remember that the dullest and most uninteresting person you can talk to may one day be a creature, which, if you saw it now, you would be strongly tempted to worship, or else a horror and a corruption such as you now meet, if at all, only in a nightmare. All day long we are, in some degree, helping each other to one or other of these destinations. It is in the light of these overwhelming possibilities, it is with the awe and the circumspection proper to them, that we should conduct all our dealings with one another, all friendships, all loves, all play, all politics. There are no ordinary people. You have never talked to a mere mortal. Nations, cultures, arts, civilizations – these are mortal, and their life is to ours as the life of a gnat. But it is immortals we joke with, work with, marry, snub and exploit – immortal horrors or everlasting splendours.

C.S. LEWIS,
"The Weight of Glory," *Screwtape Proposes a Toast*,
London: Collins (Fontana), 1965, p. 109.

I shall pass through this life but once.

Any good, therefore, that I can do

Or any kindness I can show to any fellow creature,

Let me do it now.

Let me not defer or neglect it,

For I shall not pass this way again.

ETIENNE DE GRELLET,
French missionary, precise source unknown.

Too many ... are suffering from a lack of love which leaves them feeling isolated and lonely, uncared for and unencouraged. They can feel used instead of loved, criticized rather than affirmed ... The triune God who lives eternally in relationship created us for relationships. We were made for fellowship with God and with each other. We really need each other to be fully human, fully Christian and fully effective. We need each other for comfort in times of suffering. We need each other to rejoice when we rejoice and weep when we weep. No matter how strong we are, we need to bear one another's burdens and receive help with our own burdens. We need each other's gifts. We need to hear the truth spoken in love. We need relationships which help us and nourish us as we seek to give ourselves to others. We need people to whom we can confess our sins, and with whom we can pray for healing and wholeness. We need conversations which build us up and affirm our gifts and abilities.

ROBERTA HESTENES,
"Christian Community and World Evangelization," paper given to the
"Lausanne in Manila" Congress on World Evangelization, July 11–20, 1989, p. 5.

Let [those] who cannot be alone beware of community. [They] will only do harm to [themselves] and to the community. Alone you stood before God when he called you; alone you had to answer that call; alone you had to struggle and pray; and alone you will die and give an account to God. You cannot escape from yourself; for God has singled you out. If you refuse to be alone you are rejecting Christ's call to you, and you can have no part in the community of those who are called …

But the reverse is also true: Let [those] who are not in community beware of being alone. Into the community you were called, the call was not meant for you alone; in the community of the called you bear your cross, you struggle, you pray. You are not alone, even in death, and on the Last Day you will be only one member of the great congregation of Jesus Christ, and thus your solitude can be only hurtful to you …

We recognize, then, that only as we are within the fellowship can we be alone, and only [those who are] alone can live in the fellowship.

DIETRICH BONHOEFFER,
Life Together, New York: Harper & Row, 1954, p. 77.

Each person we meet leads us to a unique experience of our own persona in a way no other person can. When you open yourself to another person, it is not a situation of one plus one equals two, but one plus one equals a new universe.

RICHARD CURRIER and FRANCIS GRAM,
Forming a Small Christian Community: A Personal Journey,
Mystic, CT: Twenty-third Publications, 1992, p. 12.

[Sociologists talk about] "social networks". Your social network consists of everyone you know. Imagine a set of points some of which are joined by lines. The points are people, or sometimes groups, and the lines tell you who interacts with whom. Each person is in touch with a number of others, some of whom may know each other. There is no common boundary to the network (unless a tribe in Papua New Guinea hasn't been discovered yet ...!).

One problem in modern industrial societies is that people move further away from their "home town" or childhood village, and they move more often. Social networks therefore replace "communities." We know more people more superficially ... As we move house (on the average every three to five years in some middle-class suburbs) we leave friends behind and are sometimes hesitant to make close friends in the new location, knowing we'll have to leave them behind too. So marriage is becoming more important to satisfy needs some of which would be met by the wider community in traditional cultures. But the "catch 22" here is that marriage is becoming more fragile, due to the disintegration of [societal] values ... This is the terrible price we pay for a flexible economic system.

ROWLAND CROUCHER,
"The Importance of Christian Community,"
LIVE! More Meditations and Prayers for Christians, Melbourne: JBCE, 1993, pp. 174–175.

When a community welcomes people who have been on the margins of society, things usually go quite well to begin with. Then, for many reasons, these people start to become marginal to the society of the community as well. They throw crises which can be very painful for the community and cause considerable confusion, because it feels so powerless. The community is then caught in a trap from which it is hard to escape. But if the crises bring it to a sense of its own poverty, they can also be a grace.

There is something prophetic in people who seem marginal and difficult; they force the community to become alert, because what they are demanding is authenticity. Too many communities are founded on dreams and fine words: there is so much talk about love, truth and peace. Marginal people are demanding. Their cries are cries of truth because they sense the emptiness of many of our words … but sometimes marginal people can become a focus for unity, because they … can force the community to pull itself together.

JEAN VANIER,
Community and Growth, Sydney: St Paul, 1979, pp. 204–205.

When the judgment comes what will King Jesus say to each of us? Will he ask if we have been "born again"? Will he ask what awards we have received or what influential people we have known? It seems not. He will ask, "Did you feed the hungry? Did you clothe the naked? Did you visit me in prison?" What is striking about this parable is that the blessed of the Lord seem unaware of what they have done. They seem surprised to hear Jesus say, "As you cared for the least of my sisters and brothers you cared for me." When Jesus says, "Come, O blessed of my Father, inherit the kingdom prepared for you," they ask, "Are you talking to us?" … The dying words of the German poet Goethe were "Light, light, let there be more light." When the twentieth century Spanish philosopher Miguel de Unamuno reflected on these words, he said, "It is not more light we need, but more warmth. Warmth, warmth, more warmth! We die of cold, not of darkness. It is not the night that kills, but the frost."

ANTHONY B. ROBINSON,
"At the Clothing Bank," *The Christian Century*, November 3, 1993, p. 1085.

A Prayer

Lord,
All the lonely people, where do they all come from?
Occasionally / sometimes / often I'm one of them.
I was made for relationships, community;
What others have done to me affects me;
What I have done to others has changed them;
I am a part of all whom I have met;

I cannot disentangle myself from others
Or from God.
So, Lord,
Help me to enhance the lives of those I meet by

- *treating others as I would like them to treat me;*
- *seeking for others the happiness I seek for myself;*
- *doing something helpful for others most days;*
- *being friendly even if my friendship is not reciprocated;*
- *contacting someone to cheer them up;*
- *developing the art of listening;*
- *praying for others;*
- *learning to worship so that I may gradually be disinfected from egoism;*
- *and remembering that I will meet you today, Lord, in the person who needs an encouraging word or a helping hand. Amen.*

A Benediction

May you know you are loved, and in the power of that love may you become what you were destined to be. May you find some others who can enhance your personhood, and may you do the same for them. Amen.

CAPSULE 1: Ethology and Boundaries

Just yesterday our family had to ask a homeless, dollar-less person to leave, after being with us on-and-off for a month. She has been a friend for twenty-five years, and has regularly stayed in our home, but it was time for her to make it on her own. She did not like it, but we had to be firm. (By the way, we found an alternative place for her, a church to underwrite the first two weeks' rent and meals, and a pastoral chaplain to help sort out her affairs.)

We have had various people stay with us throughout a period of thirty years. Why would we "toss someone out" like this? Because we love her, that's why. Let me explain.

Ethology is the study of the comparison between human and animal behaviour. An important concept in ethology is the notion of *territoriality*: the practice of marking a piece of ground and defending it against intruders. Animals as diverse as fish, worms, gazelles, and lizards stake out particular areas and put up fierce resistance when intruders encroach on their area. Many species use odorous secretions to mark the boundaries of their territory – the wolf, for example, marks its domain by urinating around the perimeter.

Humans are also territorial animals: our genetic endowment drives us to gain and defend territory, much as the animals do. The list of territorial behaviors is endless: in a library you protect your space with a book, coat, or notebook; you "save a place" in the theater or at the beach, reserving a spot that is "mine" or "ours"; juvenile gangs fight to protect their turf; neighbors of similar ethnic backgrounds join forces to keep other groups out; nations war over contested territory; pastors accuse others of "sheep-stealing."

Now there's good news and bad news here. Individuals and families ought to have boundaries – physical, material, emotional – and others ought to respect those boundaries. Indeed, in many ways boundaries define us. They tell us and others "what is me and what is not me." My fence tells me where my property begins and ends. My skin does the same thing for my body. Words do it in communication – particularly the word "No!", which helps others understand that I exist apart from them, and that "I am in control of me." Taking time off from involvement with people or projects helps you gain control of your own time-program. Emotionally, we need some privacy, particularly when someone else wants to abuse us. Because we fear being alone, we permit another to invade our personal space; we may have to separate ourselves from that person for a time to regain our emotional strength. And we must learn that the abusive "invader" is not the only source of love and intimacy in the world: we need to selectively "expose" ourselves to others as well.

For many humans, the desire to help others is a subtle, perhaps unconscious, ploy to invade their space to satisfy some of our own needs. We "need to be needed." The love we give is "need love," not "gift love." Many people-helpers want to be "little messiahs," saving everyone from themselves.

But on the other hand, people need people. "Bear one another's burdens, and in this way you will fulfill the law of Christ" (Galatians 6:2). We must try to develop the skill of knowing when it is appropriate to be helpful, and when we can best help by leaving a person (or a crowd) alone. I love the statement in Luke 5:15–16, which describes Jesus' response to the crowds that followed him to be taught and healed: "But he would withdraw to deserted places and pray." He knew when it was best for others to leave them alone, and when it was best for his own emotional and spiritual nurturing to enjoy solitude with his Father-God.

So I have responsibility for my garden, but not for others'; I nurture what is mine, but I don't have to take responsibility when others' lives are messed up. We must not trespass into territory where we don't properly belong. And we have a right to exclude others from our private space or our family's territory if they would not be helpful there.

But this can be selfish if taken too far. As a result of our fallenness, this planet and its inhabitants have substituted "territoriality" ("my space – keep out!") for "hospitality" ("my space – you're welcome!"). The Bible has many stories and injunctions about reversing this effect of the Fall. We are to house the homeless, feed the hungry, clothe the naked, welcome the stranger. We'll be asked questions about all this at the "Great Judgment," Jesus warned (Matthew 25). Knowing the fine balance between being helpful and being "spattered all over the wall of needfulness" is something to be learned through hard experience.

2

How to be an easier person to live with

Happy is everyone who fears the Lord, who walks in his ways (Psalm 128:1).

This is the day that the Lord has made; let us rejoice and be glad in it (Psalm 118:24). Take delight in the Lord, and he will give you the desires of your heart (Psalm 37:4). My soul shall rejoice in the Lord, exulting in his deliverance (Psalm 35:9). Do not be grieved, for the joy of the Lord is your strength (Nehemiah 8:10).

My heart is glad, and my soul rejoices; my body also rests secure … You show me the path of life. In your presence there is fullness of joy; in your right hand are pleasures forevermore (Psalm 16:9, 11).

Blessed are the poor in spirit, for theirs is the kingdom of heaven. Blessed are those who mourn, for they will be comforted. Blessed are the meek, for they will inherit the earth. Blessed are those who hunger and thirst for righteousness, for they will be filled. Blessed are the merciful, for they will receive mercy. Blessed are the pure in heart, for they will see God. Blessed are the peacemakers, for they will be called children of God. Blessed are those who are persecuted for righteousness' sake, for theirs is the kingdom of heaven. Blessed are you when people revile you and persecute you and utter all kinds of evil against you falsely on my account. Rejoice and be glad, for your reward is great in heaven, for in the same way they persecuted the prophets who were before you (Matthew 5:3–12).

Then he looked up at his disciples and said: Blessed are you who are poor, for yours is the kingdom of God. Blessed are you who are hungry now, for you will be filled. Blessed are you who weep now, for you will laugh. Blessed are you when people hate you, and when they exclude you, revile you, and defame you on account of the Son of Man. Rejoice in that day and leap for joy, for surely your reward is great in heaven; for that is what their ancestors did to the prophets (Luke 6:20–23).

Happy are those whose transgression is forgiven, whose sin is covered (Psalm 32:1). Happy are those who do not follow the advice of the wicked, or take the path that sinners tread, or sit in the seat of scoffers (Psalm 1:1). How happy is the one whom God reproves; therefore do not despise the discipline of the Almighty (Job 5:17). The precepts of the Lord are right, rejoicing the heart; the commandment of the Lord is clear, enlightening the eyes (Psalm 19:8).

All the days of the poor are hard, but a cheerful heart has a continual feast (Proverbs 15:15). Happy are those who consider the poor; the Lord delivers them in the day of trouble (Psalm 41:1). We must support the weak, remembering the words of the Lord Jesus, for he himself said, "It is more blessed to give than to receive" (Acts 20:35).

I have said these things to you so that my joy may be in you, and that your joy may be complete (John 15:11). Rejoice in the Lord always; again I will say, Rejoice (Philippians 4:4).

A cheerful heart is a good medicine, but a downcast spirit dries up the bones (Proverbs 17:22).

Happy people are easier – much, much easier – to live with.

Just about everybody wants to be happy. You dream of happiness, you plan for it, and perhaps pay any price to achieve it. Searching for happiness, one person will make a lot of money; another will give all their money away. In the same search a woman will have five or six children; another enters a convent. Ask the average person what he or she wants out of life, and the chances are they'll reply without hesitation, "I just want to be happy."

Where do you find happiness? Bumper stickers tell us Happiness is a German Shepherd, Being Single, Being a Grandmother, Being Italian, Dreaming in Color, or whatever. Happiness is being a non-conformist, according to Emerson. Rousseau said it is a good bank account, a good cook and a good digestion.

Although we know in theory that happiness is in the mind, many people lead lives of quiet desperation. Sure, most people are about as happy as they make up their minds to be; certainly, if you "keep your face towards the sunshine, the shadows will fall behind you." But there's still a vague unease … The old Scottish proverb can invite us to "Be happy while y'er leevin' for y'er a long time dead," but the blues still come uninvited – and overstay their welcome.

Jesus doesn't offer you happiness, but he promises you'll be "blessed." Indeed, he essentially promised three things to his followers: constant trouble, constant joy, because of his constant presence. The purpose of life is not to be happy, but to be useful, to be loving, to be unselfish, to have made a difference. Happiness is a *by-product* of having worthwhile attitudes and doing worthwhile things. Happy people serve others, have goals, are close to nature, are in touch with the child within.

And yet, and yet … Deep within just about all of us is the elusive promise of joy, somewhere. As C. S. Lewis put it memorably: "All your life an unattainable ecstasy has hovered just beyond the grasp of your consciousness. The day is coming when you will wake to find, beyond all hope, that you have attained it, or else that it was within your reach and you have lost it forever" (C. S. Lewis, *The Problem of Pain*, London: Collins (Fontana), 1957, p. 136).

Happiness, as the song says, is different things to different people. The *Oxford English Dictionary* defines it as "the state of pleasurable content of mind which results from success or the attainment of what is considered good."

Happy people are "free" people. The fundamentalists are not really free. They try to be free from complexity, but they are not free from fear or doubt. The theological liberals may be free of dogma, but they are not free to be sure about too many things. The Pentecostals may be emotionally free in some ways, but they are not free from stress ...

Happiness – whether you're a Christian or not – is not attained by trying hard to be happy. Happiness is "serendipitous." Serendipity is the art of making happy discoveries while looking for something else. The most beautiful adventures, said Robert Louis Stevenson, are not those we go to seek. You can only be happy, according to George Orwell, when you do not assume that the object of life is happiness.

Happiness is where we find it, rarely where we seek it. It is the by-product of what happens in three relationships – with God, with others, and with self.

With God. Happiness and peace cannot flourish apart from God, because it is ultimately from God that such gifts derive.

With others. Confucius said, "Those who wish to secure the good of others have already secured their own."

With self. Ultimately, your real self-worth is in yourself, not in the things you do or the offices you hold. Being rich or famous doesn't make you happy. Just before he died, Aristotle Onassis came to a realization of the futility of dedicating one's life to the making of money. Voltaire wrote, "I wish I had never been born."

Happiness is not in the ideas others have about you. After all, a diamond remains a beautiful and precious stone whether embedded in a crown or thrown into the garbage bin. Happiness is enjoying living with yourself. It's the art of being yourself. Happiness is being your own best friend.

But – and this is an important footnote – all authentic Christian spirituality, from the first century onwards, encourages both self-affirmation and self-denial. You are an unrepeatable miracle of God's creation, made in his image. However, you must not just live for yourself. This, of course, is in remarkable opposition to the "I gotta be me" message of many secular self-esteem gurus.

Happiness comes from fulfilling the primary purpose of life – to love God and to love others. The happy person has something to do, someone to love, somewhere to call home and something to hope for. You may not yet be the happiest or best-put-together person you know – but the Lord hasn't finished with you yet!

Selected Quotations

[Bishop Fulton Sheen] put his arm around my shoulders and said, "God loves you. And you know something? So do I." I found tears in my eyes. It was the love power of that man ...

Jesus Christ loves you. Your mother loved you; your father loved you; your wife loves you; your husband loves you. But nobody loves you as Jesus loves you. And that makes us happy, because it tells us we are of infinite worth and value. If you are loved like that by the Son of God, then you have a value that is beyond any material thing. And your life will be continuous into eternity because value, in the highest form, never deteriorates. Love! Love! Love! That is the secret of happiness.

NORMAN VINCENT PEALE,
"Meet the Happiness Giver," *Creative Help for Daily Living*, Part III, Vol. 31, No. 9,
New York: Foundation for Christian Living, 1980, p. 34.

A day so happy. Fog lifted early, I worked in the garden. Hummingbirds were stopping over honeysuckle flowers. There was no thing on earth I wanted to possess. I knew no one worth my envying ... Whatever evil I had suffered, I forgot. To think that once I was the same man did not embarrass me. In my body I felt no pain. When straightening up, I saw the blue sea and sails.

CZESLAW MILOSZ,
"Gift," 1973. Quoted in *Newsweek*, October 20, 1980, p. 54.

The three greatest enemies of happiness [are] ... worry, boredom, and self-centredness ... Christianity slays them all! Worry? ... Even though the worst should happen, even though your whole scheme of things were to collapse ... nothing, absolutely nothing can pluck you ... out of the great Father's keeping! Boredom? ... Christianity [fills] your life full with the glory of a friendship whose wonders are unending ... Self-centredness – Christianity finishes that. How? By taking you, once and for all, right out of yourself ...

Why be a Christian? The Christian life is happier than any other. [But] the Christian life is also harder than any other ... The life in Christ is holier than any other ... [And] the Christian life is more hopeful than any other.

JAMES STEWART,
"Why Be a Christian?" in *The Gates of New Life*, Edinburgh: T & T Clark, 1956, pp. 23–29.

[A girl from Mauritius, highly educated, entered Mother Teresa's society in India.] "The next day I sent her to work in a home for the dying. For three hours she lovingly cleaned a woman who had been picked up on the street. She came home radiating joy. 'I have been touching the body of Christ for three hours,' she told me."

[To her fellow-workers among lepers:] "Be kind and merciful. Let no one come ɔ you without coming away better and happier. Be the living expression of God's kindness, kindness in your face, kindness in your eyes, kindness in your smile, in your warm greeting" ...

"Joy is prayer – Joy is strength – Joy is Love ... God loves a cheerful giver! You give most when you give with joy. The best way to show our gratitude to God and the people is to accept everything with joy. A joyful heart is the normal result of a heart burning with love ... Never let anything fill you so much with sorrow as to make you forget the joy of Christ risen ... We all long for heaven where God is, but we have it in our power to be in heaven with him right now. To be happy with him now means loving as he loves, helping as he helps, giving as he gives, serving as he serves, rescuing as he rescues, being with him twenty-four hours, touching him in his distressing disguise."

MOTHER TERESA
in Peter Dwan, *Apostle of the Unwanted (Mother Teresa)*,
Melbourne: ACTS Publications, 1969, pp. 5, 10–11, 19–20.

For the happiest life, days should be rigorously planned, nights left open to chance ...

Every now and then you run across radiantly attractive people and you're delighted to find they adore you, till you realize that they adore just about everybody – and that's what's made them radiantly attractive.

MIGNON McLAUGHLIN,
"The Second Neurotic's Notebook," quoted in *Reader's Digest*, date unknown.

Christians are free of vindictiveness because they trust God's justice; but they are free for blessing because they know God's goodness.

EDMUND P. CLOWNEY,
The Message of 1 Peter, Leicester: Inter-Varsity Press (UK), 1988, p. 141.

Prayers

Make me, Lord, obedient without complaint, poor without regret, patient without murmur, humble without pretence, joyful without foolishness, truthful without disguise.

THOMAS AQUINAS,
cited in *Praying with the Saints*, Dublin: Veritas Publications, 1989, p. 64.

Eternal God, you dwell in light unapproachable, beyond the power of our thought to comprehend or our imagination to portray. Yet you are revealed to us in the beauty of the world we live in, in the truth our minds discover, in the inward presence of your Spirit, and above all in Christ, your Son. With reverent hearts we worship you.

We bring our fragmentary lives into the presence of your wholeness. We bring our transient thoughts into the light of your eternity. We bring our restless spirits into the calm strength of your everlasting purpose.

We have complained about the circumstances that have fretted us, about enemies who have wronged us, and even about the justice of your order that has hurt us. Teach us, nevertheless, we earnestly ask, to search our own lives, to see that each has our own destiny, each soul its own heaven and its own hell. Send us back into our souls to find there, by your grace, peace and power and adequacy to conquer life. May we be victors and not victims. Amen.

ROWLAND CROUCHER

Eternal God, grant us this day and every day such readiness and delight in following Christ, that whether our lives are short or long we shall have lived abundantly. Amen.

A New Zealand Prayer Book, Auckland: Collins, 1989, p. 106.

A Benediction

May God, from whom to be turned is to fall; to whom to be turned is to rise; and in whom to stand is to live forever: may this God grant us in all our duties his help, in all our problems his guidance, in all our dangers his protection, in all our sorrows his peace, through Jesus Christ our Lord. Amen.

Adapted from a prayer of St Augustine, cited in *Praying with the Saints*,
Dublin: Veritas Publications, 1989, p. 22.

3

How to get along with other people

In everything do to others as you would have them do to you
(Matthew 7:12). Forgive, if you have anything against anyone
(Mark 11:25). "Love your neighbor as yourself." Love does no wrong
to a neighbor (Romans 13:9–10).

We urge you ... to admonish the idlers, encourage the faint-hearted,
help the weak, be patient with all of them (1 Thessalonians 5:14).

If then there is any encouragement in Christ, any consolation from
love, any sharing in the Spirit, any compassion and sympathy, make
my joy complete: be of the same mind, having the same love, being
in full accord and of one mind (Philippians 2:1–2). The Lord is near
(Philippians 4:5).

Be angry but do not sin; do not let the sun go down on your anger
(Ephesians 4:26).

No one [should] wrong or exploit a brother or sister ... For God did
not call us to impurity but in holiness ... Now concerning love of the
brothers and sisters, you do not need to have anyone write to you, for
you yourselves have been taught by God to love one another
(1 Thessalonians 4:6–9).

He has told you, O mortal, what is good;
and what does the Lord require of you
but to do justice, and to love kindness. (Micah 6:8)

I give you a new commandment, that you love one another. Just as I have loved you, you also should love one another. By this everyone will know that you are my disciples, if you have love for one another (John 13:34–35).

Finally, all of you, have unity of spirit, sympathy, love for one another, a tender heart, and a humble mind. Do not repay evil for evil or abuse for abuse; but, on the contrary, repay with a blessing. It is for this that you were called – that you might inherit a blessing (1 Peter 3:8–9).

In the brilliant film *Kramer vs. Kramer*, the divorced father has to explain to his five-year-old son that he's just lost the custody battle between himself and the boy's mother. Soon the child will be going to live with her. The little boy sobs out what for him are questions of ultimate concern: "Where will I sleep? Where will I put my toys? Why can't I stay with you too?"

The movie is about three people. Two grown-ups – a man and a woman – find that they cannot live their lives together. Their little boy, therefore, has to have his life messed up too. Where does such a vicious circle begin? Why is it not possible for humans to live together without conflict? What can we do to stop the chain reaction of grief being handed on to another generation?

Oscar Wilde believed that "other people are quite dreadful; the only possible society is oneself." Wrong, Oscar, and sad. How can we get along with those we live with?

You begin by knowing who the real "me" is. If you don't like yourself, you won't enjoy living with others either. When I ask people in counseling "What do you like about yourself?" I often get a "nothing" response.

Some of us avoid responsibility for our behavior with the excuse "Well, nobody's perfect." True, but you don't have to opt out of growing; nor do you have to live with the negative self-fulfilling prophecies you or others have heaped on yourself. At the deepest level, your identity, your perception of who you are, has derived from what others have communicated to you about you. It's on the esteem of others that you base your own self-esteem. With the help of a caring friend, learn to accept yourself. You're an unrepeatable miracle of God's creation. If you want to get along with others, you had better start with the person inside your own skin!

Then, affirm the uniqueness of others. They, too, are who they are as a result of the mix of verbal inputs into their lives by significant others, plus the accidents of life they have experienced, plus their own success or otherwise in determining to become a whole person. The Christian approach here is simple, and it works: pray to your and their Creator God for a gift of love to view the other as one precious to God and made in his image. You can't pray this prayer sincerely for too long without beginning to appreciate the other!

Next, let's be lovingly honest with one another. One of the great middle-class sicknesses of our time is affability. We're so nice to each other it's sickening. We play games to cover our true feelings. Rather than "walking in the light" we leave one another to stumble in the darkness about who we are and who they are. But then, if we can't "speak the truth in love" without the risk of creating greater hurt rather than healing, we might have to (a) learn "win–win" conflict resolution skills, and/or (b) follow the advice on my desk calendar the other day: "Never miss an opportunity to make others happy, even if you have to leave them alone to do it."

We exist in homes, families and communities in order to care for each other, as well as to be cared for by others. However, "care" has ambiguous connotations. For example, when a Mafia boss tells his henchmen to "go take care of somebody," that somebody had better watch out. He's about to be made an offer he can't refuse! Actually, our English word "care" goes back to a Gothic root, *kara*, meaning "to lament, weep with, grieve." So caring should mean we become aware of the other in ways that stir deep feelings, and out of these feelings, resolve is born to care for them in appropriate ways. This means breaking out of the circle of selfishness and making our lives a resource to others.

This is the meaning of the Good Samaritan story. Every "good Samaritan" says to the other: "What happens to you makes a difference to me." Just as God makes an unconditional covenant to commit himself to us no matter what happens, so we forgive "seventy times seven" and serve the other, even if we are not thanked, or our labors are not returned. This is authentic caring.

Again, let's take a journey back to the first few chapters of Genesis. There we find a wonderful story about God desiring communion with the creatures he had made. When Adam sinned, that fellowship was broken. God arrived in the garden for their usual fellowship time, but Adam was hiding. The "Fall" was a fall from fellowship, not only between humans and God, but between humans themselves. Cain killed his brother Abel, and we've had to work very hard to maintain fellowship, particularly where our fallenness has led us to create barriers between persons and groups. And yet, though God in the Old Testament is characteristically sovereign and holy in his "apartness" from sinners, his statement to Moses – "I will be with you" (Exodus 3:12) – indicates his desire to commune with his covenant people. The Divine Presence within Israel was symbolized in the ark, the cloud, the guiding angel, and later in the Jerusalem Temple. As Psalm 23 tells us, he feeds us, cares for us, protects us, guides us, and encourages us.

In the New Testament, the Greek noun *koinonia* simply means "sharing" and is translated variously as "communion," "communication," "community," "fellowship," "partaking," "contribution," and so on. An ancient inscription put up by a husband in memory of his wife: "I shared (*koinonia*) all life with you alone." Thus "fellowship" in New Testament usage is the sharing of something with others in a community, not merely the act of associating with them.

The outpoured Spirit had created a community that broke through the barriers of language, culture, race, sex – even possessions (see Acts 2:42; 4:32, 35; Galatians 3:28; Colossians 3:11). The new joy and mutual love of the early Christians emanated not from a divine mandate, but from their high conception of being "in fellowship." It was nothing short of a miracle! They experienced a sense of oneness, unity, togetherness unlike anything they had known before. People didn't just associate with a few "cronies"; Jesus said tax-collectors and other disreputable people did that. The foundation of *koinonia* is nothing less than the Incarnation: Jesus sharing his life with us.

Again, we repeat: the Christian good news is about God's acceptance of us even before we change. He loves us unconditionally. This was essentially the difference between Jesus and the Pharisees. Jesus accepted and loved people before they had changed; indeed, he loved them into change. The Pharisees rejected people who were alien, sinners, until they had changed and mended their ways. With Jesus, acceptance preceded repentance; with the Pharisees, it was the other way around. So we are to accept one another as God accepts us – as people who are made in his image, who are like him! (Romans 5:6–8, 15:7). This doesn't mean we'll ignore or gloss over others' mistakes or sins, but it does mean we'll recognize their Godlikeness before we barge in to "fix" things. Jesus said to the woman caught in adultery "Neither do I condemn you" before he said "Go your way, and from now on do not sin again" (John 8:11). Jesus understood others.

We'll all meet difficult people from time to time. Jesus did. He didn't get along with everybody. He condemned injustice and god-lessness, and if you're going to do that, you're going to get crucified by the unjust and the godless. If we're "change agents," then we'll suffer at the hands of those who benefit by things staying the way they are.

On the other hand, what do we mean by a "difficult person"? Who of us is not abnormal in some sense? Who decides what is normal, who is difficult? Maybe schizophrenics are sometimes the sane ones! Perhaps we have to work harder at dealing with the log in our own eye, before we take splinters out of others' eyes!

Many interpersonal conflicts result from our idealized picture of who the other should be. Others' incompleteness reminds us of our own. This is sometimes called "transference" – transferring emotions to a person or situation which belong somewhere else. A man marries to escape a dominant mother, so when his wife nags him and reminds him of a bitter past, he over-reacts. She's trying to make him like her father, who was so helpful around the house, whereas he does nothing.

Acceptance is helped by *empathy*. Empathy is "the imaginative projection of one's personality into that of another person" – putting yourself into the other's shoes, listening deeply with mind, heart, and soul. It's not *sympathy*, which can sometimes be a selfish emotion, where you're hooked because of some unresolved emotional conflict in your own life. And it's the opposite of *antipathy*, where you judge the other for not measuring up to what you want them to be.

The church is meant to be a therapeutic community, a community of people-helpers. But to be a people-helper, one must be committed to one's own growth – physical, intellectual, social-emotional, and spiritual. It's a community of people who practice faith, hope, and love: faith that people are loved already in spite of their crabbiness; hope that with patience and acceptance we and others can grow and change; and love, by which we cover a multitude of faults and desire only the good of others. The challenge is to see Jesus in others, and practice "being Christ" to them. And that's tough work: overcoming prejudices is the hardest work of all!

Selected Quotations

From what I have learned in my own marriage, and seen in others, there are not many questions more important than this: "Am I willing to train myself away from selfishness toward the point where I honestly care how the other person feels?"

CHARLIE W. SHEDD,
Letters to Philip on How to Treat a Woman, Old Tappon, NJ: Fleming H. Revell, 1968, p. 19.

If you share your bread
in fear,
mistrustfully,
undaringly,
in a trice
your bread
will fail.
Try sharing it
without looking ahead,
not thinking of the cost,
unstintingly,
like a child of the Lord
of all the harvests in the world.

DOM HELDER CAMARA,
A Thousand Reasons for Living, London: Darton, Longman & Todd, 1984, p. 98.

A famous English preacher named Alexander Whyte was very disturbed one night because his closest friend was at the point of death. Whyte was praying earnestly to God that this man might be spared when suddenly a Voice said to him, "How serious are you about this one's survival? Would you be willing to divide with him the number of years you have left to live upon this earth?" With that, Whyte reports getting up off his knees in a cold sweat, for suddenly intercession had become more than a matter of words. Now it was the precious substance of his own life that was at stake. He pondered this question very deliberately for a while and dropped back to his knees and said, "Yes! I hereby relinquish half of the time I have left, if this will enable my friend to survive." He got up with no idea what the ultimate outcome of this agreement would be ...

Here I am with a given pool of physical and emotional and psychic vitality. How will I spend it? How much of it will I keep for myself and how much of it will I make available to others?

JOHN CLAYPOOL,
from an unpublished sermon, "How Much of Yourself Will You Give?"

Carl Sandburg talks about the "zoo" inside each of us – there's a pig and a lion and a tiger and a gentle deer. We have all kinds of feelings within us: we are responsible for some of them and not others. But although there is a zoo in me, I am keeper of that zoo!

For example, it is not wrong to be angry, but what you do with your anger could be very harmful. Jesus got angry sometimes. And if you want to get mad at me, that's O.K. I should pray for the maturity to handle our conflicts constructively. Just as friction between certain types of rocks produces sparks of light, so it is the friction of our individualities rubbing against each other that illuminates who we really are. There is a sense in which I do not really know you nor you me until we get to a point where we differ ...

So the words "ought" or "should" mustn't generally be used in relation to feelings. Our feelings are like toothache – they're there – and no amount of exhorting will make a toothache or the feelings go away ...

When you are more in touch with your own feelings, you'll be more compassionate with others ...

ROWLAND CROUCHER,
from an unpublished sermon, "Getting Along with the People You Live with."

25

To Victor, who agrees with me in nothing and is my friend in everything.

CARLYLE MARNEY's
dedication at the beginning of his book *Faith in Conflict*, Nashville: Abingdon Press, 1957.

Some families readily express hostility and anger, but fail to express tenderness, love and appreciation. Other families appear to have unwritten rules that allow the expression of kindness, concern and positive feelings, but then suppress irritation and exasperation, shame, self-doubt and expressions of disagreement, dislike and requests for what one wants for oneself. Healthier families [are] able to express a wide range of feelings ...

"Letting it all hang out" [is not recommended]. It is the range of feelings that can be expressed without attacking other members that seems to create human development and intimacy. It may be because the family members can modulate the intensity of their negative feelings that they are able to express whatever they wish. In fact, the modulation of intense feeling is one of the prerequisites of effective conflict management.

MOIRA EASTMAN,
Family: The Vital Factor, Blackburn, Vic.: Collins Dove, 1989, pp. 65–67.

Christianity is a community event. As Christians we have always believed that the life of faith is not a private enterprise but a communal venture. Over the past several decades in the Church we have come to renewed awareness of this fact. One of the most significant efforts within the Church today is the movement of Christians to understand themselves as the people of God and to experience their relations with one another as a life together in community.

EVELYN EATON WHITEHEAD and JAMES D. WHITEHEAD,
Community of Faith: Models and Strategies for Developing Christian Communities,
New York: Seabury Press, 1982, p. xi.

An Irish tenant farmer who died last century left a widow and three little children. This was before the days of social security. The man who owned the farm needed the house to get another field hand, and so this poor widow was literally turned out into the road with no resource whatsoever for herself and her family. She went to the nearest town and began to go from door to door explaining her plight and offering to do any work to provide for her children. However, person after person turned her away, saying, "I have problems of my own. What happens to you is of no concern to me." After four days of no food and sleeping out of doors in the park, the youngest child's body was weakened and she woke up with a burning fever. By noon all three of the children were sick, and before the sun went down this little neglected family was the centre of an epidemic of diphtheria that spread to the whole town. Only at that point did it become clear that this woman's plight was the concern of the larger community. Their failure to deal with the problem at one point in time meant they had to deal with it later in a worse form.

SOURCE UNKNOWN.

Forgiveness breaks the chain of causality because the one who forgives you – out of love – takes upon themselves the consequences of what you have done. Forgiveness, therefore, always entails sacrifice.

The price you must pay for your own liberation through another's sacrifice, is that you in turn must be willing to liberate in the same way, irrespective of the consequences to yourself.

DAG HAMMARSKJÖLD,
Markings, Faber, 1964. Quoted in Michael Hollings, *Hearts Not Garments*,
London: Darton, Longman & Todd, 1982, p. 82.

Of the Seven Deadly Sins, anger is possibly the most fun. To lick your wounds, to smack your lips over grievances long past, to roll over your tongue the prospect of bitter confrontations still to come, to savour to the last toothsome morsel both the pain you are given and the pain you are giving back – in many ways it is a feast fit for a king. The chief drawback is that what you are wolfing down is yourself. The skeleton at the feast is you.

FREDERICK BUECHNER,
Wishful Thinking, London: Collins, 1973, p. 2.

According to the Bible, we are to love others as ourselves (Luke 10:27), and as God loves us (John 4:11). In other words, there is an intimate connection between our love for ourselves and our love and esteem for God and others. When we fail to love ourselves, all of our relationships suffer. We fail to love our mates, our children, or our neighbors properly. Think of your own life. Remember the last time you were feeling miserable and were angry with yourself, discouraged, or depressed? How did you relate to your mate, children, and friends at that time? Were you loving, sensitive, and kind? I doubt it. When we are uptight about ourselves, we are usually uptight with others. We take our frustrations out on them.

BRUCE NARRAMORE,
You're Someone Special, Grand Rapids: Zondervan, 1978, p. 119.

I was amused to read of the adjustments Paul and Nellie Tournier worked through in their first years of marriage. "I'm an optimist and she's a pessimist," Paul Tournier reported in *Faith at Work* magazine (April, 1972). "She thinks of every difficulty, misfortune, and catastrophe that might happen, and I cannot promise her that such things will not happen. But God is neither optimist nor pessimist. The search for him leads one beyond his own personality and temperament to a path that is neither optimism nor pessimism.

"Little by little I have learned that God speaks to everybody – men and women, adults and children, blacks and whites, the rich and the poor. To discover the will of God, you must listen to him in everyone. Of course, I prefer to have God speak directly to me, rather than through my wife, and yet in truly seeking his will I must be persuaded that he speaks as much through her as through me; to her as much as to me."

Quoted in Philip Yancey, "Marriage: Minefields on the Way to Paradise,"
Christianity Today, February 18, 1977, p. 27.

Prayers

In the Ravensbruck Nazi concentration camp – where an estimated 92,000 men, women, and children were murdered – a piece of wrapping paper was found near the body of a dead child. On the paper was written this prayer:

> *O Lord, remember not only the men and women of good will, but also those of ill will. But do not only remember the suffering they have inflicted on us; remember the fruits we bought, thanks to this suffering: our comradeship, our loyalty, our humility, the courage, the generosity, the greatness of heart*

which has grown out of all this. And when they come to judgment, let all the fruits that we have borne be their forgiveness.

RICHARD FOSTER,
Prayer: Finding the Heart's True Home, London: Hodder & Stoughton, 1992, p. 238.

Accompany me today, O Spirit invisible, in all my goings, but stay with me also when I am in my own home and among my kindred. Forbid that I should fail to show to those nearest to me the sympathy and consideration which thy grace enables me to show to others with whom I have to do. Forbid that I should refuse to my own household the courtesy and politeness which I think proper to show to strangers. Let charity today begin at home.

JOHN BAILLIE,
A Diary of Private Prayer, London: OUP, 1936, p. 89.

Jesus, friend of sinners, you call us to love our enemies, to do good to those who hate us, to bless those who curse us, and pray for those who treat us badly.

Jesus, reconciler,
when someone slaps us on the cheek, you call us to offer the other;
when someone takes our coat, you bid us give our shirt as well;
when someone takes what is ours, we may not demand it back.

Jesus, Son of God, our friend and brother, when we love our enemies and do good we are children of God, who is kind to the wicked and ungrateful.

Jesus, teacher without peer, you have turned the world upside down.

A New Zealand Prayer Book, Auckland: Collins, 1989, pp. 121–122.

Lord, we come before you, not alone,
but in the company of one another.

We share our happiness with each other –
and it becomes greater.

We share our troubles with each other –
and they become smaller.

We share one another's griefs and burdens –
and their weight becomes possible to bear.

May we never be too mean to give,
nor too proud to receive.

For in giving and receiving
we learn to love and be loved;
we encounter the meaning of life,
the mystery of existence –
and discover you.

TERRY C. FALLA,
Be Our Freedom, Lord, Adelaide: Lutheran Publishing House, 1981, p. 158.

Lord Jesus, we hold our families before you; we are ashamed because so many of them are broken or are about to break. How foolish we must look in your sight as we express ourselves so harshly to one another! Lord, forgive us, and help us to make the necessary repairs on our families. We know that we cannot do much by ourselves, we need the help of your Holy Spirit. So please bring his power into our hearts. And, O Holy Spirit of Christ, work mightily among those who have heard the gospel again, and bring many of them to faith.

God the Father, look with your compassion and pity upon those who are living within families in which there is much tension and suffering. Use the message of your grace to help those who are discouraged, and enable them to see that through your power there is hope that their families can become good places to live.

We pray in the name of Jesus. Amen.

"A Good Place to Live," *The Radio Pulpit* (publisher and date unknown).

Lord, speak to me, that I may speak in living echoes of your tone; as you have sought, so let me seek your erring children. Freely I have received, may I freely give.

Help me to remember that a cancerous cell expects the rest of the body to nourish it: may I nourish others, and contribute to their well-being, without being concerned too much about any reciprocity.

In relating to others, help me to adjust to them sometimes; to be flexible when I ought to adapt to them; to be courageous when I am called upon to do or say something difficult to help another; to live in hope, that little by little I can have a part in the ongoing process of the divine redemption of the human race.

Reveal your gifts to me, and the limits of my abilities. I can't do everything to help everyone, but I can do something to help someone. Give me, please, wisdom to know how to help without getting all messed up; and how to help without messing others up.

Thank you, Lord. Amen.

A Benediction
May God grant you the serenity to accept the things you cannot change, the courage to change the things you can, and the wisdom to know the difference. Amen.

4

So what is
a "family"?

For this reason I bow my knees before the Father, from whom every family in heaven and on earth takes its name (Ephesians 3:14–15).

Then the righteous will answer him, "Lord, when was it that we saw you hungry and gave you food, or thirsty and gave you something to drink? And when was it that we saw you a stranger and welcomed you, or naked and gave you clothing? And when was it that we saw you sick or in prison and visited you?" And the king will answer them, "Truly I tell you, just as you did it to one of the least of these who are members of my family, you did it to me" (Matthew 25:37–40).

Whoever does the will of God is my brother and sister and mother (Mark 3:35). And if you greet only your brothers and sisters, what more are you doing than others? Do not even the Gentiles do the same? (Matthew 5:47). For it is better to suffer for doing good, if suffering should be God's will, than to suffer for doing evil (1 Peter 3:17).

Ascribe to the Lord, O families of the peoples, ascribe to the Lord glory and strength (Psalm 96:7). All the ends of the earth shall remember and turn to the Lord; and all the families of the nations shall worship before him. For dominion belongs to the Lord, and he rules over the nations (Psalm 22:27–28).

So then you are no longer strangers and aliens, but you are citizens with the saints and also members of the household of God (Ephesians 2:19).

The family is currently the focus of intense study. Political conventions, sociologists and churches are trying to define and redefine "family." You would think that's easy – "mum, dad, and the kids." But sometimes there's mum and the kids, dad and the kids, two de factos with or without kids, mum and her kids and boyfriend or new husband and his kids, grandparents and kids, two homosexuals or lesbians, "blended" families, households including aging parents, childless parents with adopted children and so on. Many groupings want to be known as "family." And what about the Nayar people of south-west India, where women took as many as twelve "lovers" for sexual relations and bearing children; or the Menangbekau of Sumatra, where brothers and sisters form the residence group and husbands visit for sexual purposes; or the Sambia of Papua New Guinea, where boys leave their mothers from the age of seven and form homosexual relationships until marriage? (Michael Gilding, *The Making and Breaking of the Australian Family*, Sydney: Allen & Unwin, 1991, p. 2).

The variations seem endless ...

In all societies, some sort of "family" cares for children, educates them, forms their character, and develops their moral commitment and sense of worth. The nuclear family (mum, dad, and kids) is the norm in Western cultures, but this way of doing family is historically quite recent. It is a product of the industrial age, the growth of cities, and the need to be mobile to relocate for work. Before the Industrial Revolution, most families were self-sufficient economic units, but today few Western families produce everything they need. It's no longer "profitable" to have many children, so we limit the size of our families. In Great Britain in 1870, for example, the average number of children per family was six. Now it is only two. Further, until the eighteenth century in Europe, people generally lived and died in the village in which they were born. Now families are more mobile: in some large cities of the United States, the average family moves to a different house every two years. The idea of a grandparent or single relative sharing the home (fairly common until the 1930s and '40s) is now rarer.

So TV talk-shows discuss "Will marriage last?" and "Will this be the last generation to live in families?" The ideal of the two-parent family where a man and a woman promise life-long fidelity to each other seems to be disappearing, if you read yuppie journals or watch Hollywood soapies. An Australian politician recently defined "family" as any group of people living together with a common purpose. A posse of drug-pushers would qualify under that definition.

There have been two major attempts to "abolish" the family in this century. The first, in Leninist Russia, collapsed in less than twenty years. Marx had said the family was "antiquated" and predicted it would vanish along with capitalism but by the time of Stalin, all anti-family legislation had been reversed and Marenko, one of Stalin's advisors, was speaking of the family as a "small collective."

A second, less doctrinaire, experiment is in the Israeli *kibbutzim*. But here again there is evidence of the family reasserting itself: mothers demand time off from work to spend with their own offspring; permanent conjugal relationships between the sexes are observed. Indeed, the *kibbutz* operates as a substitute family. Members regard one another as "kin" and therefore are reluctant to intermarry with members of the same *kibbutz* since this would be a kind of psychological incest.

Actually, there have been two recent revolutions in family life, one in the eighteenth and early nineteenth centuries, the other since the 1960s. In the first, the nuclear family broke free of the restraints of village and kin. In today's revolution, the declining stability in family life and resulting increase in social chaos has been caused by:

• The sexual revolution and easily available contraception from the 1960s. • The "Me decade" in the 1970s, with its emphasis on self-actualization and individualism. • The rise of the feminist movement. • Women entering the work force in greater numbers and tasting more and more economic independence (and pressuring governments to pay for day-care facilities for their toddlers – or even babies). • Young people staying at school longer to gain an education. • Easier divorce. • A higher profile by homosexuals.

• Maternity and paternity leave. • Increase in the post-war standard of living (with the temptation to bestow material goods on children as a way of showing love and affection). • Pluralism – parents hesitating to offer any clear guidance on behavior or belief. • The right to "do your own thing" – fulfilling personal goals outside the long-term stability of marriage and family.

In his chapter "The Fractured Family" in *Future Shock*, Alvin Toffler wrote: "The family has been called the 'giant shock absorber' of society – the place to which the bruised and battered individual returns after doing battle with the world, the one stable point in an increasingly flux-filled environment. As the super-industrial revolution unfolds, this 'shock absorber' will come in for some shocks of its own" (London: Pan Books, 1970, p. 219). Ten years later, in *The Third Wave*, he predicted "a high variety of family structures ... From now on the nuclear family will be only one of the many socially accepted and approved forms" (London: Pan Books, 1981, p. 225).

It can be argued that illegitimacy is the single most important problem of our time – more serious than drugs, poverty, or illiteracy. Actually, it is the driving force behind all of those other social ills, setting in motion a chain reaction in which family breakdown is perpetuated from one generation to the next. When families fall apart, societies disintegrate. Parallels can be drawn between the explosion of crime in the black community in the United States in the 1960s and the explosion of crime in the white community now. Both trends correlated with illegitimate births.

Governments are being urged to initiate "national family policies," so the question "What is a family?" is not simply academic. The shape of such policies will depend on whose philosophy of the family they agree to. "Family" is defined differently by various cultural and sub-cultural groups, and by pressure groups with competing agendas.

The Australian Festival of Light, for example, offers this conservative definition: "The family is the natural and fundamental group unit of society comprising mother (female), father (male), and children, which begins with marriage – the union of one man and one woman to the exclusion of all others, undertaken voluntarily as a life-long partnership, and solemnized and registered according to law" (media release, Australian Festival of Light, January 30, 1981).

Here's another definition, this time from the Australian Family Association's Aims and Objects, 1993–1994: "The family ... is composed essentially of a father, mother, and children; in a wider but still necessary relationship, of grandparents, grandchildren, aunts, uncles; a kinship group of human beings linked by ties of blood, marriage, and adoption, structured to bear and rear children, to care for the young, the sick, and the old and other human needs ... The family is the basic unit on which human societies are built and is the prime agency for the total development of children, i.e. the transmission of moral, ethical, and cultural values, and for the ongoing social and emotional support for all its members. Its natural purpose is to serve as the chief functioning mechanism for the primary delivery of social services in the fields of nurture, education, health, and welfare ..."

A more liberal definition would include most primary intimate groups of people: one or more individuals who have responsibility for and care of one or more children or dependants.

The Australian Anglican Church's Social Responsibilities Commission, in its "Manifesto for the Family 1985," suggested a middle course: "[Family is] one or two adults and one or more children. The church is not primarily concerned with maintaining a particular form of family as the only right form."

Conservatives preach that the relationship between religion, morality, and the family is a very close one: contempt for the family goes hand in hand with contempt for religion and traditional morality. But it could be argued that the family as the basic unit of society is not simply a product of a particular set of religious and moral values. It is the basic social unit in all cultures, regardless of religious beliefs. Indeed, family seems to be more carefully protected in certain non-Christian societies in Asia and Africa than in the so-called "Christian" societies of the West.

Conservatives like to call themselves "pro-family" and are suspicious of government competence to "interfere" with the family; governments tend to aggravate problems rather than solve them. They urge governments to return to "family values" and provide tax relief for families. The political left, on the other hand, identifies more readily with such groups as the unemployed, single mothers, street kids, homosexuals, feminists, and so on. As a Christian I am both sympathetic to and suspicious of some aspects of these extreme views.

Since Cain and Abel we have bemoaned the decline in family life. I believe there were no "good old days" when people were more Christian than today: at times when the family was a "stable" institution we discriminated more against minority groups. "Protect me and mine and my mortgage" can be the ultimate middle-class renunciation of wider social responsibilities. Right-wing reactionary conservatism is often selfish: many who call for a return to "family values" are loudest in calling a halt to the immigration of refugees, for example. These same people are not as clamant about more support for unmarried parents, the elderly, singles, or the homeless. And we can't turn the clock back to a simple, pre-industrial, agrarian communalism.

On balance, however, I am more nervous when left-wing radicals attack traditional values. God has given us some instructions about home and family life, and we ignore them at our peril. It is no accident that social dislocation, homelessness, and crime on the streets increase when home life is fragmented.

Every family is affected by actions of government, and we probably need a "family impact report" for every piece of government legislation. One study at the George Washington University in the late 1970s identified 268 programs administered by seventeen Federal departments and agencies that had potential impact on families (*Newsweek*, May 15, 1978, p. 37)! So definitions are important. They affect our laws and our lives.

Selected Quotations

The word "family" entered the English language in the fourteenth century from the Latin words *familia*, "household" and *famulus*, "servant." Until the mid-seventeenth century, its usage was divided between notions of co-residence (members of a household not necessarily related by ties of blood or marriage), and kinship (persons related by blood or marriage but not necessarily living together). Between the seventeenth and nineteenth centuries these usages were amalgamated and the dominant meaning of family came to be a small kin group living in the same house ...

In the 1980s the growth of informal cohabitation and ex-nuptial births led the Australian Bureau of Statistics to incorporate unmarried couples and ex-nuptial children in their definition of family. At the same time new reproductive technology forced legal refinements of the definition, with unprecedented evaluation of the relative significance of egg, sperm, womb and post-natal care.

MICHAEL GILDING,
The Making and Breaking of the Australian Family, Sydney: Allen & Unwin, 1991, p. 3.

The family ... is not an individual living by himself or herself. It is not a group of individual single people, unrelated to each other, sharing an apartment. The family ... is one or two adults living together with one or more children and committed to their care and protection. The children may be connected by blood, adoption, or other arrangement, but the adults are committed to them.

ALAN NICHOLS,
Families – Top Priority for Government, Canberra: Acorn Press, 1986, p. 7.

The only function of the family that continues to survive all change is the provision of affection and emotional support by and to all its members, particularly infants and young children. Specialized institutions now perform many of the other functions that were once performed by the agrarian family: economic production, education, religion, and recreation. Jobs are usually separate from the family group; family members often work in different occupations and in locations away from the home. Education is provided by the state or by private groups. Religious training and recreational activities are available outside the home, although both still have a place in family life. The family is still responsible for the socialization of children. Even in this capacity, however, the influence of peers and of the mass media has assumed a large role.

Family composition in industrial societies has changed dramatically. The average number of children born to a woman in the U.S., for example, fell from 7.00 in 1800 to 2.00 by the early 1990s. Consequently, the number of years separating the births of the youngest and oldest children has declined. This has occurred in conjunction with increased longevity. In earlier times, marriages normally dissolved through the death of a spouse before the youngest child left home. Today husbands and wives generally have about as many years together after the children leave home as before ...

IDA HARPER SIMPSON,
"Family (sociology)," Microsoft (R) *Encarta Encyclopedia*, Copyright © 1993 Microsoft Corporation. Copyright © 1993 Funk & Wagnall's Corporation.

We are living under threat in this country. The threat defines itself more clearly every day: the foundations of our traditional social order are breaking up because we are losing faith in each other and in our traditional systems. Life in any society has to be built on trust: trust in each other, trust in … the law, trust in the value of our money, the security of our savings and the honesty of those we pay to administer them. These are the currencies of our lives, the symbols of our mutual dependence. Without them we become like beasts in a jungle preying upon each other for simple survival.

MORRIS WEST,
"The Sunburnt Country: broke, bewildered, besieged," *The Bulletin*,
January 25–February 1, 1994, p. 26.

A Prayer

Dear Lord and Father of all humankind, we acknowledge that you are both our master and our friend. You are our primary nurturer in a heartless world, our guide for responsible living, and our security in times of danger.

We are glad to belong to an earthly family and to your eternal family. We are nourished by the bonds of love shared by those in our families. Help us to honor every member of our families – the young and the old, the secure and the insecure, the strong and the weak, the clever and the not-so-clever, those who are easy to get along with and the difficult ones. May we keep growing into spiritual and emotional maturity. May we both delight in our own specialness as unique individuals, and honor the uniqueness of others.

Remind us that every person is very important to you and therefore should be important to us.

May we nourish relationships with both "like" and "unlike" people in our home and church families. And as we love our families – your families – may you grow in us.

For this and all your loving and good gifts we give you thanks. Amen.

A Benediction

And now may God the Father of us all, Jesus the Savior who was a special friend of children, and the Holy Spirit our guide and counselor, strengthen you and encourage you in this exciting and dangerous quest of exploring your life with others. Amen.

CAPSULE 2: How Governments Affect Families

As the twentieth century marches to a close, it will be remembered for many things by future generations. Perhaps the most loathsome historical fact will be that our century witnessed the creation of the most bloodthirsty totalitarian governments in world history.

These all-powerful governments, from Communism to Nazism, and from Idi Amin in Uganda to Pol Pot in Cambodia, tolerated no private area of life. As Mussolini put it, "Everything for the state. Nothing against the state. Nothing outside the state."

History is replete with despots, but few can rival the totalitarian leaders, from Stalin to Hitler, who sought to fold every aspect of life into the government sphere, and who treated men and women as mere pieces of dust to be crushed and reformed in their own images.

It is not surprising that every totalitarian movement of the twentieth century has not only tried to destroy the individual, but also to destroy the family – to make it a mere bureau of government. All modern totalitarian movements have tried to substitute the power of the state for the rights, responsibilities, and authority of the family. Strong families can stand against the aggression of government and protect the individual, but not without a struggle.

When all power flows to a government, with no mediating institutions between government and the individual, the result has been disaster and tragedy. In fact, in this century of bloody wars, totalitarian governments have killed more of their own people for political reasons than all the soldiers killed in all the wars of this century combined.

Often the first area of conflict between the family and gargantuan government has been over the control of children. In the United States we have seen the tendency to let government assume more responsibility for, and power over, children, even while parental rights and authority have eroded. If this trend continues, I am convinced it will be our greatest mistake as a nation!

Adolf Hitler understood instinctively how important it would be for the "Thousand Year Reich" to control the children. He said, "When an opponent declares, 'I will not come over to your side,' I calmly say, 'Your child belongs to me already ... what are you? You will pass on. Your descendants, however, now stand in the new camp. In a short time they will know nothing else but this new community.' "

JAMES DOBSON and GARY L. BAUER,
Children at Risk: Winning the Battle for the Hearts and Minds of Your Children,
Dallas: Word Publishing, 1990, pp. 97–98.

By reading the press and monitoring the media, it has been possible, I think, to identify a host of objectives that might be called "the family agenda of the left." Listed below are their goals as I perceive them.

• Convince the public that the training and development of children are far too important to be left to the whims and errors of parents. Only child-development authorities and professionals, commissioned by the government, can do the job properly. Mothers and fathers must yield control to those who are better equipped for the task of raising children. • Propagandize heavily against the use of corporal punishment as a disciplinary measure with children. Equate it with child abuse, even when administered judiciously by loving parents. Ultimately, secure legislation to outlaw the practice. • Continually emphasize an exhaustive list of "children's rights," which will provide wedges to separate kids from their parents. • Provide mandatory schooling for every four-year-old, so that young minds can be controlled. This will be accomplished first through government-sponsored childcare centres. Once established with federal funds, they should eventually drive unassisted church-based facilities out of competition. • Teach students that gay and lesbian lifestyles are no less moral than heterosexual relationships, and that they typically involve long-term monogamous commitments. Teach girls that it is just as appropriate to fall in love and have intimate relationships with another girl as with a boy (and do the same for boys). Design counseling programs for gay and lesbian students that will permit subtle recruitment services ... • Require churches, businesses, and schools to hire gays, lesbians, and others who contradict their faith. • Promote Gay-Pride celebrations in every American city, and seek equivalent legal status of families for homosexual and lesbian partners. • Expand the power of government and its bureaucracies to control every vestige of private life. • Increase the tax burden on families, forcing more women into the work force and their children into childcare facilities. • Make homemakers feel exploited, stupid and useless. Especially at the college and university level, ridicule female students who wish to marry, to have a family, or to postpone or avoid a career.

JAMES DOBSON AND GARY L. BAUER,
Children at Risk: Winning the Battle for the Hearts and Minds of Your Children,
Dallas: Word Publishing, 1990, pp. 59–60.

How then is government policy formulated these days? One of the most disturbing new trends is what I would call "government by public opinion poll." By this ... I mean the new trend of determining policy by testing through one of the commercial poll organisations what the public thinks of a particular issue, and then deciding that will be the policy ... This new style of "government by public opinion poll" is I feel regrettable. In the first place, it relies too heavily on public opinion gained in a way which may be misleading ... But secondly, it assumes that governments follow public opinion rather than lead it. This is most regressive in my view, for we must all fall then to the lowest common denominator of public policy, appealing to the worst and most selfish elements in human nature and pitting various interest groups against one another. And so we have the unwholesome scene of pensioners vying with farmers for a slice of the economic cake.

Not that I object to governments finding out what the public thinks about an issue, by some objective means. Nor do I object to every sector of the community making their own bid for popular support ...

Governments should in my opinion govern. That is what we elect them to do. That is what we want them to do. And that involves leadership from the front, standing on moral and social principle, not lagging behind some perception of what the public approve or disapprove of.

ALAN NICHOLS,
Families – Top Priority for Government, Canberra: Acorn Press, 1986, pp. 15–18.

[There are] three prevailing national responses to the trend of family fragmentation:
• Deny the problem
• Treat the symptoms
• Change the economy ...

If the family remains the crucible in which individual autonomy and freedom are encouraged and shaped, albeit in some instances imperfectly, then concern for policies that support family must be a key element of democratic liberalism. Conversely, policies that undermine families, reduce their independence and encourage their reliance upon the state ultimately threaten democracy itself ...

Preventive support services need to be a responsible government's priority ... Yet expenditure on prevention is minuscule compared to remedial programs.

KEVIN ANDREWS,
Liberal MHR, in the Melbourne *Age*, November 4, 1993, p. 15.

The Commission believes that the survival and prosperity of Australia as a nation depend on the survival and prosperity of its families. Australia is not reproducing itself, and the structure of its tax system is clearly biased against investment by couples raising the future generations of Australians. The decline over many years in the economic recognition of the family by successive governments through changes in the Australian tax and social security systems has subjected all types of families, especially sole parent, low income and large families, to increasing hardships, both financial and social. Families do not exist to serve the economy. The family is and ought to be the means by which families support themselves and support each other. Living standards of Australians have fallen over many years. The high cost of housing, escalating costs of raising children, unemployment, separation and divorce, and increasing tax burdens have contributed to the deteriorating economic position of the family ... It is inequitable that those with lesser ability to pay tax, because they have the moral and legal obligation to support dependants, should be taxed on the same basis as those who have no dependants to support. The Commission opposes any Government policy that would expect both spouses to be in paid employment in order for the family to be self-sufficient. A fair and just tax system should be based on the ability of the taxpayer to pay, that is, it should take into consideration the number of dependants that are supported by the taxpayer.

Australian Catholic Social Welfare Commission, *A Fair Go for Families*,
Blackburn, Vic.: Collins Dove, 1989, pp. 64–65.

Dr Alan Tapper, author of *The Family in the Welfare State* ..., says that two-parent families [in Australia] pay more in their taxes than they receive in benefits, and families with children now get by on an equivalent income three-fifths that of the rest of the population. He shows that the largest contributions to tax come from young married couples with children under five years of age. This explains in part why so many young couples cannot afford to have children or lose the second income in the household.

MARRIANNE CROWE,
"Empowering the Family," *The Australian Family*, Quarterly Journal of the Australian
Family Association, Vol. 13, No. 3, September 1992, p. 19.

5 | Families are not yet obsolete!

Then the Lord God said, "It is not good that the man should be alone; I will make him a helper as his partner." God blessed them, and God said to them, "Be fruitful and multiply, and fill the earth and subdue it; and have dominion over the fish of the sea and over the birds of the air and over every living thing that moves upon the earth." Now the man knew his wife Eve, and she conceived and bore Cain, saying, "I have produced a man with the help of the Lord" (Genesis 2:18, 1:28, 4:1).

Whoever does not provide for relatives, and especially for family members, has denied the faith and is worse than an unbeliever. If any believing woman has relatives who are really widows, let her assist them; let the church not be burdened, so that it can assist those who are real widows (1 Timothy 5:8, 16).

A wise child makes a glad father, but the foolish despise their mothers. Listen to your father who begot you, and do not despise your mother when she is old (Proverbs 15:20, 23:22). Love one another with mutual affection; outdo one another in showing honor (Romans 12:10).

A few years ago in Melbourne two homeless young people sleeping in a large industrial waste disposal bin woke to find themselves being tipped into a compactor unit behind a truck. The driver heard their screams and managed to pull one of them to safety. The other died under the waste …

Why were they homeless?

All the studies show the majority of people are still in favor of marriage, but younger people want more independence and freedom within it. Most women are not content any longer to see their primary roles in terms of "raising the kids and helping hubby with his job." An Australian Institute of Family Studies survey (1991) found that eighty percent of women and seventy percent of men wanted to maintain a sense of "independence" in intimate relationships. Indeed, thirty-eight percent of women said that if they could not continue to grow as an individual in the relationship, they should not stay in it. A lower thirty-two percent of men said they would opt out of a stifling relationship.

Men are having to adjust to the increasing number of options open to women, particularly in terms of opportunities for a wider variety of jobs and further education. Women are saying, more fervently as each decade passes, "I too have needs and rights." And men also have more options. For example, they can be a "househusband" rather than the sole breadwinner. Certainly personal development by adults is a good thing, but the net result is that in Western families children are less important than they used to be.

Relating to a mate and running a home are two of the most complicated tasks humans undertake – with very little, if any, training. And it's getting harder. In the last few centuries, the major function of the family has shifted from that of economic survival to emotional sustenance. In the last few decades, marked shifts in values have certainly contributed to the liberation of individuals, but they have also eroded the resilience of the family to handle crises. Whereas couples used to expect marriage to provide economic support, security, and social status, now they are seeking rather the satisfaction of their personal and emotional needs.

The foundation of our society is in the family. If the foundation is weak here, society crumbles. As goes the family, so goes the nation. A nation of secure families will see this solidarity reflected in crime statistics. A happy family will provide the basis for an individual to be secure. The most important thing we can do for the next generation is not only to reduce the debt they will inherit, or leave them a cleaner earth, but to help them, through healthy and happy family life, to become better-put-together people than their parents were.

Historically, families are the primary "socializing" contexts. In families children learn their identity, what the culture's important values are, and how to accept responsibility in such matters as work and sex. In families we learn to relate meaningfully to others, and to respect others' privacy and property. The family is the only department of health, education, and welfare that works: moral values learned in the family setting cannot be adequately duplicated in any other way.

A roof over one's head doesn't necessarily provide a family. Rather "home and family" is living in the mind of someone else who cares for you. Family, ideally, is an experience of selflessness, where love is absolute and limitless. Family is where those who can give love give it, and those who need love receive it.

Three general principles about the family can be found in the Bible. (1) Marriage and family are human institutions, but ordained by God. (2) Sex is "good" because it is also ordained by God, designed for both procreation and pleasure within a legally constituted marriage. (3) Women and men have equal dignity, and different divinely ordained roles in marriage and family life.

Over the centuries, at least four major cultural emphases have influenced how we think about these three principles. First, the Bible gives us, side-by-side, two models of how men and women relate: a patriarchal model, dominant in most of the world for most of history, and an egalitarian model, exemplified by Christ's teaching and relationships and inherent in the apostolic understanding of the good news breaking down old hierarchies (Galatians 3:28). Second, Augustine and later Catholic tradition tended to regard sex as primarily for procreation, and sometimes as a "necessary evil." Third, notions of romantic love entered the scene from the sixteenth century. Fourth, modern individualism sees sex and family as means of self-expression.

Over recent centuries, many functions of the traditional family – from teaching skills and developing work habits to instilling approved social values, from care of the sick to support of the poor, from preparation of food to instruction in leisure activities – have passed out of the home into the hands of institutions and professional providers. The authority of the father is now shared by teachers, doctors, social welfare workers, and other "experts"; mothers tend to find leisure and vocational interests outside the home (but surveys show the majority of men and women would prefer mothers to stay at home while the children are small).

What is highly disturbing is that you are more likely to be hit, physically injured or killed in your own home, by a member of your own family, than anywhere else or by anyone else. Family feuds account for thirty-six percent of all murders in Australia. A Catholic priest in a downtown area in the English city of Liverpool no longer dares to preach on the "ideal family," because of the number of suicides and cases of depression likely to follow such an attempt.

Selected Quotations

If the family fails then all the other institutions of society will fail. The family is that basic unit of society which undergirds all else. Every influence which weakens the family and makes it more difficult for it to do its job will ultimately weaken society. All that is done to build strong, healthy, happy and effective families will increase the possibility of a strong and healthy society. Any effort to deal with the problems we face without dealing with their roots within the family is shortsighted.

KENNETH CHAFFIN,
Is There A Family In the House?, Minneapolis: World Wide Publications, 1978, p. 15.

Hollywood no longer reflects – or even respects – the values of most American families. On many of the important issues in contemporary life, popular entertainment seems to go out of its way to challenge conventional notions of decency. For example:

- Our fellow citizens cherish the institution of marriage and consider religion an important priority in life; but the entertainment industry promotes every form of sexual adventurism and regularly ridicules religious believers as crooks or crazies.
- In our private lives, most of us deplore violence and feel little sympathy for the criminals who perpetrate it; but movies, TV and popular music all revel in graphic brutality, glorifying vicious and sadistic characters who treat killing as a joke ...

- Nearly all parents want to convey to their children the importance of self-discipline, hard work, and decent manners; but the
  entertainment media celebrate vulgar behavior, contempt for all
  authority, and obscene language – which is inserted even in
  "family fare" where it is least expected.

MICHAEL MEDVED,
Hollywood vs. America, New York: HarperCollins, 1992, p. 10.

We know now what some of the goals are in the proper development
and implementation of a national public policy for families and
children – • families should be given every chance to lead a decent
life according to their chosen values; no family in Australia should be
permitted to fall below the Poverty Line; • every child deserves both
economic and emotional security. If this can be gained through one
caring parent rather than through two conflicting ones, support
should be available to suit the circumstances; • parents should be
taught how to educate their future citizens; it cannot be left to
chance, and we cannot presume parental competence; • any interference on the part of public authorities in family matters should be
demonstrably necessary; the onus must be on the authorities, not on
the families, to show their actions are not harmful and they are
clearly beneficial; • families must have the power to make decisions
over their own lives, and in the context of their local communities,
and this power should not be taken away and given to experts; • the
family should not be seen as an isolated unit, but as always being
inextricably linked to broader communities.

ALAN NICHOLS,
Families – Top Priority for Government, Canberra: Acorn Press, 1986, pp. 65–66.

According to one recent analysis, many of our perceptions about
family life have come from some widely accepted but largely inac-
curate myths about marriage and the family. These myths influence
our behavior, affect our marriages, and often are carried into counseling without anyone ever acknowledging their existence.

Myth #1. Families and marriages in the past were more stable,
better adjusted, and happier than they are today. Most of us have a
tendency to idealize the past ... We fail to realize that desertion by

spouses, child beating, sexual unfaithfulness, marital failure, and harassment in the home were common in the past (even though they were more often hidden) just as they are common now ...

Myth #2. There are firm boundaries between the family and the rest of life. This has been called "the myth of separate worlds." It assumes that the family is a freestanding, independent, self sufficient entity that is not much affected by social pressures, the economy, politics, relatives, the places where family members work, the values portrayed by the media, or the policies of government ...

Myth #3. There is a typical ... Christian family. This "myth of the monolithic family form" assumes that we know what the family is supposed to look like. Often this typical family picture is drawn from our images of families in the past, or from books, observations of our own parents, sermons, popular lectures, or even the speeches of politicians. Many tend to assume, for example, that the typical family is middle class, monogamous, with a father who works to provide for the family and a mother who stays at home, children who go to neighborhood schools, grandparents who are nearby and supportive, with each family living in a single family house.

Myth #4. All families have similar experiences. This is the assumption that all family members have common needs, common interests, and common backgrounds. Many of the problems that couples bring to counseling are because the husband, wife, or other family members have very different expectations for their families and bring different experiences to their family problems ...

Myth #5. Most baby boomers have little commitment to marriage, marital harmony, sexual fidelity, and effective parenting ... This myth is far from the truth. The divorce boom of the late sixties and early seventies appears to be on the decline. With increased interest in their families, baby boomers are giving greater attention to marriage, relationship building, parenting skills, and what has come to be known as "cocooning."

MAXINE BACA ZINN and C. STANLEY EITSEN,
Diversity in Families, New York: HarperCollins, 1990, excerpts pp. 9–20.

Evidence of the fact that families pass on success and failure is found in the history of divorce in families. I collected the family histories of 2,000 students at the University, getting the marital histories of the grandparents, parents, and aunts and uncles. The study revealed that if neither set of grandparents had divorced, only fifteen percent of their children had divorced; if one set of grandparents had divorced, twenty-four percent of their children had divorced; but if both sets of grandparents had divorced, thirty-eight percent of their children had divorced. Other studies have shown a very close relationship between the failure of parents in marriage and failure of their children in marriage.

JUDSON LANDIS,
"The Family and Social Change: A Positive View," a lecture in the University of California's symposium on "The Family's Search for Survival," San Francisco, 1964, p. 5.

Economic factors affecting families include • increases in the rate and duration of unemployment; • increasing proportion of the population reliant on below the poverty line unemployment benefits; • Aboriginal people bear a disproportionate burden of unemployment; • sole parent families have become increasingly reliant on inadequate social security payments because of a lack of access to employment; • increases in the proportion of the population reliant on social security incomes; • declines in real disposable incomes of families with children; • high housing costs; • increased participation by women in the workforce.

Heart and Hearth: families and shelter consultancy report No. 5,
International Project on Family and Community, Australia, May 1987, pp. 12–13.

The question of whether the family is a safe place for women and children has to be asked and answered, particularly by the church which has placed so much emphasis on the sacrament of marriage and on family life … Confronted with cases of women and children exposed to danger in their homes, fear of violating the sacrament of marriage and the ideal of Christian family life has often paralyzed the churches into inactivity. Both church and community have turned a blind eye to the reality of such situations on the pretext that no one has the right to interfere in a couple's private life.

ARUNA GNANADASON,
No Longer A Secret, Geneva: WCC Publications, 1993, p. 44.

For me, no family that destroys women and maims children can be tolerated; it cannot be supported when it grants men the right to destroy and maim. If crime happens in the family – and the evidence proves it does – then the family promoting it must be ended. No one desiring peace, order and good government, love, tenderness and care can tolerate any abuse meted out on women, children – or, for that matter, men. Governments promoting the "family life" revealed in analyses of the family in law and society today are deliberately promoting crime. And they are promoting crime against the very unit they allegedly hold so dear: the Australian family.

JOCELYNNE SCUTT,
Even in the Best of Homes, Melbourne: Penguin Books, 1983, p. 7.

One night during the Middle Ages, two warriors in armor were riding along, each thinking there was no one else for miles around. They happened upon each other at a particularly dark spot. Both were startled and each misinterpreted the movements of the other as gestures of hostility. So they began to fight, each believing he was under attack and must defend himself. The conflict grew more intense until one knight finally succeeded in unhorsing the other. Then, with one mighty effort, he drove his lance through the fallen man's heart. The victor dismounted and limped over to the adversary he had just killed. He pulled back the face mask, and there to his horror, in the pale moonlight, he recognized his own brother! He had mistaken a kinsman for an enemy and had destroyed him!

JOHN R. CLAYPOOL,
Opening Blind Eyes, Oak Park, Ill.: Meyer Stone Books, 1987, p. 103.

Movies and television programs tend to portray families as either delightfully benign "Ozzie and Harrietisms" or centers for continual family conflict. Most families in movies, plays, novels, or soap operas are either a mess, and the source of endless conflict and tragedy, or a mirage of perfectly peaceful and delightfully benign daily living. Somewhere in between is where most of our families really live. Few of the heroes and heroines of our media are family people. The "real" movie hero has long ago left his parents. He saves the town or the ranch, is tempted to settle down, but is naturally driven by the need for freedom and rides off on a horse, for whom he shows more concern than for the people around him. A potential love looks wistfully at his back as the almost always male hero rides into the sunset. The message is clear. Women can stay on the ranch with the family, where the skies are not cloudy all day, while the almost always male hero goes out to start and fight new wars. The family means female submission to what must be done to keep the family going, and freedom from family means adventure and hero status for the male, who may drop in on one of his several families once in a while. The television family situation comedy is often about a father's futile and comic attempt to keep some semblance of order and control over "his" household while he tries to carry on in his "real" work, his career. The wife is seen as guardian of the family, a stable and mature officer in charge of supplies, cleaning, and caring. If she has a career, she is expected to add this work to her family obligations.

PAUL E. PEARSALL,
The Power of the Family, Garden City, New York: Doubleday, 1990. p. 9.

A Prayer

Lord, today/tonight our minds roam around the world – your world – as we pray for people in families and communities everywhere. Bring peace to those who live with domestic discord and among warring peoples. Be the special friend of women and children in violent homes; and bring comfort to women and girls raped in war zones. Feed the hungry, house the homeless, clothe the naked: and do some of these ministries through our family. We pray for women everywhere, who carry the greater burden of fostering and maintaining family life. We pray for mothers in poor villages and communities, many of whose skills will never be fully developed, and some of whom will die in childbirth because of inadequate medical help. And we pray for men and fathers: may they see their roles as much in the home and family as in the public sphere. Comfort those who are finding it very difficult to provide food for their families and pay the bills ...

Lord, we pray for families and communities that are coming apart because people have not been able to get along. For homes fractured by separation and divorce; for single parents battling against huge financial and emotional odds to keep their families together; for parents of angry young people in trouble with the law; for those in prison and for their relatives; for some who minister selflessly to the sick and dying. Lord, be especially close to these who struggle sometimes to see meaning and purpose in their lives.

Bless those individuals and groups that feel marginalized and have difficulty coping – indigenous tribal people who have been victimized by the superior power of those who invaded their ancestral lands; the mentally ill, who languish in painful loneliness in institutions and in their own private worlds; the physically disabled, for whom otherwise simple tasks are very difficult; those who are chronically ill and perhaps near death.

Lord, guide our governments and leaders as they make policy dealing with social security, taxation, housing, health, education, and family law.

Lord, you feel the pain of your children. Help us to feel it too, and do what we can to lessen the pain of someone, somewhere.

For your love's sake. Amen.

A Benediction
May Jesus Christ who befriended the poor and healed the sick; who preached good news and opposed injustice; who enjoyed family life and the fellowship of female and male friends; who sorrowed with the grieving and laughed with partygoers; enable you to do in your world what he did in his. For his glory. Amen.

CAPSULE 3: Why Families?

THE FAMILY offers us a place to belong. A true home is the place, the people, where you are welcome at any time. An effective family is where each member accepts some responsibility for the welfare of all the other members.

THE FAMILY is where intimacy is experienced. Belonging to a loving family offers love, warmth, affection, shared concerns and interests – through the whole of our lives.

THE FAMILY is the basic unit of society. It is our culture's main unit for passing on important values, for economic security, for personal nurture and support.

THE FAMILY is where children are loved into maturity. Here they develop the basic skills and attitudes for successful living. They learn that they are special and unique, and are free to become the creative, fulfilled people God intended them to be.

THE FAMILY gives us our identity. You tell people who you are by giving them your name – Bill Smith, Mary Brown – the name you derived from the Smith or Brown family.

SOURCE UNKNOWN.

6

How do happy families get to be that way?

Let the peoples praise you, O God; let all the peoples praise you. The earth has yielded its increase; God, our God, has blessed us (Psalm 67:5–6).

We do not live to ourselves, and we do not die to ourselves (Romans 14:7). How very good and pleasant it is when kindred live together in unity! (Psalm 133:1).

Likewise, tell the older women to be reverent in behavior, not to be slanderers or slaves to drink; they are to teach what is good (Titus 2:3). Let deacons be married only once, and let them manage their children and their households well (1 Timothy 3:12). At the same hour of the night he took them and washed their wounds; then he and his entire family were baptized without delay (Acts 16:33).

With all humility and gentleness, with patience, bearing with one another in love, making every effort to maintain the unity of the Spirit in the bond of peace (Ephesians 4:2–3). Let your father and mother be glad; let her who bore you rejoice (Proverbs 23:25).

So, whether you eat or drink, or whatever you do, do everything for the glory of God (1 Corinthians 10:31). And my God will fully satisfy every need of yours according to his riches in glory in Christ Jesus (Philippians 4:19).

I pray that, according to the riches of his glory, he may grant that you may be strengthened in your inner being with power through his Spirit, and that Christ may dwell in your hearts through faith, as you are being rooted and grounded in love. I pray that you may have the power to comprehend, with all the saints, what is the breadth and length and height and depth, and to know the love of Christ that surpasses knowledge, so that you may be filled with all the fullness of God (Ephesians 3:16–19). For we now live, if you continue to stand firm in the Lord (1 Thessalonians 3:8).

Families are fundamental to a healthy society. There is no greater gift than to be in a close, loving family. Families are the laboratories where all the components for living are mixed into a nurturing or a volatile brew. They are the place we learn who we are, where and whether we belong, whether we have significance and competence. By the age of two children begin to talk to and treat others as they have seen the Big People do it. That's scary! As someone put it, "Sometimes in a modern home the TV set is better adjusted than the kids!"

A good analogy is that of the symphony orchestra. Successful family living means that each player has his or her own unique instrument to play, and special skills with which to do it, but everyone has to subordinate their individual virtuosity so that the whole symphony is played with a beautiful harmony. But sometimes there will be a concerto for "solo instrument and orchestra," and the other performers will join the audience in the applause!

In happy families:

- Parents realize the best thing they can do for children is to love each other, show affection, and listen carefully to each other. The way parents relate is the single most powerful socializing factor in any child's history.
- "Blood is thicker than water" (or, as the Spanish version goes, "An ounce of blood is worth more than a pound of friendship"). In

happy families there is strong emotional support in times of crisis. Remember Robert Frost's famous line: "Home is the place where, when you have to go there, they have to take you in."

- Who makes what decisions is clear. "Authority" is a matter of firm, gentle strength, but is increasingly shared with children as they grow older. An ancient Chinese proverb says, "Govern a family as you would cook a small fish – very gently."

- The policy of "being helpful" takes precedence over "doing your own thing." You often hear, "What can I do to help?" Fathers and mothers teach their children practical skills, like personal hygiene, cooking, fixing things, cleaning, gardening, how a car works.

- There's laughter and games and jokes (but not at the expense of the sensitive members).

- "What is mine" and "what is ours" is clear, but in the best families there is more in the latter category! Everyone has a little place to call their own, but too much "split-level isolation" isn't encouraged.

- Everyone submits to appropriate social disciplines. This extends from conforming to a tidiness regimen, to keeping the volume of one's music down (that is, you don't invade others' space either visually or auditorally).

- Dinnertime is special most nights. Turn the TV off (videotape anything important, like the evening news); put on your phone-answering system. Say or sing grace. Allow each person to talk about their day. Have a few rules: when one is talking others listen; no quarrels, no ridicule; be consoling if someone spills something. As the kids grow older, have some passionate discussions – about world events, life's great questions, what's good/bad about your country, their school, and so on.

- Sexual behavior is regulated. Happy families are not prudish, but they are not "exhibitionistic" either. Adults, in my view, should keep overtly sexual behavior private. And each child is privileged to have some privacy.

- People are allowed to "be themselves." Parents don't have to succeed vicariously through their children's performances. In happy families everyone wins. And the family itself doesn't have to anxiously grade itself for performance either.

Happy families are possible but they don't just happen. They are the product of selfless hard work, disciplined loving, and a lot of patience. Yours can be one of them.

Selected Quotations

Some form of family meets a basic human need for relationships with other people who care. Despite bitter revilement by some and interesting experiments in alternative ways of living by others, nobody ... has yet come up with a long-term alternative that works. Families are important because they provide people with a sense of personal identity and with other people whose basic concern can be taken for granted.

PENELOPE LEACH,
Who Cares?, Harmondsworth, Middlesex: Penguin Books, 1979, pp. 12–13.

What is a family, anyhow? I think the family is two things: a nest, and an altar. Nest building is our best hope of trying to perpetuate the species, and to defend ourselves from going mad in the world's chaos. The family is also the altar at which human beings worship their own archetypes, and offer up sacrifices of themselves – from Abraham to Mrs Portnoy.

SHANA ALEXANDER,
"The Silence of the Louds," *Newsweek*, January 22, 1973, p. 34.

Families are the building blocks of a strong society because family is the strongest factor influencing human development and competence.

We know what are the characteristics that distinguish families who build human competence from the families who undermine and destroy competence and confidence, and these factors all relate to the way family members relate to one another and to the outside world. Families create social capital, that is why they are vital.

Let us look for a moment at some of the evidence of the impact of families on human growth and development.

Family outweighs any other factor in influencing intellectual growth and development, success in schooling, mental and physical health, social awareness and responsibility, moral growth, social skills.

Families mediate social stresses to individuals, and have an amazing power to ameliorate or exacerbate socially induced stress.

Families have a strong impact on the economic viability of family members.

MOIRA EASTMAN,
"Families – the Building Blocks of a Strong Society," in *The Australian Family*, Quarterly Journal of the Australian Family Association, Vol. 12, No. 4, December 1991, pp. 23–24.

[There are] seven characteristics of a functioning family: 1. It has a legitimate source of authority, established and supported over time. Mother and father have the right to make the rules, and the children have the right to be heard. Families cease to function when parents abdicate their role and give their parental work to one or more of the children. It is especially difficult if one parent forms an alliance with the children against the other parent. 2. It consistently operates on a stable rule system. Families need consistent structure. Children and adults function best when family guidelines are clear and fair to all. Difficulties arise when rapid or unexpected changes take place. 3. All members are affirmed, loved and appreciated. No human being can have a quality existence without being nurtured. This is the "stuff" of which relationships are made. 4. It has effective and stable child-rearing practices. Strange as it may seem, few people are born with all the knowledge necessary to rear children. Stranger still, each child is unique, and each family system different. There has to be constant upgrading, relearning and adapting. But this principle does not conflict with the need to have a consistent approach that recognises the dignity of each family member. 5. It works at maintaining the marriage. Many parents feel that they need to invest the major portion of their nervous energy in their children. But the most important relationship needs maintenance and nurture. 6. It has a set of goals to which the family and each member works. This calls for making decisions together, cooperating and supporting each other. But cohesion does not mean conformity, and unity does not mean uniformity. 7. It is adaptable enough to accommodate normal developmental challenges as well as unexpected crises. Each year brings the family to a new stage in its development. Children grow and mature. Family practices that worked for juniors will not work for teenagers. And the types of intimacies that satisfied the newly married may not be sufficient for the more mature.

R.J. and D.S. BECVAR,
Systems Theory and Family Therapy, Lenham: University Press of America, 1982, p. 82.

Almost everyone belongs to a family, or at least has belonged to a family at some stage during their life. Sons and daughters, brothers and sisters, mothers and fathers, step-parents and siblings, in-laws, foster parents, live-ins and de factos, aunties and uncles, cousins, grandmothers and grandfathers, and even Godmothers and Godfathers, all contribute to that human patchwork quilt we call "family" ...

The family [is] a social institution: regulates sexual intercourse, assigns responsibility for children, conserves lines of descent, orders wealth and inheritance, assigns roles for the division of labour for everyday living, supports the roles of its members in the external economy, participates with other institutions (church, state, school, economy, mass communications, etc.) in the socialization of the coming generation, plays a role in the physical and psychological welfare of family members. "The family," understood as a special relationship between its members: contains voluntary members (parents) and involuntary members (children), forms and expresses the identity and character of all of its members, and can grow or decrease both naturally (birth and death) and socially (adoption, separation and divorce, remarriage). Families therefore are networks and not just households and change form, shape and content over time. People move in and out of relationships and change their status in existing relationships. Consequently families are continually being reconstituted ...

From the very beginning of life we are shaped by the strong and intimate attachments which form within our family. We receive our identification this way. We begin to grow personally in this environment. Our father, mother, brothers and sisters play an important role in this development, and the absence of any of these family members makes a difference. This is not to suggest that there is such a thing as an "optimal" family or a "deficit" family, since human beings are adaptable and flexible. But what is essential for all of us is the intimate, accepting and forgiving environment which we call "family."

ALAN NICHOLS, JOAN CLARKE, and TREVOR HOGAN,
Transforming Families and Communities: Christian Hope in a World of Change,
Sydney: AIO Press, 1987, pp. 5–6.

Social order is impossible unless the conduct of individuals is predictable. In human beings, predictability of conduct depends on the development of a stable character and of reliable habits. Everything we know about social psychology indicates that both have their origins in family life …

The family, today as always, remains the institution in which at any rate the very great majority of individuals learn whatever they will ever learn about morality. It is very unlikely that this will change. Once again, this means that the family has a political function of the greatest importance, especially in a democracy.

BRIGITTE and PETER BERGER,
The War Over the Family, New York: Anchor Press, 1983.
Quoted in *The Australian Family*, Vol. 13, No. 1, March 1992, p. 7.

One of the most persistent myths in our society is that the normal and healthy family does not experience problems and stress. This myth remains despite the fact that every significant study of the family demonstrates that the normal family does not always live in perfect harmony, does get ruffled at times, and does not always cooperate with one another. The difference between the healthy and destructive family is not the absence of problems but how those problems are seen and dealt with.

KENNETH CHAFFIN,
Is There a Family in the House?, Minneapolis: World Wide Publications, 1978, p. 31.

"Show us the Father," the disciples asked Jesus. Good families should do that, helping us to experience a loving God who understands our problems, who knows all about our sense of loss, rejection, powerlessness, the struggle to survive, who loves us as his own children.

The Bible is full of wisdom about family living. The creation ordinance is foundational (Genesis 2:24), but the Fall distorted family relationships (Genesis 3:16). Humans are made in the image of God – and we become more like God as we grow into loving, truthful, responsible people. Marriage and family are signs of God's love for his people. The Mosaic law was family-centered – for example, the prohibition of adultery and the command to honor parents. When God became one of us in Jesus Christ, he was born into a family and raised and cared for in that family (Luke 2:51–52). Jesus' followers, the apostles, affirm a stable family life within the family of the church (Ephesians 5:22–6:4); we are to care for members of our family (1 Timothy 5:8). Some who forbade marriage or encouraged extramarital sexual relations are strongly rebuked (1 Corinthians 7:2; 1 Timothy 4:3). Earth is the place where God wants us to bear the family likeness of his Son (Romans 8:28f), and heaven will be a grand family reunion, where we shall belong to a spiritual, eternal family rather than a biological family (Matthew 22:30).

ROWLAND CROUCHER,
excerpts from an unpublished sermon.

Prayers

Are we sensitive to others?

Does a teacher show his love for his students
by giving them the answers to their problems
for fear they'll make a mistake?

Does a mother show her love for her baby
by refusing to teach him to walk for fear he'll fall?

Does a father show his love for his son
by forbidding him to go out for fear he'll get into trouble?

We learn
to give, by receiving;
to love, by being loved;
to forgive, by being forgiven;
to tolerate, by being tolerated;
to accept, by being accepted …

I give you a new commandment:
love one another, just as I have loved you,
you must also love one another.

TERRY C. FALLA,
Be Our Freedom, Lord, Adelaide: Lutheran Publishing House, 1981/1987, pp. 342–344.

O God, from whom every family in heaven and on earth is named, the pattern of all parenthood, who rules in love as our Father and who, like a mother, nurtures and protects us, we worship you.

Give us a special gift of love for all in our families. As parents and children may we never graduate from the school of Christ.

Watch over all our loved ones this day and this night. May the angels assigned to each of them do a good job! Keep them safe from harm and danger; supply their material, emotional, and spiritual needs; guide them in your way; comfort them in sorrow; heal them in times of tension or bitterness; and bring each of them at last to your heavenly home.

We ask this of you, the life, the truth, the way. Amen.

A Benediction

May God, who created us as sexual beings and designed marriage, family, and community for our wholeness and the well-being of children, loved ones, and friends, make your home a colony of heaven. May his peace rule in your hearts; may his grace enable you to accept one another as you have been accepted; may his love empower you to serve and forgive others. For Christ's glory and our wholeness. Amen.

CAPSULE 4: Extended Families

I'm at airports frequently, and notice that when a crowd of people is farewelling someone they are almost always from a minority ethnic group. I believe we have lost something vital in highly industrialized countries, where we live further away (geographically and emotionally) from in-laws and others who can enrich our own family life. Surely it's time to re-tribalize, and the contemporary revolution in business towards a greater emphasis on information and service industries may be a bonus for the family. It has generated a "work-from-home revolution" (aided by faxes and modems): perhaps this will help us create the village community again. (However, a warning: I work principally with pastors, most of whom "work from home." These people are not necessarily "present" to any greater degree to their families simply because their study is under the same roof! You have to work hard to separate "work" from "family" in these contexts.)

The approach of this book is that no family can provide for all the needs of its members. The extended family rather than the nuclear family is the best model (and always has been). Let's work hard to bring surrogate extended families into being: every kid, for example, should have a "grandma" and "grandpa" who is or is not biologically related to them. Margaret Mead was right: we are expecting our nuclear families to do the impossible. The single mum up the road; the retired couple around the corner; the young boy trying to play cricket by himself; the latchkey kids across the street waiting until their parents come home after dark – we could form extended families in our own neighborhoods.

A study of sixty-four Australian families found that there are times when every family needs outside support. Two kinds of families – those of immigrants whose relatives were overseas and those in which the parents had grown up in unhappy homes – tended to suffer through inadequate access to others in an extended family group. Many families, preserving their autonomy, do not seek help when perhaps they should; others are overwhelmed with problems, and sink into apathy and passivity. (See Jean McCaughey, *A Bit of a Struggle: Coping with Family Life in Australia*, Fitzroy, Vic.: McPhee Gribble/Penguin Books, 1987, pp. 216–217, 226.)

Here's a quote I like from well-known Australian pro-family crusader Dr John Court: "The nuclear family is not the kind of family which will survive until 2000, nor indeed would I want to fight for it. It is the extended family which has a long history of stability and the backing of Christian teaching" (John Court, "The Family in the Year 2000," ANZAAS Symposium, University of Adelaide, August 1975, p. 2).

The local church is ideally placed to enrich family life. In chapter 22 we will look at some ways in which that can happen.

Think about this:

Even though the nuclear family will continue, the lessons of the commune should not be lost on the American family. Father should not be expected to be the lone, isolated source of male psychological support in the family. Children should not be brought up in rows of houses where nobody knows or cares about their neighbors. Nor should children deprived of their own father or mother be deprived of fathering or mothering in general.

Thus, we do not advocate communes, but we do advocate communities, complete with a firm sense of social-fathering and -mothering. Reestablishing the community of families might involve measures as diverse as a larger involvement in community social-fathering ... or even the revival of the old architectural concept of houses grouped around a town square. It would mean increasing the availability of block clubs, civic groups, and special-interest groups, and breaking society into geographical sub-groups to which the individual family can relate as a unit ... Above all, it would mean encouraging men to become aware that they have the power as fathers and as social fathers to keep the bonds between family and society strong (Henry Biller and Dennis Meredith, *Father Power*, New York: David McKay Co. Inc., 1974, p. 360).

7

The ten marks of a happy marriage

So God created humankind in his image, in the image of God he created them; male and female he created them (Genesis 1:27). And the rib that the Lord God had taken from the man he made into a woman and brought her to the man. Then the man said, "This at last is bone of my bones and flesh of my flesh; this one shall be called Woman, for out of Man this one was taken." Therefore a man leaves his father and his mother and clings to his wife, and they become one flesh (Genesis 2:22–24). For this reason a man shall leave his father and mother and be joined to his wife, and the two shall become one flesh (Matthew 19:5).

Let him kiss me with the kisses of his mouth! For your love is better than wine, your anointing oils are fragrant, your name is perfume poured out; therefore the maidens love you. Draw me after you, let us make haste ... We will exult and rejoice in you; we will extol your love more than wine; rightly do they love you (Song of Solomon 1:2–4).

Do you not know that wrongdoers will not inherit the kingdom of God? Do not be deceived! Fornicators, idolaters, adulterers, male prostitutes, sodomites, thieves, the greedy, drunkards, revilers, robbers – none of these will inherit the kingdom of God. And this is what some of you used to be. But you were washed, you were sanctified, you were justified in the name of the Lord Jesus Christ and in the Spirit of our God (1 Corinthians 6:9–11).

Let marriage be held in honor by all, and let the marriage bed be kept undefiled; for God will judge fornicators and adulterers (Hebrews 13:4). You shall not commit adultery (Exodus 20:14). You have heard that it was said, "You shall not commit adultery." But I say to you that everyone who looks at a woman with lust has already committed adultery with her in his heart (Matthew 5:27–28).

Wives, be subject to your husbands as you are to the Lord (Ephesians 5:22). Husbands, love your wives, just as Christ loved the church and gave himself up for her (Ephesians 5:25). In the same way, husbands should love their wives as they do their own bodies (Ephesians 5:28). Each of you, however, should love his wife as himself, and a wife should respect her husband (Ephesians 5:33).

You've probably heard the old saying about some marriages being made in heaven. Have you also heard the comment by a less starry-eyed wit: "Marriage is nature's way of preventing us fighting with strangers!"? Marriage is beautiful, fulfilling – and difficult.

After thirty-five years of marriage, and 11,000 hours of pastoral counseling, I've learned a lot about good and bad marriages. I've identified ten marks of a good marriage, which I share in this chapter, and ten myths about marriage, which I outline in the next. But first, here's my definition of marriage:

Marriage is a covenantal relationship between a man and a woman in an emotional, physical, moral, and spiritual union, exclusively and for life. The husband and wife take each other and forsake all others.

Marriage is not just an arrangement to clarify inheritance. It has been called a dramatic act in which two strangers come together to redefine themselves.

The ten marks of a happy marriage are as follows:

1. *Commitment.* Some couples like their wedding service to be traditional, others "freer." But three solemn declarations must be there somewhere: I am not married to anyone else; I take you to be my lawful wedded wife/husband; forsaking all others I will be lovingly committed to you for life.

When I counsel a couple before marriage, we talk about their vows (they usually compose their own). Some young people are wary of commitment and view marriage as a trap. But you can't have a satisfying marriage relationship without commitment – a commitment of one imperfect person to another imperfect person. Marriage is not simply a fifty-fifty affair: it's 100 percent give, both ways!

Commitment is more than an obligation to permanent residence or sexual fidelity. For Christians commitment is not just "being there year after year in the easy chair." It is more than a promise not to go away. It ought to include, above all, a commitment to grow, to become the persons God intended us to be. "Growing" couples set growth goals – to read a good book and discuss it; to go away every year on a retreat; to pray together; to do a course together. One couple said in their wedding vows: "In this marriage I want to grow as a person, I want to help you grow as a person, and I want to see our relationship of love, companionship, and support grow deeper, larger, and stronger. With the help of God, I commit myself to that."

2. *Loving acceptance.* The most fundamental idea in Christianity is about "grace" – I am loved before I change. God loves me as I am. He doesn't love anyone else more than he loves me, and nothing I can do can increase his love for me. Our society, on the other hand, teaches us that worth is something you earn. At school those with higher grades are more highly esteemed than "dunces." In the army those with fewer stripes take orders from those with more. But in God's family, the prodigal is valued as highly as the loyal son.

So too in marriage. I love my wife before she changes, or whether she changes or not. Nothing is unforgivable. Nothing will stop me loving her: she can count utterly on that. So a good marriage is the union of two good forgivers: it is "three parts love and seven parts forgiveness."

3. *Respect.* If acceptance and love are reactions to a "sinning other," respect is our response to another's "God-likeness." The person we are relating to is made in God's image; he or she is like God. So I should treat my spouse with courtesy and dignity even when I don't feel like it. Little habits of helpfulness actually feed respect. It is an honor to serve one who is like God. But marriage calls upon us to transcend that need: the partner's needs and pleasures must take equal if not superior status to our own.

4. *Maturity and responsibility* are necessary for resolving differences, carrying through promises, sharing finances, and modeling a Christian lifestyle for our children. I take responsibility for resolving personal issues, not dumping them on my partner. I take responsibility for my own happiness.

If our motivation for marriage is to "live happily ever after" we are setting ourselves up for trouble. If you came into the marriage unhappy, chances are you'll stay that way. Happiness is a by-product of self-respect, solving problems responsibly, and doing worthwhile, interesting, and useful things.

5. *Intimacy.* Marriage is "incarnation." When God wanted to communicate his love for us he sent Jesus to embody that love. Jesus loved people as God loves us. He loves us even though he knows us intimately.

So it is in a good marriage. As we are utterly transparent with one another – we have already promised to love "for better or for worse" – we learn to know and love the other *with* their imperfections and faults, not after their removal!

But if you're unsure of your parent's love, you may marry to find a kind of paternal/maternal love from your partner, which complicates the relationship. Here we must be very honest. Most women, I believe, are engaged in a life-long search for a strong nurturing father-figure; most men marry a wife to find a responsive nurturing mother-figure.

Now you are allowed to have your own feelings about all this, and to express them: "feelings are neither right nor wrong." Figure out which feelings, wishes, and thoughts come from within yourself, and which from your partner. Marriage fights are usually more about the past than the present! For example, if our parents were tidy perfectionists, we'll have to figure out why we're the same – or the opposite!

6. *Conflict resolution.* A survey among 700 marriage counselors found that "communication breakdown" headed the list of marital problems. And communication most frequently breaks down in situations of conflict.

Conflict arises because we bring different biographies, needs, interests, values, and lifestyles to our marriage. The trigger for a "conflictual explosion" may include loss of a job, arrival of a new baby, an illness, moving to a new house, or taking an aged parent into the home. Marriage breakdowns do not happen because of "differences"; they happen because a couple can't handle those differences. Relationships do not cause conflict; they bring out whatever incompleteness we have within us anyway.

Conflict is a contest of wills, but it ought not to be viewed as a power struggle or as a question of who is right or wrong. Gentle assertiveness is called for: "speaking the truth in love" and asking about feelings that underlie the difficulty. Discuss with dignity and sensitivity to the other's needs.

Resolution may allow one partner or the other to have a "veto" in certain areas. In our marriage, Jan has veto power in the kitchen, I do with the cars (except for their colour!). In contrast, the issue of my ministry-time away from home was resolved in a family conference: I would not be away more than a third of the time and would forgo preaching engagements at least once a month to attend our local church with my wife and family.

Some things important to you you'll have to concede. Jan and I compromise on our leisure: I like competitive sports and swimming but she prefers walking, so we walk more than we swim. And don't complain too much: your "fussing" can be viewed as trivial by the other.

7. *Money.* "The silver is mine, and the gold is mine, says the Lord of hosts" (Haggai 2:8). Here Jan and I began our thinking by agreeing that all we own belongs to God anyway. We are "joint stewards" with him of our home, our savings, our possessions. We happen to believe that a joint bank account is an appropriate token of our togetherness, so we've always had one.

"When money is tight, couples fight." As an ex-wives' tale puts it: "They won't have incompatibility as long as he has income and she has pattability." Sometimes one partner is more of a spendthrift than the other; sometimes the bread-winner is tightfisted about offering money for housekeeping. I believe it is demeaning for one partner to control the finances against the wishes of the other: this is a result of immaturity or insecurity. Some couples may need financial counseling: in your church an accountant or bank manager will be delighted to help. Draw up a plan together. Be willing occasionally to touch up the plan as circumstances change. And decide mutually to live more simply!

8. *Gender roles and sex.* You may have heard the song "Let's Talk About Sex, Baby!" Do that (although the subject of commitment should come first). Think with your brains, not just your hormones!

Sex is part of God's creation, which he pronounced "very good" (Genesis 1:31). Sexual relations are more than physical: they are also emotional, spiritual, and moral. In 1 Corinthians 7:1–5 Paul talks about the willing surrender of husband and wife to each other to create "coupleness." There's a lot of help around about a wholesome Christian approach to sex, to guard us against either a lustful hedonism or a prudish asceticism.

Sex is more than the union of bodies; it is also about roles. So sort them out. With women freer to pursue careers, role-expectations by men of women and women of men are dramatically changing. What household chores should be done by whom? Expectations are usually connected back to what our parents did – who fixed what, who put out garbage and vacuumed floors and got up to the sick kids at night. Everything ought to be negotiable on such issues.

9. *Spirituality.* God was the first marriage celebrant. He invented marriage. The engagement ring I bought Jan thirty-five years ago had two small diamonds and one larger one to depict the "eternal triangle" – one man, one woman, one God.

Try to worship together regularly; pray with and for each other. Having a Christian commitment that is both real and similar to each other's is a healthy indicator of future marital harmony. That ought not to preclude each partner relating to God uniquely. However, when one is a committed church-going Christian and the other isn't, there's usually (though not invariably) trouble. Talk this issue out very, very carefully before you marry. Some couples have reluctantly called their wedding off when the Christian partner takes seriously the biblical injunction about not being joined with an unbeliever: in my experience, only one in eight or nine men will become a Christian after marriage if they weren't before.

In a truly Christian marriage the order of priority is always God first, spouse second, children third, church/job next. But in a well-ordered and committed life, all these "loves" enrich one another.

10. *Have regular marriage check-ups* at a marriage enrichment or marriage encounter weekend, or with a counselor. Jan and I are currently talking to an experienced counseling couple about our relationship. The issues include: What are our feelings about each other at the moment – and about those close to us? How can we accommodate to each other's differing sexual drives? How much "quality time" should we have with our grandchildren? With Jan's part-time and my full-time ministries, how do we apportion chores, or share each other's vocations?

And remember: a good marriage is both a mystery and a miracle. It depends less on finding the right partner than on being the right partner.

Selected Quotations

Marriage is a holy undertaking marked by at least three characteristics:

(1) It is completely public. The two persons meet with their friends in the "sight of God and this company," to let all the world know what their vows are ... From its earliest days, the Christian church has [affirmed] the public nature of marriage, recognising that it is public because it involves consequences for the total society. A secret marriage is, therefore, from the Christian point of view, a contradiction in terms.

(2) In the Christian system, marriage is a commitment and not a mere contract. It is not a deal or a bargain, but an experience of total self-giving "for better, for worse, for richer, for poorer, in sickness and in health": and not for a term or the moment, but "so long as we both shall live." Here is one of the most profound ideas that can enter the human mind ...

(3) The third element is the acceptance of chastity ... Chastity means celibacy before and outside of marriage, and it means fidelity within marriage. This is a tough position to take, but Christian faith would not be what it is today on any other basis.

D. ELTON TRUEBLOOD,
"The Family in Crisis," Closing address at SBC Convention in Atlanta, Georgia,
June 1978. Quoted in *The Australian Baptist*, July 26, 1978, p. 7.

Biblical teaching supports the family and the conditions necessary for its strength and efficient functioning. Sexual permissiveness, either before or after marriage, is not compatible with the family structure. Love and caring concern involve respect, honesty, giving and responsibility for each other's happiness and welfare. The "seven deadly sins" – pride, anger, lust, gluttony, envy, greed, laziness – endanger marriage and love. The contrasting Christian virtues are humility, meekness, purity, temperance, brotherly love, generosity and zeal.

CLAIRE ISBISTER,
The Christian Doctor Speaks on the Family, Homebush West, NSW: Lancer Books, 1984, p. 31.

Middle-aged men without wives are actually twice as likely to die during a 10-year span as men with wives.

JEAN SELIGMANN,
"For Longer Life, Take a Wife," *Newsweek*, November 1990, p. 44.

Transference is a complex notion in psychotherapy, but put simply it occurs when feelings and behaviors originally experienced with significant people (particularly parents) in one's childhood are relived in one's current relationships. So the emotions of love, hate, anger are experienced with one's spouse, counselor, pastor or various authority figures. "I hate it when you come across like that: it's just like my mother used to do!" [or] "I'm not going to do it just because [the authority-figure] says so: they're not going to boss me around!" may be indications of transference occurring. Understanding how you and your partner came to be the persons you are is incredibly important. In the immortal words of St Francis, we too should regularly pray, "Lord, grant that I may seek more to understand than to be understood."

ROWLAND CROUCHER,
from a seminar, "How to Help Your Friend: An Introduction to Counseling."

The free and loving exchange of nakedness that takes place between a husband and wife is just one of the spectacular ways in which the divine ordinance of marriage actually sets about to reverse the curses of original sin. Marriage attacks original sin, in effect, at its visible root, in the shame of nakedness, and defeats and heals this shame by directly confronting it on the safe and holy ground of a covenant relationship. For a husband and wife to be naked together is like a kind of radiation treatment, the healing rays of which can be felt at the center of the soul. It is, as nearly as possible, a return to the very last statement the book of Genesis makes about mankind's state of innocence in Paradise: "The man and his wife were both naked, and they felt no shame" (Genesis 2:25).

MIKE MASON,
The Mystery of Marriage, Portland, Oreg.: Multnomah Press, 1985, p. 120.

Love by itself is not enough, it must be verified through words, through actions, and by affection. Everybody needs it and no one ever outgrows it. "I LOVE YOU."

BRUCE LESLIE,
Seven Things Men Should Know About Women,
Burwood: New Hope Christian Counselling Service, n.d., p. 13.

Intimacy is fostered by celebration. Develop traditions around birthdays or your wedding anniversary each year. Do something special, though it doesn't have to be expensive. (But be wary of "surprise happenings": some people don't appreciate surprises; they'd prefer to have something they know about to look forward to.)

ROWLAND CROUCHER,
from an unpublished wedding talk.

Some years ago when I was studying people sixty-five years old and older I asked them at what period in life they had been happiest and why they had been happiest at that time. By far the largest percentage said they were happiest during the period after marriage and before their children had left home. The things they most often mentioned as bringing greatest happiness had to do with marriage and parenthood. Last year a study was made of over 2,000 alumni of a West Coast liberal arts college to determine what had brought greatest personal satisfaction to these college graduates as adults. By far the most common thing mentioned was family relationships. For both men and women, career or occupation ran a poor second to the family in bringing personal satisfaction to them.

JUDSON LANDIS,
"The Family and Social Change: A Positive View," a lecture in the University of California's symposium on "The Family's Search for Survival," San Francisco, 1964, p. 1.

Sex is used differently by men and women in a love relationship. Many women view sharing as being close and men view being close as something sexual. Women view sex as one way of being close and too many men view it as the only way to be close. For women, tenderness, touching, talking and sex go together. For some men, sex is sufficient, especially if they do not know how to relate in other expressions of intimacy.

Most men substitute sex for sharing. Sex is an expression of emotion and also substitutes for emotion. As one woman expressed her feelings about sex with her husband, "To me being close means sharing and talking. He thinks being close is having sex. Maybe that's the difference in the way we love. When he's upset or mad or insecure he wants sex ... When I get home from work and I'm wound up with a lot of baggage, I want to talk about it. When he comes home that way, he doesn't want to talk, he wants sex. When I'm sad, what I need is a shoulder to cry on and someone to hear me out. When he's sad, he wants to be seduced out of his feelings."

H. NORMAN WRIGHT,
Questions Women Ask in Private, Glendale, Calif.: Regal Books, 1993, p. 149.

Talking to some modern young women who are now the age I was when I married, I am convinced that we gained rather than lost by waiting to our wedding night to consummate our love for one another. The myth that says that you don't know whether you'll "fit" one another or not unless you try beforehand, is no more than a myth and has no medical basis. Few couples achieve fully satisfactory sexual relations from an emotional point of view outside the security of a loving and committed relationship.

"What have you gained," I asked a younger friend, "by sleeping with those boys?" She was rightly defensive as my words were ill chosen and tactless. She replied: "Well at least I've had many experiences of love – you haven't."

Later, on my own, I wept for her: "Poor kid ... you've let men use you as an object, and you think that is love. You say 'there's sex for love and sex for kicks' – but you don't really know what love is. Love isn't sleeping with a man – or another woman for that matter. Love is giving yourself totally to another person with every part of your being."

ANNE TOWNSEND,
Now and Forever: Christian Marriage Today, London: Fount Paperbacks, 1986, p. 19.

A Prayer

Lord, the giver of all good gifts, the source of all love, the one who blessed a wedding at Cana and is still blessing marriages, we pray for our relationship. Help us to be true to the vows we have made to be faithful to one another for life. Help us daily to rekindle the flame of love. May we be patient and gentle, ready to trust each other, giving strength to each other.

Thank you for happy times: help us to be continually grateful. And for sad times: may we learn to trust you more.

Be with us in our troubles, and help us to bear one another's burdens, so fulfilling the law of Christ.

When we hurt one another, help us to forgive. Remind us that simple gifts enrich our life together. As we communicate, may we have a gift of understanding; in our decision-making, give us wisdom; in our sexual union, may we experience uninhibited joy; in our work, give us creativity and commitment.

May your presence dwell in our home. May our home be a place of refuge for the lonely; a place of welcome for the homeless; a place in which the children delight to find peace and joy.

Lord Jesus, bless us so that we will be a blessing to one another and to others. Amen.

A Benediction

God the Father make you holy in his love; God the Son enrich you with his grace; God the Holy Spirit strengthen you with joy. The Lord bless you and keep you in eternal life. Amen.

8 | Ten myths about marriage

Male and female he created them, and he blessed them and named them "Humankind" when they were created (Genesis 5:2). Then the Lord God said, "It is not good that the man should be alone; I will make him a helper as his partner" (Genesis 2:18). God blessed them, and God said to them, "Be fruitful and multiply, and fill the earth and subdue it; and have dominion over the fish of the sea and over the birds of the air and over every living thing that moves upon the earth" (Genesis 1:28).

For this is the will of God, your sanctification: that you abstain from fornication; that each one of you know how to control your own body in holiness and honor, not with lustful passion, like the Gentiles who do not know God; that no one wrong or exploit a brother or sister in this matter, because the Lord is an avenger in all these things, just as we have already told you beforehand and solemnly warned you. For God did not call us to impurity but in holiness (1 Thessalonians 4:3–7). Let marriage be held in honor by all, and let the marriage bed be kept undefiled; for God will judge fornicators and adulterers (Hebrews 13:4). But because of cases of sexual immorality, each man should have his own wife and each woman her own husband. The husband should give to his wife her conjugal rights, and likewise the wife to her husband. For the wife does not have authority over her own body, but the husband does; likewise the husband does not have authority over his own body, but the wife does. Do not deprive one another except perhaps by agreement for a set time, to devote yourselves to prayer, and then come together again, so that Satan may not tempt you because of your lack of self-control (1 Corinthians 7:2–5).

For thus said the Lord God, the Holy One of Israel: In returning and rest you shall be saved; in quietness and in trust shall be your strength (Isaiah 30:15).

The eye cannot say to the hand, "I have no need of you," nor again the head to the feet, "I have no need of you" (1 Corinthians 12:21). And though one might prevail against another, two will withstand one. A threefold cord is not quickly broken (Ecclesiastes 4:12).

A couple wanted a quiet wedding, so the pastor agreed to have it in the manse. One matter, however, was overlooked. At the precise moment the question was asked, "Do you take this man to be your lawful wedded husband?" a voice came from the clock behind them: "Cuckoo! Cuckoo!" Seven times! The bride never did quite regain her composure. Some brides and bridegrooms never do.

A cynic said, "Marriage is an institution, but who wants to spend their lives in an institution?" Marriages are held together by mutual service, a lot of patience, giving the benefit of the doubt, and by the gifts of apology and forgiveness. All of which isn't easy.

Here are ten common misunderstandings about marriage which surface in my counseling room:

1. *"People marry because they love each other."* In Western cultures we "fall in love" then marry. In other societies, you marry then learn to "love" your mate.

True love is measured by the degree to which the satisfaction or the security of the other person becomes as significant as one's own satisfaction or security. Romantic love is quite different – it's a mix of psychosexual or biochemical drives, plus a hunger for nurture and approval, and the almost mystical experience of eliminating psychic boundaries with another. Surprisingly, some marriages are strong even if the couple are not "in love": they may have a shared companionship and contentment that is mutually satisfying.

True love (what I call realistic love) is enhanced in the "everydayness" of marriage, two people sharing common interests, doing interesting things together. The flame of married love is nurtured by kindness, consideration, adjustment to the other's difficult habits, little surprise gifts, and agreeing on important values. The best marriages result from hard work: as one humorist put it, "Every marriage has three rings – engagement ring, wedding ring and suffering." Life is more than a Mills and Boon romance or a soap opera where everything ends up fine without solid hard work.

Neglect kills marriages fast, so plan ways to enjoy times together. Jan and I block out a day a week for each other, enjoying our grandchildren, occasionally seeing a good movie, walking, eating out, maybe just reading together, talking about "how we are," reviewing our goals, and evaluating our relationship. We're planning for the time when our youngest children will have left and we'll be alone. We'll then have maybe twenty or thirty years (nearly half our married life) "for better, for worse, and for lunch"!

2. *"Partners help each other solve deep problems."* If you expect your spouse to make your life right for you, you'll almost certainly be disappointed. Some expect their partner to meet most of their needs. As we have said, it is impossible to make another person happy. Each partner must take charge of their own gratification and fulfillment.

Somewhere I found this wise statement: "The wife's primary responsibility is to know herself so well and to respect herself so much, she gives herself to her husband without hesitation ... The primary responsibility of the husband is to love his Lord so deeply and to like himself so completely, he gives himself to his wife without hesitation ... The wife's primary role is to model true femininity ... character traits that are precious to God and impressive to her husband ... The husband's role: to model genuine masculinity ... unselfish and sensitive leadership that strengthens the home and gives dignity to the wife."

3. *"In happy marriages they do everything together."* In a good marriage maybe they do seventy to eighty percent of their leisure activities together, but there is room for individual growth and privacy as well.

4. *"True lovers can read each other's thoughts."* This is a half-truth and it's a problem, particularly in the sexual area. "If my partner understood me he or she would soon find out what satisfies me." One cannot automatically experience another's feelings. Don't expect your spouse to read your mind or your body: teach him! Teach her!

On the other hand, "you'll never understand the opposite sex so don't try" is too pessimistic. Males and females have more in common than they might realize: our humanness, giving and receiving love, the desire to be appreciated, and the need for respect and honor are all shared by the sexes.

Should marriage partners "tell each other everything"? Counselors are divided on this one. Some I counsel are working through issues of impure thinking (perhaps relating to matters such as pornography or sado-masochism) but feel that their naive wives would probably not understand. If I were pressed I'd say 99.5 percent can be shared. Perhaps there are rare exceptions, motivated by love and integrity rather than deceit. Should married partners say what they think when they think it? Not necessarily. Sometimes critical feedback may be destructive if not couched in love and bathed in prayer. You don't have a right to "let it all hang out." Attacks may generate counter-attacks – or "passive aggressive" responses where the other becomes a saboteur. Sometimes it's important to think of things far enough ahead not to say them.

5. *"He or she will change after we're married."* Not necessarily; in fact, not likely! As the saying goes, lots of girls would make better wives if they weren't trying to make better husbands (and vice versa).

Disagreements do not necessarily mean a poor marriage. On the contrary, in almost all cases when people say "We've never had a disagreement throughout our married lives," I'm suspicious. Sometimes that's a sign of a sick marriage. If one wants the in-laws to share holidays and the other doesn't, that's O.K. Some compromise will be necessary. If a concert would be exciting to one and utterly boring for the other, again you'll need "plan B"! A good marriage survives these episodes.

6. *"If the man is a good provider, that's the main thing."* Many men think they can show their love by working, earning, and spending. They are

hurt when their hard efforts to bring home the bacon and pay the bills aren't appreciated. But women would prefer men who listen and resonate with their feelings. Even the Beatles knew that "money can't buy me love." Orange County in California has about the highest per capita income in the world, but its divorce rate is over seventy percent.

7. *"Children will make our marriage better."* If the marriage isn't happy, the coming of children won't fix that. All you'll have now is an unhappy marriage plus a baby. The psychological and financial expenditure of caring for a child often exacerbates the tensions between the couple. By the way, it's wise to read some books or attend some seminars on parenting before and during the time children are around! Discuss how many children you want and when, how they will be brought up, and who will stay at home when they're young.

8. *"An affair automatically spells the end of the marriage."* Not necessarily. But the line "a little adultery never hurt a strong marriage" is not true either: the "open marriages" of the 1960s were found to be a deeply flawed idea. Adultery is forbidden in the Ten Commandments not because a law-giving God doesn't want us to enjoy ourselves, but because humans need a context of fidelity and love to fulfil their God-endowed potential.

In the film *Indecent Proposal* a rich gambler offers $1 million to a desperately poor couple in exchange for a night with the wife. Even in our freer culture, there is still a widespread sensitivity to infidelity. Of course, "playing around" happens without million-dollar incentives …

If possible, when you discover that your partner has been carrying on with someone else: (1) Stay calm. (2) Feel betrayed – even mad – but condemn the behavior rather than the person. (3) Don't even think about revenge: ask why the marriage allowed this to happen. (4) Don't worry if you can't forgive your partner immediately. That's normal. Forgiveness will come later (though if it never comes I'd be worried). (5) Find a counselor and seek therapy. An "affair" need not be the end of the marriage, but some new, honest negotiating will be necessary to get the marriage onto a secure foundation again.

The problem with infidelity is in the meaning of that word: one is participating in a lie. The loss of honesty and the spinning of a web of deception destroys loving trust. Even so-called "harmless flirting" cheapens the relationship and is a sign of disrespect: that habit should be broken.

9. *"It's better to hang on in a destructive marriage."* Again, not necessarily. While God hates divorce, God is not a legalist either. I've counseled women married to psychopaths where everyone was being destroyed, and, yes, had to agree after many bashings and the children being traumatized that the least of all evils was to leave the perpetrator of violence. In less destructive situations, sometimes the shock tactic of a trial separation may be called for, but only, I feel, as a last resort after all else has failed, and only with the guidance of a skilled counselor.

10. *"Christian couples should pray together."* Yes, maybe, but usually they don't. One usually prays "better" than the other, and because we inhabit a sick competitive culture and forget we should pray to our Father as a child would, we get embarrassed about our poor flow of words. So I frankly don't know what "better" means. If you "pray as you can, not as you can't" and we respect each other's uniqueness, it should be possible to pray meaningfully together.

Probably there's a deeper reason, however. Praying couples soon find that integrity is called for if the prayer is not phony. God looks on the heart. He understands our deepest motives. Unless the marriage relationship is utterly transparent, praying becomes a form of ritualized verbosity.

How often should you pray together? As often as you like. Maybe pray separately in the mornings and together at night, or vice versa. You may choose to share your own personal prayer journey with your partner.

Selected Quotations
We learn about marriage from our parents, the media, from married friends, or from marriage enrichment courses. But learning from your parents can be hazardous, if their marriage wasn't good. Well-known Australian "biker" evangelist John Smith asked a few hundred school-

kids, "How many of you would marry if you knew your marriage would be about as good as your parents'?" Only six or seven said yes. So the others will have to learn about marriage from somewhere else …

If they're going to learn from TV or the movies, then they'd better ask: "What values is Hollywood portraying? Is love ever more than sexual attraction or temporary emotion? Were deep commitment, faithfulness, unselfishness, and respect for one another part of the plot?" Sometime analyze the songs about love on the radio: probably ninety percent will say "I need you, baby … I can't live without you … Hold me tight … set me alight …" or whatever. Most will be about romantic love rather than realistic love.

ROWLAND CROUCHER,
from an unpublished sermon.

Love at first sight is a physical and emotional impossibility. Why? Because love is not simply a feeling of romantic excitement; it goes beyond intense sexual attraction; it exceeds the thrill at having "captured" a highly desirable social prize. These are emotions that are unleashed at first sight, but they do not constitute love. I wish the whole world knew that fact. These temporary feelings differ from love in that they place the spotlight on the one experiencing them. "What is happening to Me? This is the most fantastic thing I've ever been through! I think I am in love!" You see, these emotions are selfish in the sense that they are motivated by our own gratification. They have little to do with the new lover. Such a person has not fallen in love with another person; he or she has fallen in love with love! …

Real love, in contrast to popular notions, is an expression of the deepest appreciation for another human being; it is an intense awareness of his or her needs and longings for the past, present and future. It is unselfish and giving and caring.

JAMES DOBSON,
Emotions – Can You Trust Them?, London: Hodder & Stoughton, 1980, pp. 55–57.

Romantic love is the single greatest energy system in the Western psyche. In our culture it has supplanted religion as the arena in which men and women seek meaning, transcendence, wholeness, and ecstasy. As a mass phenomenon, romantic love is peculiar to the West.

We are so accustomed to living with the beliefs and assumptions of romantic love that we think it is the only form of "love" on which marriage or love relationships can be based. We think it is the only "true love."

But … in Eastern cultures, like those of India or Japan, we find that married couples love each other with great warmth, often with a stability and devotion that puts us to shame. But their love is not "romantic love" as we know it. They don't impose the same ideals on their relationships, nor do they impose such impossible demands and expectations on each other as we do …

For romantic love doesn't just mean loving someone; it means being "in love." This is a psychological phenomenon that is very specific. When we are "in love" we believe we have found the ultimate meaning of life, revealed in another human being. We feel we are finally completed, that we have found the missing parts of ourselves. Life suddenly seems to have a wholeness, a super-human intensity that lifts us high above the ordinary pain of existence. For us, these are the sure signs of "true love." The psychological package includes an unconscious demand that our lover or spouse always provide us with this feeling of ecstasy and intensity. With typical Western self-righteousness we assume that our notion of "love," romantic love, must be the best. We assume that any other kind of love between couples would be cold and insignificant by comparison. But if we Westerners are honest with ourselves, we have to admit that our approach to romantic love is not working well.

Despite our ecstasy when we are "in love," we spend much of our time with a deep sense of loneliness, alienation, and frustration over our inability to make genuinely loving and committed relationships. Usually we blame other people for failing us; it doesn't occur to us that perhaps it is we who need to change our unconscious attitudes – the expectations and demands we impose on our relationships and on other people.

ROBERT A. JOHNSON,
The Psychology of Romantic Love, London: Arkana, 1983, pp. xi, xii.

Christian marriage counselors usually define love more in terms of actions and decisions than feelings. We know God's love because he did something, not because he felt something. We are exhorted to love our spouses whether we feel like it or not. People who report that they no longer love their mates are urged to engage in a series of loving behaviours with the implicit promise that feelings will follow. The correct assumption behind this thinking is that the truth of God's Word is to be the basis for our actions. We are not to be led by our erratic emotions, but are to follow biblical instruction whether our feelings agree or rebel.

LARRY CRABB,
The Marriage Builder, Homebush West, NSW: ANZEA, 1992, p. 113.

People fall in love, but they decide to stay in love. Emotions change like the weather, but love must be a determined commitment. "Husbands, love your wives, just as Christ also loved the church" (Ephesians 5:25). "Encourage the young women to love their husbands" (Titus 2:4). We must commit to love in a self-sacrificial way whether or not the love is reciprocated.

JERRY WHITE,
The Power of Commitment, Colorado Springs: NavPress, 1985, p. 88.

> I love you,
> Not only for what you are
> But for what I am
> When I am with you.
>
> I love you,
> Not only for what
> You have made of yourself
> But for what
> You are making of me.
>
> I love you,
> For the part of me
> That you bring out;
> I love you,
> For putting your hand
> Into my heaped-up heart

And passing over
All the foolish, weak things
That you can't help
Dimly seeing there,
And for drawing out
Into the light
All the beautiful belongings
That no one else had looked
Quite far enough to find.
I love you because you
Are helping me to make
Of the lumber of my life
Not a tavern
But a temple;
Out of works
Of my every day
Not a reproach
But a song.

ROY CROFT,
in Charles Swindoll, *Growing Strong in the Seasons of Life*,
Portland, Oreg.: Multnomah Press, 1983, pp. 67–68.

Codependency is a compulsion to control and rescue people by fixing their problems. It occurs when a person's God-given needs for love and security have been blocked in a relationship with a dysfunctional person, resulting in a lack of objectivity, a warped sense of responsibility, being controlled and controlling others (three primary characteristics); and in hurt and anger, guilt, and loneliness (three corollary characteristics). These characteristics affect the codependent's every relationship and desire. His goal in life is to avoid the pain of being unloved and to find ways to prove that he is lovable. It is a desperate quest.

PAT SPRINGLE,
Rapha's 12-Step Program for Overcoming Codependency, Dallas: Word Books, 1990, p. xiii.

It goes without saying that in marriage, two wills are in operation at the same time. Sometimes, and especially in the early months of the marriage, the two wills are spontaneously congruent, and experienced as one. But as time goes by and early ecstasies are succeeded by routines and demands, what was experienced as a gift must be developed as an art. The art is willed passivity ...

Learning the art of willed passivity begins with appreciating the large and creative part passivity plays in our lives. By far the largest part of our life is experienced in the mode of passivity. Life is undergone. We receive. We enter into what is already there. Our genetic system, the atmosphere, the food chain, our parents, the dog – they are there, in place before we exercise our will ...

But there are different ways of being passive: There is an indolent, inattentive passivity that approximates the existence of a slug; and there is a willed and attentive passivity that is something more like worship. St Paul's famous "Wives be subject to your husbands. Husbands love your wives, as Christ loved the church and gave himself up for her" (Ephesians 5:22–25) sets down the parallel operations of willed passivity.

EUGENE H. PETERSON,
The Contemplative Pastor: Returning to the Art of Spiritual Direction,
Carol Stream, Ill.: Christianity Today, Inc., and Word, Inc., 1989, pp. 112–114.

When I married, I did not expect John to understand me to the degree which I now expect ... I find now that I want my husband to understand all that there is to know about me. I don't want any part of me to be hidden – even my secret hurts and vulnerability. Armed with such understanding, I want him to anticipate certain things which will cause me pain. But I need to realize that such a demand is probably unrealistic – the media have taught me first to want him to know these things and then to expect him to know them intuitively, without my even telling him.

ANNE TOWNSEND,
Now and Forever: Christian Marriage Today, London: Fount Paperbacks, 1986, p. 36.

Deep sharing is overwhelming and very rare. A thousand fears keep us in check ... the fear of breaking down, of crying; that the other will not sense the importance with which this feeling or memory is charged ... How painful it is when such a difficult sharing falls flat either on ears too preoccupied or mocking, ears that in any case do not sense the tremendous significance of what we are saying. It may happen between a man and wife. The partner who has spoken in a very personal way without being understood falls back into terrible emotional solitude. It is impossible to overemphasize the immense need men have to really be listened to, to be understood. No one can develop freely in this world and find a full life without feeling understood by at least one person. Misunderstood, he loses his self-confidence, he loses his faith in life or even in God.

PAUL TOURNIER,
Marriage Difficulties, Crowborough, E. Sussex: Highland Books, 1984, pp. 21–22.

[Based on an informal survey of six hundred people who had maintained successful marriages, psychologist James Dobson arrived at "three tried and tested, back to basics recommendations" for reducing the chances of divorce and for maintaining marital stability:]

- A Christ-centered home where the husband and wife are deeply committed to Jesus Christ;
- A committed love in which nothing short of death is permitted to come between the couple (in contrast to the idea that "I'll stay with you as long as I feel love for you"); and
- A never-ending willingness to work at maintaining good communication.

People are not looking for perfect marriages, but [for] marriages that keep working. But even these less-than-perfect marriages have evaded many in the baby boom generation. Marital instability has been taken for granted in this low-commitment era, and divorce has come to be seen as a reasonable way to get out of an unhappy marriage. As a result, the United States has the highest divorce rate in the world.

JAMES C. DOBSON,
Love for a Lifetime: Building a Marriage That Will Go the Distance,
Portland, Oreg.: Multnomah Press, 1987, pp. 49–66.

R.C. Sproul once said that "If you imagined your mother married to your father-in-law, and your father married to your mother-in-law, you'd have a good picture of the dynamics of your marriage." I grew up in a home where my dad was a "Mr Fix-it." When anything broke, he fixed it. Johnny grew up in a home where his dad wasn't interested in fixing things. It was his mother's job to call the repairman. One of our first misunderstandings as newlyweds was when an appliance broke. I kept hinting for Johnny to fix it, but to no avail. Finally in a fit of exasperation, I said, "Why haven't you fixed it?" He responded, "Why haven't you called the repairman?" I must admit that in the years since, he has become a better Mr Fix-it, and I have called in a repairman a few times as well!

SUSAN ALEXANDER YATES,
And Then I Had Kids, Milton Keynes: Word (UK), 1992, p. 79.

A Prayer for Husbands

Lord Jesus, gentle and strong, who related with tenderness to women, to children, and to the marginalized, but also with prophetic anger to the enemies of God's love, give me a big dose of gentle strength for my wife. Help me to love her as you loved the church, a love that was willing to endure the ultimate sacrifice of death.

Help me to meet my wife's needs for genuine affection, for honest communication, for little surprises and common courtesies. Help me to listen to her feelings, not merely her words; to understand the differences between us that enrich our life together; to be willing to accept her as she is without wanting to change her.

Help me as I look into her eyes to give her the gift of openness, trust, and security.

Help me to work hard to support her and the family financially. If my earnings are inadequate, give me the gift of creativity to figure out ways of earning more or spending less.

Help me, however, to put my wife and family first. May I be faithful in giving the gift of listening time, the gift of my interested presence, and the gift of my learning and skills to those I love.

Sometimes I feel so inadequate. I confess my sins of neglect, of the idolatry of my vocation, of being second best when at home. Lord, forgive me. I commit myself to you and to my wife and family. May I really believe that "success" is unimportant anywhere if it is not a goal of my life at home.

I pray in your strong name. Amen.

A Prayer for Wives

Jesus, tender lover of women and children, of his friends and the friendless, I come to you for a special gift of love for my husband and family. Lord, help me to respect him, not because he's perfect (you and I know he isn't), but because he's made in your image, and because you have commanded wives to respect their husbands, as you have also commanded husbands to love their wives.

Lord, I offer to you and to him my beauty – the beauty of a quiet, serene spirit and the beauty of my mind and my emotions and my body. Help me to be interested in the things he's interested in and be willing to share those interests with him.

Help me, Lord, to be willing to be an excellent sexual partner for him. Help us to talk freely about how we "tick" so that our sexual life will be satisfying and enjoyable.

May our home be a haven of peace in a turbulent world, a place of quiet rest when life is too noisy and stressful. Help me to have the grace and strength to be a secure mother of our children; help us both to plan fun times together as a family. Help me to be interested in my husband's work and achievements; to be an interesting conversation-mate; and, above all, help me to pray for him, for us, and for our family regularly.

I offer my life to you, Lord. May I bring joy to you as I live in obedience to your perfect will. Amen.

A Benediction

The riches of God's grace be upon you,
that you may live together in faith and love
and receive the blessings of eternal life.
May almighty God,
who creates you, redeems you and guides you,
bless you now and always. Amen.

9
Parenting: the most complex job on earth

Now the man knew his wife Eve, and she conceived and bore Cain, saying, "I have produced a man with the help of the Lord" (Genesis 4:1). Adam knew his wife again, and she bore a son and named him Seth, for she said, "God has appointed for me another child instead of Abel, because Cain killed him" (Genesis 4:25).

For it was you who formed my inward parts; you knit me together in my mother's womb. I praise you, for I am fearfully and wonderfully made. Wonderful are your works; that I know very well. My frame was not hidden from you, when I was being made in secret, intricately woven in the depths of the earth. Your eyes beheld my unformed substance. In your book were written all the days that were formed for me, when none of them as yet existed. How weighty to me are your thoughts, O God! How vast is the sum of them! I try to count them – they are more than the sand; I come to the end – I am still with you (Psalm 139:13–18). Know that the Lord is God. It is he that made us, and we are his; we are his people, and the sheep of his pasture (Psalm 100:3). Your hands have made and fashioned me; give me understanding that I may learn your commandments (Psalm 119:73).

You shall put these words of mine in your heart and soul, and you shall bind them as a sign on your hand, and fix them as an emblem on your forehead. Teach them to your children, talking about them when you are at home and when you are away, when you lie down and when you rise. Write them on the doorposts of your house and on your gates, so that your days and the days of your children may be multiplied in the land that the Lord swore to your ancestors to give them, as long as the heavens are above the earth (Deuteronomy 11:18–21).

And whoever does not provide for relatives, and especially for family members, has denied the faith and is worse than an unbeliever (1 Timothy 5:8). If any of you put a stumbling block before one of these little ones who believe in me, it would be better for you if a great millstone were fastened around your neck and you were drowned in the depth of the sea (Matthew 18:6).

Train children in the right way, and when old, they will not stray (Proverbs 22:6).

First, the bad news. My city's major paper (Melbourne's *Age*, January 20, 1994, p. 7) carried this headline: "Schoolyard bullies often graduate to crime, says psychologist." Its opening wisdom: "Violent parents breed violent children who are likely to be school-yard bullies and eventually criminals, according to a Canadian psychologist specializing in child behavior." Professor Kenneth Rubin (University of Waterloo, Ontario) claimed that bullying children are over-represented among juvenile delinquents, and that parents are responsible for how well or how badly their children were brought up. While children depend on their peers for how they dress, how they wear their hair and how they speak a pretty rough equivalent of the Queen's English, they mirror their parents' ability to form relationships. Children who are not accepted by their peer groups because they are aggressive, or alternatively withdrawn, generally would develop some psycho-social problems.

Isn't it amazing that we need qualifications for doing just about everything else in society, yet we allow virtually anyone, almost without regard for their mental or moral aptitude, to try their hand at raising young human beings? At school we learn the three Rs, how to smoke a cigarette behind the toilets without coughing too much, and (these days) how to test the strength of a condom, but the most important subject of all – education for future parenthood – is conspicuously absent. Parenthood is for amateurs! Until recently, the extended family was there to provide guidance and support. With increasing mobility, the extended family has all but disappeared.

Surveys around the world tell us the happiest people are children or parents in a happy family. The reverse is also true: unhappy families breed unhappy people. A father was summoned by the police. His youngest son had been charged with possessing and selling hard drugs. As the man walked out later, shaken and devastated, he said to his wife, "I've had it with life; the first half is ruined by your parents and the second half by your children."

Parents are there in place of God. Historic Christian wisdom has always maintained that our children are more God's than ours; they have been entrusted to us to care for them during the few short years of their inability to properly care for themselves. We care for them through "tender love" all the time and "tough love" sometimes: tender love because the fragile plant may be crushed if we are rough with it; tough love when the child ought to learn something for their own good which will never be forgotten.

But we never – well, hardly ever – need to yell at children. Continually raising our voice is often a sign of insecurity in us and breeds insecurity in our children. Figure out the ground rules, have a policy of fairness, and request obedience just once before disciplinary action. Let me say all that in other words: give a command once, quietly (unless they're deaf), and expect it to be obeyed. Punish if it isn't – from the earliest age. If this kind of predictable discipline is enforced, for most children after the age of four or five you won't have too many problems. (The strong-willed child is sometimes a special case!)

As the popular poster puts it, we have two gifts to give our children: one is roots, the other is wings. We work hard so that our sons and daughters are rooted in integrity, honesty, and love. Then we encourage them to take wings and fly on their own because they have mastered basic life-skills and self-esteem. Our objective as parents, then, is to do very little for our children that they can do for themselves.

Your family is the most precious possession you have. Take time to recognize how important each member of the family is to you, and communicate that. You'll be surprised at how many family "problems" evaporate when you give the gift of time, and communicate warmth and love and trust.

Selected Quotations

Who of us is mature enough for offspring before the offspring themselves arrive? The value of marriage is not that adults produce children but that children produce adults.

PETER DE VRIES,
in Robert I. Fitzhenry (ed.), *Chambers Book of Quotations*,
Edinburgh: W&R Chambers Ltd., 1986, p. 125.

The choice to have children is regarded as the biggest and most far-reaching decision a couple can make. The length of the commitment is so daunting for a start. It has been pointed out that we can have ex-spouses and ex-jobs, but not ex-children. Becoming a parent is a major turning point for most people.

WENDY GREEN,
The Future of the Family, Oxford: Mowbrays, 1984, p. 93.

Parents teach in the toughest school in the world – The School for Making People. You are the board of education, the principal, the classroom teacher, and the janitor, all rolled into two. You are expected to be experts on all subjects pertaining to life and living. The list keeps on growing as your family grows. Further, there are few schools to train you for your job, and there is no general agreement on the curriculum. You have to make it up yourself. Your school has no holidays, no vacations, no unions, no automatic promotions, or pay raises. You are on duty or at least on call twenty-four hours a day, 365 days a year, for at least eighteen years for each child you have. Besides that, you have to contend with an administration that has two leaders or bosses, whichever the case may be – and you know the traps two bosses can get into with each other. Within this context you carry on your peoplemaking. I regard this as the hardest, most complicated, anxiety-ridden, sweat and blood producing job in the world. It requires the ultimate in patience, common sense, commitment, humor, tact, love, wisdom, awareness and knowledge. At the same time, it holds the possibility for the most rewarding, joyous experience of a lifetime.

VIRGINIA SATIR,
Peoplemaking, Palo Alto, Calif.: Science & Behavior Books, 1972, p. 197.

However reluctant we may be to admit it, so much of our future is bound up in our children. They are a part of our immortality, a positive commitment to life. That is why we have to be so careful that we do not lay upon them our unfulfilled dreams and ambitions.

WENDY GREEN,
The Future of the Family, Oxford: Mowbrays, 1984, p. 109.

Robert L. Fulghum, in his book *All I Really Need to Know I Learned in Kindergarten* (Villard Books, 1989), says it well:

"Most of what I really need to know about how to live, and what to do, and how to be, I learned in kindergarten. Wisdom was not at the top of the graduate school mountain, but there in the sandbox at nursery school. These are the things I learned: Share everything. Play fair. Don't hit people. Put things back where you found them. Clean up your own mess. Don't take things that aren't yours. Say you're sorry when you hurt somebody ... Learn some and think some and draw and paint and sing and dance and play and work every day some. When you go out into the world, watch for traffic, hold hands, and stick together. Be aware of wonder ... Think of what a better world it would be if we all – the whole world – had cookies and milk about three o'clock every afternoon and then lay down with our blankets for a nap. Or, if we had a basic policy in our nation and other nations to always put things back where we found them and clean up our own messes. And it is true, no matter how old you are, when you go out into the world, it is best to hold hands and stick together." Holding hands and sticking together – that's really what you're doing as you teach your youngster to draw, paint, sing, dance, play, and work.

CARYL WALLER KRUEGER,
Working Parent, Happy Child: You Can Balance Job and Family,
Nashville: Abingdon Press, 1990, pp. 306–307.

Love is likely to get a bit out of hand when children are around. Watch it: tell your own you love them if you must, but not too often. Without love, a home is a house; too much love and it is bedlam. In other words, love them, but don't smother them. Like fire, love is a good servant but a bad master. It can swamp everything and impair judgment. I like kindness better, because it is more convenient. Love is demanding, kindness is not; love is wild and uncontrolled, kindness is gentle and without obligation. Children understand kindness. For most mothers, love is instinctive. Kindness needs some prompting. As for patience, you really have to work on that: there is too little of it in the world. It is "second layer country," involving thought and time, but with the promise of a dividend, a closer understanding with your child. It is one of the hardest lessons to learn in parenthood.

KEITH SMITH,
How to Get Closer to Your Children, Surry Hills, NSW: Waratah Press, 1985, p. 58.

Statistics show that most parents who abuse their children were abused themselves. While it is true that parents tend to treat their children as they were treated, no parent wants to abuse their children. Abuse has consequences, not only for the child, but also for the parent … Abusive parents carry the weight of the millstones of guilt, fear, confusion, and regret.

LYNDA D. ELLIOT and VICKI L. TANNER,
My Father's Child: Help and Healing for the Victims of Emotional, Sexual, and Physical Abuse, Brentwood, Tenn.: Wolgemuth & Hyatt, Publishers, Inc., 1988, pp. 141–142.

Some overprotected kids remain babies or are afraid of the world. Others "go underground" and do the opposite of what their parents value. Coping with overprotective parents is a must if you are growing into a person who knows what is right or wrong for yourself. Self-worth and independence, which you will need for the rest of your life, can be achieved only by standing up to this problem … By taking steps to grow up, you will help yourself move toward the full, happy life you deserve. It's not a selfish thing to do, though. Becoming more independent can also help your parents move toward their own maturity. Move a little distance from your parents' ever-enveloping arms. Take a look at your strong self. That way, you can approach your mother and father with love, using your dignity and self-esteem. You will be liberated to lead your life without guilt. And the extra reward is that your parents will be liberated in the process.

MARGOT WEBB,
Overprotective Parents, New York: Rosen Publishing Group, 1990, p. 156.

Children are constantly looking for evaluation and feedback from parents. "Daddy, look how strong I am!" "Mommy, see how I tied my shoes!" "Look at my school report; I did better at math!" When children are unsuccessful in building self-respect, it is almost certain that either the parents have sent the message, "You are worthless," or they have not sent any message at all. Sometimes it is a combination of both.

ARCHIBALD D. HART,
Children and Divorce, Dallas: Word Publishing, 1982, p. 111.

One in three Britons eat their main meal on their laps in front of television, according to a new study of eating habits. Little more than half the people surveyed eat at the table, according to the report by market analyst Mintel.

The Sunday Age, Melbourne, January 1, 1994, p. 11.

It belongs to the centre of the Christian message that children are not properties to own and rule over, but gifts to cherish and care for. Our children are our most important guests, who enter into our home, ask for careful attention, stay for a while and then leave to follow their own way … The awareness that children are guests can be a liberating awareness because many parents suffer from deep guilt feelings towards their children, thinking that they are responsible for everything their sons or daughters do. But children are not properties we can control as a puppeteer controls his puppets, or train as a lion tamer trains his lions. They are guests we have to respond to, not possessions we are responsible for.

HENRI NOUWEN,
Reaching Out, Glasgow: Collins Fount, 1976, pp. 75–77.

Babies are not the helpless, innocent creatures they appear to be. Beneath that wrinkled, rosy exterior lurk the mind and instincts of a seasoned guerilla fighter, determined to force you, the parent, into unconditional surrender. No holds barred, no weapon too ghastly to be used against you. Predawn attacks are commonplace; assaults with loaded diapers and ear-piercing battle-cries are just the beginning of the struggle. But what is this war about? What does the little monster want? Just this: your total and unquestioning obedience to every gurgle and yell; the rearrangement of your entire life to suit his or her schedule; and twenty-four hour attention. During the first year, your baby will try to lay the foundations for a whole childhood of making you jump.

PETER MAYLE,
Baby Taming. Quoted in Carol Tannenhauser and Cheryl Moch (eds),
In Celebration of Babies, New York: Ballantine Books, Fawcett Columbine, 1987, p. 71.

Rearing a family is probably the most difficult job in the world. It resembles the merger of two business firms, putting their respective resources together to make a single product. All the potential headaches of that operation are present when an adult male and an adult female join to steer a child from infancy to adulthood. The parents in a nurturing family realize that problems will come along, simply because life offers them, but they will be alert to creative solutions for each new problem as it appears. Troubled families, on the other hand, put all their energies into the hopeless attempt to keep problems from happening; when they do happen — and, of course, they always do — these people have no resources left for solving them. Perhaps one of the distinguishing features of nurturing parents is that they realize that change is inevitable: children change quickly from one stage to another, nurturing adults never stop growing and changing; and the world around us never stands still. They accept change as an unavoidable part of being alive and try to use it creatively to make their families still more nurturing.

VIRGINIA SATIR,
Peoplemaking, Palo Alto, Calif.: Science & Behavior Books, 1972, pp. 17–18.

As Professor Rutter, Professor of Child Psychiatry in London, said at a conference in preparation for the International Year of the Child: "The importance of the family as a formative influence on a child's personality needs no arguing ... it is a matrix in which the child develops, the area where his strongest emotional ties are formed, and the background against which his most intense personal life is enacted."

KEVIN ANDREWS,
"The Family, Marriage and Divorce," in *The Australian Family,* Quarterly Journal of the
Australian Family Association, Vol. 13, No. 4, December 1992, pp. 19–20.

Parents, what on earth are you supposed to be doing? Six things:

1. Acting as God's representatives (until the time your children can begin to know Him for themselves).
2. Acting as providers for their spiritual, physical and emotional needs.
3. Acting as their trainers/instructors in Christian values and common sense.
4. Living with them as their friends.
5. Acting as correctors when they go off the narrow path.
6. Living as examples before them of what God wants them to grow up to be.

KATHY BENCE,
Turn Off the TV: Let's Have Fun Instead!, London: Marshall Pickering, 1990, p. 111.

Prayers

Father,
shield the children from my weaknesses,
protect them against my attempts to
round them off or square them away ...

Let me understand them when they are
bearing burdens they cannot share with me
nor let me help carry ...

Let me not pry when I see them suffering
from sins unpublished
but deep with inner shame ...

Let them be brave and safe
but if they cannot be both
let them be brave ...

Let me share their tiny tragedies
and terrible heartaches
their soaring delights and
silent revelations
if they want me to

and as they want me to ...
Let their confidence be established in you ...

ROBERT A. RAINES,
"Shield the Children," in *Lord, Could You Make It a Little Better?*,
Waco, Tex.: Word Books, 1972, p. 52.

Father in heaven, pattern of all parenthood and lover of children, we pray for
our homes and families. Sustain and comfort them in need and sorrow. In times
of bitterness, tension and division, draw near to heal. May parents and children
together be learners in the school of Christ, daily increasing in mutual respect
and understanding, in tolerance and patience, and in all-prevailing love;
through Jesus Christ our Lord. Amen.

TIMOTHY DUDLEY-SMITH,
in Tony Castle (ed.), *The Hodder Book of Christian Prayers*,
London: Hodder & Stoughton, 1986, p. 211.

O Thou who hast set the solitary in families, I crave Thy heavenly blessing also
for all the members of this household, all my neighbours, and all my fellow
citizens. Let Christ rule in every heart and his law be honoured in every home.
Let every knee be bent before him and every tongue confess that he is Lord.
Amen.

JOHN BAILLIE,
A Diary of Private Prayer, London: OUP, 1936, p. 49.

A Benediction
May God who comforts us when we are down, and chastens us when we need
his discipline, bless you in your parenting. May you know he is near you when
you're in deep water; may you have his wisdom when little people make your
existence so complex; and at the end of the day, after some successes and many
mistakes, may you be willing to stand humbly before him and honestly say, "I did
my best." Amen.

CAPSULE 5: Some Ideas for Family Fun

- Once a year, every year, go on a good, fun-filled holiday. For example, visit a farm, arrange a house-swap, or stay with distant relatives.
- On your holiday take a bird-book and identify all the birds in an area.
- Put together a special album of each child's photos from baby onwards.
- Write a love-note to your child at least once a year – perhaps on birthdays – beginning "I'm glad I'm your Mum/Dad because …"
- Encourage the kids to go to a Christian adventure holiday camp (if possible, plan ahead and ensure their friends attend too).
- At least once a week, have an after-dinner discussion time. Begin by choosing one of the following: "The best thing about our home and family is …" "If our family could do anything at all I'd like to suggest …" "I'd like to help …" "I think our church is …" "When I grow up I …" "For our next holiday …" "If I could change something in our world I'd …" "In a book I've been reading …"
- On birthdays, Mother's Day, Father's Day, develop your own traditions (like special breakfast-in-bed, that person does no work at all, "This Is Your Life" etc.).
- Get to know an Aborigine (in the United States a native Indian; in the United Kingdom someone from the Caribbean) and invite their family to dinner.
- Enjoy your own special traditions on Christmas Day (in the afternoon we play a special version of family cricket in which all ages can have fun), and Easter (like a family communion Good Friday evening).
- Sponsor a poor overseas child and write to him or her.
- Visit a book fair and buy some books.
- Do occasional day trips to amusement parks, zoos, national parks, or community festivals.
- Have the kids' friends over for a pool party or slumber party.
- Go to a good movie.
- Go for a walk/bike ride in the park.

- Have a family barbecue, hot dog roast, roasted marshmallows, etc.
- Ask an expert on something to accompany your family (and perhaps a few other families) on an excursion. Ideas: astronomy, stamp-collecting, birdwatching, identifying insects, fishing, bushwalking, cross-country skiing.
- Make your own Christmas cards.
- Give each family member a section of the garden to cultivate. Give away or sell excess vegetables, fruit, flowers.
- Ask the neighbors in for dessert and coffee.
- Go to half-a-dozen Saturday garage sales (plan what you want so you don't do too much "impulse buying").
- Memorize the order of the books of the Bible (New Testament first).
- Do something each month for someone, such as babysit, mow lawns, or do shopping or odd jobs for an elderly widow.
- Arrange a make-a-pizza and pot-luck soup night (guests bring various ingredients).
- Organize a progressive dinner: go to different families for each course.
- Have a family project each year – for example, to help a mission. One year you could add on to your house a self-contained bungalow to accommodate a homeless person.
- Get a book from the library to teach you how to make candles.
- Learn a craft and sell the products – spinning and weaving, copper engraving, leathercrafting, woodworking, specialty photography, gemstone jewellery, calligraphy, pottery, macrame, painting.
- Raise a guide dog puppy for a year.
- Go to a pick-your-own-fruit farm, then make jams, preserves, and so on.
- Help one another collect something – anything!
- Set aside part of your garden for a bird sanctuary (bird-bath, bird-feeders, and flowering trees).
- Visit an antique market and get an expert to describe why certain items are valuable.
- Arrange prayer-partners: each one prays for another each day; rotate weekly.
- Encourage each family member to read everything by their favorite author, and share the wisdom with the others on Family Night.

- Read a story.
- Make and fly a kite.
- Create your own crossword puzzle.
- Learn a new card game.
- Buy Scrabble and play "Take Two." Rules: Turn all the pieces over and start with seven each. When the first person completes a crossword with all their letters, they say "Take two" and everyone takes two more letters. When all the letters are gone and someone has completed a crossword, they yell "Stick 'em up!" and they're the winner. Great for kids older than about ten.
- Make a banner on a biblical theme for the church hall.
- Create a diorama in a shoebox. Paint the backdrop, then scour the house for bits and pieces for furniture and props.
- Build a doll's house for young girls.
- Offer to make three months' supply of colouring-in pages for kids in church.
- Play "I Spy."
- Form an orchestra: for those who don't play a musical instrument, have a box of do-it-yourself percussion instruments.
- Construct mobiles from a coat-hanger.
- Chase up your family history (a book from the library will help you).
- Create a jigsaw puzzle from a favorite picture glued onto cardboard.
- Adopt a missionary and/or a Third World village and write to them. Get some advice about what not to write about or send.
- Board a foreign student for a year.
- Eat a Third World meal.
- Go camping or caravanning.
- Make an indoor garden.
- Cultivate silkworms and learn how to spin silk.
- Buy a pet – but don't put any into cages if they're safe and better off roaming around.
- Make a compost pen: get instructions about how to do it properly.
- Grow mushrooms.
- Build a treehouse.
- Go pony-trekking.
- Start a nursery (for plants, not toddlers!).

- Plan a landscaping project for your garden (or part of the church's).
- Visit another church.
- Buy a book of Bible stories and read some of them. (Don't major on blood and gore stories. Be selective, and tell the kids why: since Jesus has come, the Old Testament has to be understood in the light of his teaching.)

(Some of these ideas have been derived/adapted from Kathy Bence, *Turn Off the TV: Let's Have Fun Instead!*, London: Marshall Pickering, 1990. There are many more in that excellent little book. I have also derived ideas and suggestions from our four children and two of our grandchildren, Abbie and Coralie.)

CAPSULE 6: What the Experts Say About Disciplining Children

Children must be taught respect and responsibility. They must be brought under parental authority. And most of them need to be spanked now and then. But we are not limited to one disciplinary technique, nor will a single formula fit every situation or every human being. There will be times when a child should be required to spend ten minutes sitting on a chair. Or a privilege may be taken away or the child may be sent to bed an hour early … And occasionally, I have found it useful to talk to a repentant child and grant him or her unexpected and undeserved mercy. Children are infinitely complex.

Ultimately, the key to competent parenthood is in being able to get behind the eyes of your child, seeing what he sees and feeling what he feels. When he is lonely, he needs your company. When he is defiant, he needs your help in controlling his impulses. When he is afraid, he needs the security of your embrace. When he is curious, he needs your patient instruction. When he is happy, he needs to share his laughter and joy with those he loves.

Thus, the parent who intuitively comprehends the child's feelings is in a position to respond appropriately and meet the needs that are apparent. And at this point, raising healthy children becomes a highly developed art, requiring the greatest wisdom, patience, devotion and love that God has given to us.

JAMES DOBSON,
Discipline While You Can, Eastbourne, E. Sussex: Kingsway, 1987, pp. 120–121.

A few guidelines for balanced discipline:

Make the punishment fit the crime. Don't overreact to minor infractions, and take seriously the mistakes which carry long-term implications.

Logical consequences make the most sense and also teach valuable lessons, such as: "If you don't put away your toys, I'll have to put them up for a couple of days." "Since I don't like to see you act that way, why don't you sit in the other room until you're through pouting?"

"Pick your battlegrounds." This simple phrase expresses the need for you to decide which areas are important enough to "battle" over.

This is particularly true of teenagers. Since discipline takes a lot of thought and energy, you may decide not to battle over "cleaning your plate," or whether your daughter can wear makeup to school.

Distinguish between accidents, disobedience, and defiance. Even though accidents may be devastating to you personally, don't deal with them as harshly as disobedience or defiance … The most serious infraction is defiance, and therefore deserves the harshest consequences. If my daughter looks me right in the eye and pours the juice on my computer right after I tell her to take her juice back to the kitchen, that is defiance. For that a young child might be spanked or restricted to her room. An older child might even have to work to replace the computer he or she has ruined (a logical consequence of the defiant action) …

Punish the deed, not the doer.

Remember when your parents used to say, "This is going to hurt me more than it will hurt you," just before they spanked you? Even though it drove you crazy at the time, I believe the message behind those words is valid. The message is "Because I love you, I have to do this. But it hurts me, too."

When you react to your child's misbehavior, be careful to express your love for the child while also making your displeasure with the deed clear. Often you'll want to modify your immediate reaction. "You're acting like a stupid idiot" might become "I know you are very capable, but the way you're acting right now isn't very smart." "Shut up!" could be stated, "I want to listen to you, but could you please stop talking right now so that I can think?"

THOMAS WHITEMAN,
with Randy Petersen, *The Fresh Start Single Parenting Workbook*,
Nashville: Thomas Nelson Publishers, 1993, pp. 87–89.

Dr Spock and I are in opposite camps on many issues … However on the issue of discipline, I do not find myself in disagreement with his views. [In a TV program we both] endorsed the use of corporal punishment when appropriate. And if his earlier writings are examined carefully, one can find the recommendations for parental control represented, but not emphasized, therein. Very little was written which would earn him the title of "Ultimate Permissivist," although he recommended following permissive feeding schedules. (I certainly agree that babies should be fed when they are hungry, regardless of the clock or some arbitrary feeding plan.) Throughout his book, I feel he took a rather reasonable approach to parent-child relationships.

[In an article in *Redbook* magazine Dr Spock wrote:] "A child – let's say a girl – instantly detects parental hesitancy, parental guilt, parental crossness. These attitudes challenge her to resist requests and to demand more privileges. Her peskiness in turn makes the parent increasingly resentful inside, until this finally explodes in a display of anger – great or small – that convinces the child she must give in. In other words, parental submissiveness doesn't avoid unpleasantness; it makes it inevitable ..."

The parent who is most anxious to avoid conflict and confrontation often finds himself screaming and threatening and ultimately thrashing the child. Indeed, child abuse may be the end result.

This leads to *the* most common error in disciplining children, and perhaps the most costly. I am referring to the inappropriate use of *anger* in attempting to control boys and girls ...

There is no more ineffective method of controlling human beings (of all ages) than the use of irritation and anger. Nevertheless, *most* adults rely primarily on their own emotional response to secure the cooperation of children. One teacher said on a national television program, "I like being a professional educator, but I hate the daily task of teaching. My children are so unruly that I have to stay mad at them all the time just to control the classroom." How utterly frustrating to be required to be mean and angry as part of a routine assignment year in and year out.

JAMES DOBSON,
Discipline While You Can, Eastbourne, E. Sussex: Kingsway, 1987, pp. 98–99.

There are three important goals to keep in mind whenever you try to resolve conflicts between children or between a child and a parent:
- Everyone must win – no one must seem to lose.
- Understanding each other's point of view is more important than reaching agreement.
- Self-respect is more important than self-preservation.

Each of these goals has an important function. No one likes to be a loser or to feel in the wrong. Small children do not have the capacity to accept failure without "losing face," so whenever there is a conflict each party to the conflict should come out feeling they haven't lost their sense of value.

ARCHIBALD D. HART,
Children and Divorce, Dallas: Word Publishing, 1989, p. 170 .

A widow shared with us her feelings when she learned that her eighteen-year-old unwed daughter was pregnant – a situation prevalent enough today. Her first reaction was resentment, grief, shame and anger – anger against her daughter, anger against God. She felt put upon by the Lord and betrayed by her daughter. In the midst of her anguish she prayed and after a while she found an unexplainable strength, so that she was able to speak calmly to her daughter: "I want you to know I love you unconditionally. I'm not going to say I'm not hurt or humiliated or approving the action that brought your pregnancy about. But you're my child and I love you." Further prayer brought the widow to a new level of consciousness, enabling her to see within *herself* dark areas of pride, possessiveness, false values, and a spirit exhausted by sin. She saw the redemptive power of repentance and love, God triumphing in the midst of sin, and loving her unconditionally as she loved her daughter. Because of the daughter's humiliation, the family was drawn together, their love for one another increased, their faith was revitalized and assumed a wholly new and higher dimension.

MARY CLARE VINCENT,
The Life of Prayer and the Way to God,
Still River, Mass.: St Bede's Publications, 1982, pp. 23–24.

10

"Be a man!" But what exactly does that mean?

Then the Lord God formed man from the dust of the ground, and breathed into his nostrils the breath of life; and the man became a living being. And the Lord God planted a garden in Eden, in the east; and there he put the man whom he had formed ... The Lord God took the man and put him in the garden of Eden to till it and keep it (Genesis 2:7–8, 15).

Then Moses summoned Joshua and said to him in the sight of all Israel: "Be strong and bold, for you are the one who will go with this people into the land that the Lord has sworn to their ancestors to give them; and you will put them in possession of it. It is the Lord who goes before you. He will be with you; he will not fail you or forsake you. Do not fear or be dismayed" (Deuteronomy 31:7–8).

The God who has girded me with strength has opened wide my path. He made my feet like the feet of deer, and set me secure on the heights. He trains my hands for war, so that my arms can bend a bow of bronze. You have given me the shield of your salvation, and your help has made me great. You have made me stride freely, and my feet do not slip (2 Samuel 22:33–38).

O Lord, who may abide in your tent? Who may dwell on your holy hill? Those who walk blamelessly, and do what is right, and speak the truth from their heart; who do not slander with their tongue, and do no evil to their friends, nor take up a reproach against their neighbors; in whose eyes the wicked are despised, but who honor those who fear the Lord; who stand by their oath even to their hurt; who do not lend money at interest, and do not take a bribe against the innocent. Those who do these things shall never be moved (Psalm 15:1–5).

A gentle tongue is a tree of life, but perverseness in it breaks the spirit. Scoffers do not like to be rebuked; they will not go to the wise. Better is a little with the fear of the Lord than great treasure and trouble with it. Without counsel, plans go wrong, but with many advisers they succeed. To make an apt answer is a joy to anyone, and a word in season, how good it is! (Proverbs 15:4, 12, 16, 22–23). It is good for one to bear the yoke in youth (Lamentations 3:27).

I am distressed for you, my brother Jonathan; greatly beloved were you to me; your love to me was wonderful, passing the love of women (2 Samuel 1:26). Two are better than one, because they have a good reward for their toil. For if they fall, one will lift up the other; but woe to one who is alone and falls and does not have another to help (Ecclesiastes 4:9–10).

A man may beget a hundred children, and live many years; but however many are the days of his years, if he does not enjoy life's good things, or has no burial, I say that a stillborn child is better off than he (Ecclesiastes 6:3).

There's an old Celtic motto: "Never give a sword to a man who can't dance." Although the sword has been, from ancient times, a potent phallic symbol, there is now a wider wisdom in this saying. Men, particularly those who are fathers, suffer more "role confusion" in our Western cultures than any other group, with the possible exception of teenagers. And yet their importance in developing the self-esteem of their daughters, and in initiating their sons into manhood, can't be overestimated.

111

For some time I've had a thin file labeled *Men* and a very fat one labeled *Women*. But that's changing: from the mid-1980s the burgeoning American "men's movement" has been addressing the severe role conflicts in the modern male.

Robert Bly begins his seminal book *Iron John*: "We are living at an important and fruitful moment now, for it is clear to men that the images of adult manhood given by the popular culture are worn out; a man can no longer depend on them. By the time a man is thirty-five he knows that the images of the right man, the tough man, the true man which he received in high school do not work in life. Such a man is open to new visions of what a man is or could be ... We know that our society produces a plentiful supply of boys, but seems to produce fewer men" (*Iron John: A Book About Men*, New York: Vintage Books, 1992, pp. ix, 180).

Previously, unless they were sailors or traveling merchants, men worked at or near home. The Industrial Revolution changed all that. Then in the 1960s women invaded the work force, and in the 1970s they were demanding equal pay and status. At the same time the counter-culture mounted the first overt challenge to male sovereignty: the hippies were a put-down of the success-driven "organization man" of the 1950s, and the Vietnam protesters heaped scorn on the consecrated masculine proving ground of war. (They had studied war in college and learned, for example, that in World War I at Ypres in 1915, 100,000 young men died in one day. None saw the machine-gunners who mowed them down. For some reason these "post-war" students couldn't understand why anyone would "glory" in that.)

Little girls may either play with dolls or be a "tomboy," but little boys are not allowed to be "sissy." Because father isn't around the house much, many boys have few intimate male models. As a growing boy grasps for a definition of his maleness, it seems to be that which is not female. And media models don't help – on TV men are generally self-concerned, unemotional, preoccupied with their careers and their sexual prowess. The whole "macho" thing may cover up a deep sense of insecurity.

Here's the "composite male" I come across in my counseling. He is marginal to his family, has no deep relationships with anybody, and angrily "comes on heavy" with the kids as almost his sole contribution to parenting. He has no deep religious faith – that's something for women in church and kids in Sunday school. He's undeveloped emotionally and has never before talked to someone meaningfully about his inner life. When his wife mentions any marriage difficulties he can't see the problem (so long as she keeps the home – and sexual – fires burning). He is very reluctant to change into a caring (and cared for), growing person.

A German psychologist, Alexander Mitscherlich, has written that society has torn the soul of the male, and into this tear demons have fled – demons of insecurity, selfishness, and despair. So men do not really know who they are; they define themselves by what they do, who they know, or what they own.

Back to Robert Bly's *Iron John*. In essence Bly says that we have inherited a "responsible workaholic male" from the '50s; the '60s male, reacting to the Vietnam War, got in touch with his feminine side; then there was the '70s "soft male." The key challenge for the '80s and '90s male is to get in touch with the "hairy, primitive Wild Man" at the bottom of his psyche. This ought to happen when boys are initiated into the ranks of the men of the tribe. Modern fathers are too preoccupied to do this properly; and, anyway, our society has given them a "Dagwood Bumstead" image. Our modern psychology, says Bly, comes from two "mothers' men," Freud and Jung. So the young are angry; they "rage."

But there is positive energy buried deep within the male psyche. As Wild Man (in touch with positive sexuality and with nature as protector of the earth), Warrior (in the service of the True King, that is, a transcendent cause), Lover, Trickster (who does not "go with the flow" but reverses it), Magus (in touch with energies in the invisible world), and Grief Man (deriving great strength from the power to grieve), men can endure and achieve almost anything. But such energy comes only through "wounding" (an old tradition describes Jesus walking with a limp).

Another writer, Verne Becker, defines this woundedness in terms of passivity. Modern men, particularly in the family, respond and react rather than initiate. They feel a vague sense of loss and are alienated; they don't know how to relate to other men; they avoid responsibility, struggling with addictions or compulsions; they don't know how to get angry; they are entranced by women; they say yes too often; they have difficulty setting and defending their boundaries; they have no idea who they are on the inside, having lost touch with the core of their being buried deep in their psyche.

This passivity, writes Becker, finds its origins in several kinds of wounds: techno-wounds (since the Industrial Revolution men have left home to relate to machines, and now computers); entertainment-wounds (TV is our society's greatest passivity-creator); religious wounds (where religion does not introduce us to a deep experience of God); and eco-wounds (man's relationship to the earth has been severed). So we have a couple of generations of underfathered and overmothered sons, a suicide rate among men that is four times that of women, and a life expectancy ten percent shorter. "Men account for two-thirds of all alcoholics, ninety percent of all arrests for alcohol and drug abuse violations, eighty percent of America's homeless, and sixty percent of high school dropouts. Among minority groups the statistics are even worse … Together these data show the despair and desperation so many men feel" (Verne Becker, *The Real Man Inside*, Grand Rapids: Zondervan, 1992, p. 57).

So everything conspires to rob modern men of "masculine grandeur." We have few adequate mentoring relationships. Women have had two or three decades to sort out who they are (that process isn't finished yet), but men have a lot more work to do. Patriarchy has kept women in their place, so (as with any systemic injustice) women have had to be demanding and shrill in claiming equality with men.

I believe we should be "liberal" in our view of the equality of the sexes and "conservative" in our view of their God-given roles. Generally (but not always, for God is not a legalist) men are initiative-takers, women are responders. Sometimes (as with Deborah in the Old Testament) women are better leaders, so God doesn't mind them leading. Sometimes men are better in a subordinate role (as was Deborah's lieutenant Barak), so that's what God ordains for them.

When women who are not given leadership gifts usurp the role of leader, then there's trouble. If men refuse to be initiative-takers when God ordains that role for them, there's also trouble. Part of Eve's "original sin" was in her taking the lead in response to the serpent's offer, and one of the results of the Fall was men "ruling" over women. But the Fall is reversed in Christ. Nowhere in Jesus' teaching is there any note of women's subordination. Most of the evils of patriarchy result from our fallenness.

In Ephesians 5 we have a beautiful picture of the church as the Bride of Christ, and husbands loving their wives with Christ's love. Women ought to respect their husbands; husbands ought to love their wives enough to die for them: that's the evangelical ideal. After counseling with women for 7,000 hours, I've yet to meet one who knows her husband loves her like that and is not prepared to respect that man! The pre-Fall creation mandate, and the ideal of our re-creation in Christ, is of a man and a wife enjoying complementarity – living in unity and equality and interdependence.

Selected Quotations

Grown men are, deep down, only little boys, with more expensive toys.

BENJAMIN FRANKLIN .

The boys in our culture have a continuing need for initiation into the male spirit, but old men in general don't offer it. The priest some-times tries, but he is too much a part of the corporate village these days.

Among the Hopis and other native Americans of the South-west, the old men take the boy away at the age of twelve and ... he does not see his mother again for a year and a half.

The fault of the nuclear family today isn't so much that it's crazy and full of double binds (that's true in communes and corporate offices too – in fact in any group). The fault is that the old men outside the nuclear family no longer offer an effective way for the son to break his link with his parents without doing harm to himself.

The ancient societies believed that a boy becomes a man only through ritual and effort – only through the active intervention of the older men.

It's becoming clear to us that manhood doesn't happen by itself; it doesn't happen just because we eat Wheaties. The active intervention of the older men means that [they] welcome the younger man into the ancient, mythologized, instinctive male world ...

When women, even women with the best intentions, bring up a boy alone, he may in some way have no male face, or he may have no face at all ... A clean break from the mother is crucial, but it's simply not happening. This doesn't mean that the women are doing something wrong: I think the problem is more that the older men are not really doing their job ...

In New Guinea [they say]: "A boy cannot change into a man without the active intervention of the older men." A girl changes into a woman on her own, with the bodily developments marking the change; old women tell her stories and chants, and do celebrations. But with the boys, no old men, no change ...

ROBERT BLY,
Iron John: A Book About Men, New York: Vintage Books, 1992, pp. 14–15, 17, 19, 86–87.

When a man reaches his twenties, he sets out to make his place in the world. It is an exciting time for him as many aspects of his life begin to change. He starts to put most of his life's energy into building his career and, if he is married, into his marriage. He may be acutely aware of the burden he carries to meet his family's financial needs and may work fifty to seventy hours a week in order to provide the best of everything for the family he loves. He may jump through hoop after hoop in an effort to meet his driving need for achievement and his family's need for financial security.

In the midst of these compelling concerns, a man has little time for friends. There is no time to maintain close, caring friendships with his peers, or to develop relationships with older men who could support him in his growth as a husband and father and guide him as he navigates the twists and turns of his career. At this point in his life, a young man's energies are focused on priorities other than relationships.

Unfortunately, this is also a dangerous time for a young man. Every man needs close relationships with other men. When those relationships are lacking in a young man's life, trouble lies ahead. The emptiness a man feels inside from the woundedness of his relation-ship with his father can only be filled through relationships with other men and with God. Often, however, a man will seek to fill that masculine woundedness through relationships with women, but women cannot meet this deep emotional need. A man who shares his deeper feelings exclusively with women is either in trouble emotion-ally or is setting himself up for trouble later on.

This period of life is also risky because at this age most men ... are disconnected from their feelings. When a man is out of touch with his feelings of grief, emptiness and loss, he is simply unable to recognize the emotional needs of others around him. He cannot really identify with another person's feelings or what they are going through unless he has some understanding and connection with his own feelings. Since family relationships are emotionally intimate, an emotionally disconnected man will have a destructive impact on his loved ones.

EARL R. HENSLIN,
Man to Man, Nashville: Thomas Nelson Publishers, 1993, pp. 47–48.

[The following are some ways men tend to appear emotionally unaffected and in control of their lives]:

- Men rationalize a course of inaction by telling themselves "What good is it going to do to talk about it? That's not going to change anything!"
- Men worry internally, but rarely face what they really feel.
- Men escape into new roles or hide behind old ones.
- Men take the attitude that the "feelings" will pass and shrug them off as unimportant.
- Men keep busy, especially with work.
- Men change one feeling into another – becoming angry instead of experiencing hurt or fear.
- Men deny the feeling outright.
- Men put feelings on hold – put them in the file drawer and tend to forget what they were classified under.
- Feelings are confronted with drugs and alcohol.
- Men are excellent surgeons. They create a "thinking bypass" to replace feelings with thought and logic.
- Men tend to let women do their feeling for them.
- Men sometimes avoid situations and people who elicit certain feelings in them.
- Some men get sick or behave carelessly and hurt themselves so they have a reason to justify their feelings.

KEN DRUCK,
The Secrets Men Keep, New York: Ballantine Books, 1984, pp. 27–28.

Men, by nature, are task-oriented. Most men find it hard to come before the God who says, "Be still, and know that I am God" (Psalms

46:10). Unless they are writing something, building something, moving something, or changing something, they don't believe they are getting anywhere. Daily quiet times don't come easy for men, not even for pastors. It has to be cultivated, developed, and groomed before it becomes a natural part of the day.

BOB MOOREHEAD,
The Husband Handbook: Essentials for Growing a Successful Marriage,
Brentwood, Tenn.: Wolgemuth & Hyatt, Publishers, Inc., 1990, pp. 85–86.

It is not a very encouraging picture. We are hurting. But the hurting goes beyond the physical. It is found in our yearning for emotional intimacy with other males – sons, fathers, and friends – yet finding ourselves unprepared, unequipped, and fearful of that intimacy. The hurt is in our wanting relationships of genuine equality and mutuality with women, yet finding ourselves crippled by centuries of male sexism, and by our emotional dependencies on the opposite sex. The hurt is in our discovery that we have bought heavily into the message that our self-worth is directly dependent upon our occupational success, and yet the idol of work somehow does not deliver its promised salvation.

JAMES B. NELSON,
The Intimate Connection: Male Sexuality, Masculine Spirituality,
Philadelphia: The Westminster Press, 1988, p. 13.

God created us in the divine image, and we returned the favor, creating "God" in our own. Traditional male-constructed theism has perceived God as autonomous and unrelated. Transcendent. Wholly other. Sovereign in "his" absolute power. But there is an irony to this theological creation. Male theologians uncritical of patriarchal sexism, who themselves enjoyed and defended ecclesiastical male power monopolies, erected theologies that located all legitimate power in God and virtually none in humanity. God was imaged as male, and that meant power, control, and the demand for obedience. Many men are hungering for a fuller experience of God than this. Perhaps intuitively we sense that such a God is a "wounded father" we carry inside us, an image of God distant, cold, controlling, unavailable. We have had enough of separation. Yet healing that wounded God image is complex. The image has served what we thought was our self-interest. When God became male, males were divinized, and patriarchy had cosmic blessing.

JAMES B. NELSON,
The Intimate Connection: Male Sexuality, Masculine Spirituality,
Philadelphia: The Westminster Press, 1988, p. 45.

The Roman Stoics, who so influenced early Christianity, prized a life devoid of passion. Some early Christian Stoics, following their lead, wished that sexual intercourse (obviously necessary for the continuation of the race) might be as passionless as urinations. Medieval theologians were largely suspicious of sexual pleasure because in orgasm people seemed to lose their rationality, and to the medievalist, rationality was the key to human dignity. The Protestant Reformers of the sixteenth century abandoned the notion that celibacy was a higher virtue than married love, but they could not quite believe that sexual pleasure was good in its own right. It still remained God's enticement to procreation. The nineteenth-century Victorians simply assumed that sexual pleasure was animalistic. Each of these antipleasure chapters in the book of church history was dominated by male thought.

JAMES B. NELSON,
The Intimate Connection: Male Sexuality, Masculine Spirituality,
Philadelphia: The Westminster Press, 1988, p. 58.

The most delicate and important questions ... were about male sensibility when the child entered [the father's] world. I often found that I was one of the few people, sometimes the only one, to whom the man had spoken his feelings. He may not have done this with the woman ("I never knew you thought that" was a common interjection in the interviews), perhaps because she excluded him, or did not expect it of him or was obviously much better at such discussion herself. He hardly ever explored his private response with male colleagues at work. Conversation there was ritual, stylized, public – wages, sport, weather, holidays, politics, the job in hand ("My mates just didn't want to know," "Don't know whether they were bored or embarrassed, maybe just plain not interested"). I doubt if that was wholly so. Women inherit a culture which enables them to express intimate feelings. The mothers talk openly, freely and at length, between themselves about the minutiae and sensation of parenthood. Not every woman will use this chance, but nevertheless it is there, and the mothers are far more practised, skilled, and confident than the men in discussing and sharing the delights and depressions of parenthood. This does not mean that the fathers care or feel any less. They are anxious to express fatherhood. But they often met dilemmas. One was their lack of practice in articulating the gentler feelings, whether in word, touch or action ...

The first-time father needed a new vocabulary of expression if he was to attune his private with his public self. Perhaps the mothers, sharing intimate life, had always known this of him: voiceless love in the dark ... The tap-roots of fatherhood run deep. The image I take away is of men in tears at the birth, and yet feeling they had to disguise them. The question I most remember asking is "When did you last cry?", knowing that so often it would be countered with "Not since I was a child myself." To release the full force of fatherhood will mean breaking the masculine taboo on tenderness.

BRIAN JACKSON,
Fatherhood, London: George Allen & Unwin, 1984, pp. 134–135.

[Boys tend to] separate sexual feelings from emotional attachment ... Early in life boys have learned that sexual feelings have their own independence. Not so for the girl, for whom the explicitly sexual feelings were repressed in the early childhood experience with her mother. As Lillian Rubin remarks, "For a woman, sex usually has meaning only in a relational context – perhaps a clue to why so many girls never or rarely masturbate in adolescence or early adulthood."

JAMES B. NELSON,
The Intimate Connection: Male Sexuality, Masculine Spirituality,
Philadelphia: The Westminster Press, 1988, p. 78.

Male preoccupation with sexuality is widely assumed and has even been documented in various studies. Karen Shaner reports, for example, that men between twelve and forty-five think of sex an average of six times per hour. Between twelve and nineteen, it is twenty times per hour, or every five minutes. Such content of men's thoughts, as well as their frequency, is revealing. For the most part, the mental images of heterosexual men include the sexual "conquest" of women and fantasies of being the warrior and the victor ... While we caution against the over-generalization that all men are obsessed with predatory notions of sexuality, studies such as this confirm what we have come to recognize as normative for maleness in this culture – a mystique of masculinity that fashions images of power and sexual dominance, again and again, in the mind's eye. We believe the model of masculinity and male sexuality that men have been socialized to adopt is a violation of the biblical calling to live in justice-love and right-relatedness.

Presbyterians and Human Sexuality 1991, Louisville, Ky.:
The Office of the General Assembly Presbyterian Church (USA), p. 37.

In Genesis 3:16 the woman is being warned that she will experience an unreciprocated longing for intimacy with the man.

[The woman's] desire will be for her husband so as to perpetuate the intimacy that had characterized their relationship in paradise lost. But her nostalgia for the relation of love and mutuality that existed between them before the fall, when they both desired each other, will not be reciprocated by her husband. Instead of meeting her desire ... he will rule over her ... [In short], the woman wants a mate and she gets a master; she wants a lover and she gets a lord; she wants a husband and she gets a hierarch.

GILBERT BILEZIKIAN,
Beyond Sex Roles: A Guide for the Study of Female Roles in the Bible,
Grand Rapids: Baker Book House, 1985, pp. 55, 229.

In the last analysis a man can usually enforce his wishes upon his wife. Even if he never lays a finger on her, he will almost always be capable of bullying her to get what he wants ... We should simply face up to the fact, on the basis of Genesis 3:16 and empirical evidence, that the fall gives a man a certain power over a woman which he can easily use at her expense. His "strength" can be his wife's enslavement.

ANNE ATKINS,
Split Image: Male and Female after God's Likeness,
Grand Rapids: Eerdmans, 1987, pp. 168–169.

Am I then really all that which other men tell of?

Or am I only what I know of myself?

restless and longing and sick, like a bird in a cage,

struggling for breath, as though hands were compressing my
     throat,

hungry for colours, for flowers, for the voices of birds,

thirsty for words of kindness, of neighbourliness,

trembling with anger at despotisms and petty humiliation,

caught up in expectation of great events,

powerlessly grieving for friends at an infinite distance ...

Who am I? They mock me, these lonely questions of mine.

Whoever I am, thou knowest, O God, I am thine.

DIETRICH BONHOEFFER,
"Who Am I?" in *Letters and Papers from Prison*,
The Enlarged Edition, London, SCM Press, 1971, p. 348.

A Prayer for Men

So, Jesus, what kind of man were you?

You were strong and tender, introvert and extrovert, and had an easy familiarity both with men and women (and with children).

You knew who you were, so you didn't need anyone's approval (except your Father's).

You knew what you were on this planet to do, and you didn't hang around here after it was done.

You challenged people who were infected with their own self-importance.

You were gentle with others who did not think of themselves as important at all, whose self-esteem needed an injection of love.

You had the strength to confront the Powers, and they thought they "did you in." But such Life could never be extinguished.

You are alive in the world – your world – and in the church – your church. You are still doing your Father's will in the same way you did it in Judea and Galilee and Samaria (though now unseen).

Jesus, help me to be the man of God I was destined to be. Your Spirit is available to give me life and truth and comfort and love and power. As a modern male I need a special dose of all of these.

I ask all of this for your glory. Amen.

A Benediction

May Jesus the Messiah, Son of a woman and Son of God, who lived in the power of the Spirit and taught the truth of God his Father, and who died and rose again and ascended into heaven, and who is coming at the end of history to judge the living and the dead; may Jesus the Lord and Christ empower you to do in your world what he did in his. Amen.

CAPSULE 7: Males and Females

"Any man who says he can read a woman like a book is probably illiterate," says one gag.

In the Scriptures quietness and gentleness are emphasized in women's lives; courage and aggressiveness are underlined for men. Such "manliness" equips men to take social responsibility for groups, lead them, and protect them from harm. Now aggressiveness must not be confused with insensitivity. "Blessed are the meek," Jesus says, and here the "meek" are not the "weak," but those who have "controlled and disciplined strength."

Jesus and Paul introduced a new ethic into male–female relationships. Unlike his male contemporaries, Jesus treated women with great respect. Paul stressed that in Christ there are no more discriminating divisions between "male and female" (Galatians 3:28) and told husbands to "love your wives, just as Christ loved the church and gave himself up for her" (Ephesians 5:25). Peter similarly commanded husbands to treat their wives with understanding and respect (1 Peter 3:7). Peter added that women, too, are recipients of God's gift of life.

Men and women are different, physically and psychologically. They have different bodies, minds, emotions, and roles. The "brain sex" literature tells us that the genetic difference in DNA between men and women amounts to three percent, spread through every cell of our bodies. That is, three percent of males makes them masculine, and three percent of women makes them feminine – but we have ninety-seven percent in common. The challenge for men and women is to identify their "manliness" and "womanliness," and to become a "conscious man" and a "conscious woman." Let's not be too embarrassed, too proud, or too ashamed of our three percent!

Some writers talk about "the two sides of love." The hard side of love models strength, toughness, winning in spite of obstacles, "sticking at it" until it's finished. Movie stars like John Wayne, Clint Eastwood, and Charles Bronson have taught a generation of boys what it means to be a man in this sense. The soft side of love models nurturing qualities such as tenderness, self-sacrifice, the willingness sometimes to express emotion (for example, by crying) and to display affection (for example, by sensitive and appropriate touch or hugging). Well-put-together men display both sides of loving. Both "Sensitive New Age Guys" and construction workers who wolf-whistle passing girls can be true men, if they allow themselves to get in touch with all aspects of their masculinity.

11 | Dad, your kids need you more than you may realize!

As a father has compassion for his children, so the Lord has compassion for those who fear him (Psalm 103:13).

So deeply do we care for you that we are determined to share with you not only the gospel of God but also our own selves, because you have become very dear to us ... You are witnesses, and God also, how pure, upright, and blameless our conduct was toward you believers. As you know, we dealt with each one of you like a father with his children, urging and encouraging you and pleading that you lead a life worthy of God, who calls you into his own kingdom and glory (1 Thessalonians 2:8, 10–12).

David therefore pleaded with God for the child; David fasted, and went in and lay all night on the ground (2 Samuel 12:16). And when the feast days had run their course, Job would send and sanctify [his children], and he would rise early in the morning and offer burnt offerings according to the number of them all; for Job said, "It may be that my children have sinned, and cursed God in their hearts." This is what Job always did (Job 1:5). When you depart from me today you will meet two men by Rachel's tomb in the territory of Benjamin at Zelzah; they will say to you, "The donkeys that you went to seek are found, and now your father has stopped worrying about them and is worrying about you, saying: 'What shall I do about my son?'" (1 Samuel 10:2).

> Things that we have heard and known,
> that our ancestors have told us.
> We will not hide them from their children;
> we will tell to the coming generation
> the glorious deeds of the Lord …
> that the next generation might know them,
> the children yet unborn,
> and rise up and tell them to their children,
> so that they should set their hope in God,
> and not forget the works of God (Psalm 78:3–7).

Fathers, do not provoke your children, or they may lose heart (Colossians 3:21). Fathers, do not provoke your children to anger, but bring them up in the discipline and instruction of the Lord (Ephesians 6:4). Discipline your children while there is hope; do not set your heart on their destruction (Proverbs 19:18). [A bishop or overseer] must manage his own household well, keeping his children submissive and respectful in every way (1 Timothy 3:4).

Two events in my life as a father have indelibly imprinted themselves on my memory – and on my conscience. The first occurred one night when Jan and I were reading in bed. Our fourteen-year-old son Paul came into our room. Précised, the conversation went like this:

"Dad, you love the church more than you love the family, don't you?"

"What makes you think that, Paul?"

"Well, when we're having a family-time and someone from the church comes with a problem, you leave us to attend to them, and we may not see you any more that night. But when you're counseling someone in your study, we can't interrupt you. The church can interrupt the family, but the family can't interrupt the church. So the church is more important than the family."

What would you have said? Here was my lame response: "Paul, you and I do lots of things together. Most fathers are not around for a significant chunk of the day when they have to earn a living. I'm actually around more than most."

His response: "Yes, you're around, but I often think your head is somewhere else."

That week we installed a telephone-answering machine and put notes on the front door when we were having family-time. But it was too late for Paul. His hatred of the church persists to this day, twenty years later.

Actually, my problem as Paul's dad went deeper. He was a well-put-together kid, and although we played games together, we didn't often spend one-on-one time talking together. I didn't realize he desperately needed that. Of course he didn't ask for it (his dad was busy), but he shouldn't have had to ask. I should have realized that growing boys need to talk to their dads as the key to their initiation into manhood.

Now why didn't I know that? Simple: my own father (according to my memory) never had any worthwhile conversation with me. I can't remember ever exchanging more than half a meaningful sentence with him. He was a good man, a faithful provider, a diligent Bible student, and secretary of the little Brethren Assembly we attended three times every Sunday. But he didn't talk to me. My earliest memories of him were during the war when he came home dressed in a soldier's uniform. He was very handsome, I thought. I remember him at night studying to pass Public Service exams to get ahead because he had dropped out of school early. His father was a cleaner in a factory, and didn't talk to his son either …

My second "aha!" experience occurred halfway into a study-year in Canada. Jan went out to work and I was at home each afternoon when our younger daughters, Amanda and Lindy, came home from school. They had a snack and told me all about their day. It was wonderful! When Jan came home, however, they'd already told their stories, so over dinner I had to extract them again for Jan's benefit. Often I heard myself saying, "Darling, you've been so privileged over all these years to be there when the kids came home. I'm jealous!"

When you hear it said of some man "So-and-so's a success," what do you think of? His home and marriage? Unlikely – usually it's his career. What nurtures the family unit is in conflict with what maximizes personal development. And yet the highest happiness on earth is in marriage and family. Every man who is a happy husband and father is a successful man, even if he's failed in everything else. I like the story about a man who came to his friend Carl Jung, saying enthusiastically, "I've been promoted!" Jung said, "I'm very sorry to hear that; but if we all stick together, I think we will get through it." Another friend said ashamedly, "I've just been fired." Jung replied, "Let's open a bottle of wine; this is wonderful news; something good will happen now."

Fathers in the industrialized world have generally failed to integrate competent fathering with "breadwinning." But that's not a new problem. Robert Bly, in *Iron John*, points out that there are no good fathers in the major stories of Greek mythology, and very few in the Old Testament.

Fathers, your family is precious. Take time to recognize how important each member of the family is to you, and communicate that. All members of your family need to know that you care about them. You'll be surprised at how many family "problems" evaporate when you communicate warmth and love and trust to your family.

Quality time with children involves not merely spending time, but wasting time with them. The serendipitous moment when a child says "Hey Dad," "Hey Mum" can't be planned – you've got to be around when it happens. Modern dads are often bigamous until they're into their forties – married to their job as first priority. A spate of books about "absent fathers and lost sons" is pointing to a trend for boys not understanding what it means to be masculine because Dad isn't home enough, doing interesting and instructive things with his younger and teenage sons. Does a teenager really want his Dad? Yes, if a strong relationship was built between them in earlier years.

And so does a teenage daughter. At puberty most girls have as their Number One question: "Am I attractive to guys?" The girl's father is the representative male, and if Dad gives the message, "Hey, how did I deserve a gorgeous daughter like you? There's some lucky young fellow wandering the earth ...," the daughter's self-esteem gets a real assist. Future marital happiness for a woman depends as much on her previous relationship with her Dad as on her relationship with her husband – and sometimes more.

Selected Quotations

Child psychologist Dr Urie Bronfenbrenner was once asked, "What is the key ingredient in the successful development of a human being?" Without hesitation he replied, "Someone, some adult, has to be crazy about the kids." We all know what he meant. Our children need 100 percent of us. I can't have one eye on the television and one eye on Sarah's homework. You can't "listen" to your children when you're still replaying in your mind the big staff meeting at work. Kids have great antennae. They know where they stand in our priorities.

GARY BAUER,
Our Journey Home: What Parents Are Doing to Preserve Family Values,
Dallas: Word Publishing, 1992, p. 127.

It is little more than a month since I was handed this living heap of expectations, and I can feel nothing but simple awe … I have got a daughter, whose life is already separate from mine, whose will already follows its own directions, and who has quickly corrected my woolly preconceptions of her by being something remorselessly different. She is the child of herself and will be what she is. I am merely the keeper of her temporary helplessness.

LAURIE LEE,
"The Firstborn," quoted in Alexandra Towle (ed.), *Fathers*,
Artarmon, NSW: Harper & Row, 1986, p. 214.

David Blankenhorn of the Institute for American Values has pointed out that the phrase "good family man" has almost disappeared from our popular language. This compliment was once widely heard in our culture – bestowed, to those deserving it, as a badge of honor. Rough translation: "He puts his family first." Ponder the three words: "good" (moral values); "family" (purposes larger than the self); and man (a norm of masculinity). Yet today within elite culture, the phrase sounds antiquated, almost embarrassing … Contemporary American culture simply no longer celebrates, among its various and competing norms of masculinity, a widely shared and compelling ideal of the man who puts his family first.

DAVID BLANKENHORN,
"What Do Families Do?", paper presented at Stanford University, November 1989, p. 19.
Quoted in James Dobson and Gary L. Bauer, *Children at Risk: Winning the Battle for the Hearts and Minds of Your Children*, Dallas: Word Publishing, 1990, p. 166.

In addition to purely physical power, of course, fatherhood repre-
sents a great deal of psychological power in a child's life. Because
your child sees you as a successful, dynamic member of the world he
[or she] wants to enter, you have the power to shape significantly
what your child will become. By using the power to educate, to set
limits, to make decisions, you will influence much about your child's
personality.

Unlike personal power, nurturance, the ability to protect and
comfort a child, has been an undervalued facet of masculinity in our
society. Many men believe they may express nurturance toward their
children only by protecting them from outside dangers or by
economically providing for the family and not through a personal,
tender relationship with the child. They don't see it as masculine and
thus don't see it as a natural part of their father power.

Children, male and female, possess a natural tendency to give and
respond to tenderness – from both parents. If you allow nurturance
to be a totally feminine domain in your family, you can hurt both
your sons and your daughters. Rigid, strict, punitive fathers compel
their sons to stifle tender feelings and become harsh and unloving
themselves. Such fathers make their daughters feel that men are not
tender creatures, that only harsh men are masculine.

To associate nurturance with femininity is a common mistake in
American society. Indeed, usually we call it "mothering" instead of
"parenting" ... The father crooning to his infant may not feel himself
quite the masculine male. Rather than seeing it as weakness, you
should adopt the attitude that you are showing nurturance-from-
strength. You should realize that you are actually evidencing power
and competence by showing your children how to throw a ball or by
cuddling them.

HENRY BILLER and DENNIS MEREDITH,
Father Power, New York: David McKay Co Inc., 1974, p. 104.

Almost all the fathers who attended the birth reached an ecstatic
peak of emotion: a personal Everest. Often this was at the moment of
birth itself, sometimes it came an hour or two later as the shock
passed through their system. Then for some while afterwards, their
behavior was manic, disordered, high ... "I felt like an astronaut
who'd landed on the moon." Even the more withdrawn ones became

voluble, often drawing total strangers into eager conversation. So powerful was the feeling that almost every man cried. Some did this quite openly, some brushed away the tears or sought to conceal them. The taboo against men's tears is fierce, and for many this was the first time they had cried since they were small children themselves. We checked the accuracy of this by observing fathers at twenty successive births. Eighteen were crying. The other two were numbed; perhaps their tears came later … Most men will become fathers. They will not receive all that much of a cultural bequest to help them in the art and science of the role: how dads become dads, and how they might emerge as better ones. The old strategies are changing.

BRIAN JACKSON,
Fatherhood, London: George Allen and Unwin, 1984, pp. 121–122.

No man can possibly know what life means, what the world means, what anything means, until he has a child and loves it. And then the whole universe changes and nothing will ever again seem exactly as it seemed before.

LAFCADIO HEARN,
quoted in Alexandra Towle (ed.), *Fathers*, Artarmon, NSW: Harper & Row, 1986, p. 211.

There is considerable evidence of the impact – for good and bad – of family life on children. Consider the intense bitterness which Germaine Greer expresses towards her parents in *Daddy, We Hardly Knew You*. Cut by her father's abandonment of her to go to war, her anguish is intensified by his subsequent failure to want to know her and show her affection: "Some children can remember their fathers reciting Urdu poetry or Marlowe, or teaching them to recognise birds and butterflies, to spot trains, to play chess or cricket. But you, Daddy dear? Not a curve-ball, not a cover-drive, not a card-trick. Not a maxim. Not a saw, adage or proverb. Except, 'You're big enough and ugly enough to take care of yourself.'"

KEVIN ANDREWS,
"The Family, Marriage and Divorce," in *The Australian Family*, Quarterly Journal of the Australian Family Association, Vol. 13, No. 4, December 1992, p. 18.

Lily and I regard ourselves as our children's servants. It is for this reason that we do not expect – except in our more immature moments – any great gratitude from them. They are entitled to our service; it is our position to serve them. It is our expectation that they themselves will grow into servanthood – that having been served and having role models for service, they will be able to serve their children and the world in turn ... We would hardly serve our children well if we did everything they wanted, obeyed their every whim ... And wherever the decisions are made, that's where the locus of power resides.

M. SCOTT PECK
with Marilyn Von Walder and Patricia Kay, *What Return Can I Make?*,
London: Arrow Books, 1985, pp. 55–56.

Three hundred years ago Jonathan Edwards, a dynamic Calvinistic preacher, was largely responsible for the Great Awakening in this country ...

[He] married a godly woman, and over the past three hundred years his descendants have included: 265 college graduates, twelve college presidents, sixty-five university professors, sixty physicians, one hundred clergy... thirty judges, three Congressmen, two Senators, and one Vice President of the United States.

Sociologists have compared the effects of Jonathan Edwards' life and marriage to those of another man living at the same time: Max Juke – a derelict and ungodly vagabond who married a woman of similar character. Over the generations, their union has produced: three hundred children who died in infancy, 310 professional paupers, 440 crippled by disease, fifty prostitutes, sixty thieves, seven murderers, and fifty-three assorted criminals of other varieties.

D. JAMES KENNEDY,
Learning to Live With the People You Love, Springdale, Pa.: Whitaker House, 1987, p. 75.

Armand Nicholi, a clinical professor of psychiatry at Harvard medical school, has studied the literature on the question of parental absence and children's well-being. The literature spans over forty years of research and study. His conclusion is this: "What has been shown over and over again to contribute most to the emotional development of the child is a close, warm, sustained and continuous relationship with *both parents*" ...

Nicholi goes on to make this observation: "One other comment about this research. In addition to the magnitude of it, the studies taken as a whole paint an unmistakably clear picture of the adverse effects of parental absence. Yet this vast body of research is almost totally ignored by our society. Why have even the professionals tended to ignore this research? Perhaps the answer is, to put it most simply, because the findings are unacceptable.

"Attitudes which now prevail toward parental absence resemble those once prevalent toward cigarette smoking. For decades Americans ignored the large body of research concerning the adverse effects of cigarette smoke. We had excellent studies for decades before we began to respond to the data. Apparently as a society, we refuse to accept data that demands a radical change in our lifestyle."

"The Assault on the Family," *Family Update*, a Bi-Monthly Newsletter of the
Australian Family Association, Vol. 9, No. 3, May–June 1993.

"Clubhouse" magazine, a publication of James Dobson's *Focus on the Family*, recently asked its young readers to share what they liked most about their dad ... I was struck by how seldom these children mentioned physical possessions or material things their fathers provided them. Instead it was the simple manifestations of love and commitment that were cited most often, the very things that sometimes fall by the wayside in our increasingly fast-moving world.

"A father should be not only your dad, but your friend, too" – Samantha, age ten, Southaven, Mississippi.

"My dad's most important quality is his willingness to ask forgiveness from me when he is wrong" – Stephanie, age nine, Duluth, Georgia.

"A good dad would come to your games ... and miss work just for you" – Brook, age twelve, Roswell, Georgia.

"The most important quality in my father is that he makes me feel safe" – Erin, age nine, Kansas City, Missouri.

"A dad must discipline you when you do something wrong so you won't grow up to be a bad person" – Lisa, age thirteen, Concord, California.

"I think a dad should care about his children's grades and their lives. And it helps when your dad will study for a test with you" – Lynn, age ten, Chambersburg, Pennsylvania.

"The most important qualities of a father are that he loves and does the best he can for his kids. My dad does that all of the time ...

well, most of the time. No dad is perfect" – Alicia, age eleven, Wausaw, Wisconsin.

All of these touched my heart. But one came at me like a freight train. It was written by ten-year-old Sommer from Fergus Falls, Minnesota: "The most important thing is that my father loves my mother."

GARY BAUER,
Our Journey Home: What Parents Are Doing to Preserve Family Values,
Dallas: Word Publishing, 1992, pp. 145–146.

This morning I asked my nine-year-old son, "Do you know that I love your mother?"

"Yeah," he said.

"How do you know?" I persisted.

"You tell her all the time," he said.

"Well," I continued, "what if I lost my voice and couldn't say I loved her. Would she still know I loved her?"

"Yeah," he said. "You could write it down for her."

So I said, "OK, son, let's say I had both my arms amputated, and I can't write with my feet. Would she know I loved her?"

"Yes," he said. "I'd tell her for you."

"Wait," I said. "How would you know I loved her?"

Long pause. "By the way you treat her," he said.

It took about five minutes to get him to the point. But eventually he saw that love goes deeper than words.

JOSH McDOWELL,
"Love is Shown by Actions," in LaVonne Neff et al., *Practical Christianity,*
© 1987 by Youth for Christ/USA.
Used by permission of Tyndale House, Wheaton, Ill., 1988, p. 232.

A father needs to be willing to be finite and mortal in his children's eyes ... The image which needs to be shattered is that fathers are the ones who know all the answers, can take charge in all situations, are always right and never make mistakes. What needs to be communicated is that fathers do have a great responsibility in the home but that it is possible for fathers to misunderstand a situation, to make wrong judgments, to get their own ego involved in a situation, and to need forgiveness.

KENNETH CHAFFIN,
Is There a Family In the House?, Minneapolis: World Wide Publications, 1978, pp. 92–93.

When a father now sits down at the table, he seems weak and insignificant, and we all sense that fathers no longer fill as large a space in the room as nineteenth-century fathers did. Some welcome this, but without understanding all its implications.

These events have worked to hedge the father around with his own paltriness. D.H. Lawrence said: "Men have been depressed now for many years in their male and resplendent selves, depressed into dejection and almost abjection. Is that not evil?"

As the father seems more and more enfeebled, dejected, paltry, he also appears to be a tool of dark forces. We remember that in *Star Wars* we are given the image of "Darth Vader," a pun on dark father. He is wholeheartedly on the side of the dark forces. As political and mythological kings die, the father loses the radiance he once absorbed from the sun, or from the hierarchy of solar beings; he strikes society as being endarkened ...

In our time, when the father shows up as an object of ridicule ... on television, or a fit field for suspicion (as he does in *Star Wars*), or a bad-tempered fool (when he comes home from the office with no teaching), or a weak puddle of indecision (as he stops inheriting kingly radiance), the son has a problem. How does he imagine his own life as a man?

Some sons fall into a secret despair. They have probably adopted, by the time they are six, their mother's view of their father, and by twenty will have adopted society's critical view of fathers, which amounts to a dismissal.

ROBERT BLY,
Iron John: A Book About Men, New York: Vintage Books, 1992, pp. 98–99.

As University of Utah psychologist Michael Lamb puts it, "Fathers are not merely occasional mother-substitutes: they interact with infants in a unique and differentiable way." Whereas mothers tend to talk to or cuddle with their kids or play with dolls, blocks and puzzles, fathers naturally engage in physical activities ... As a result of these different playing styles, children often look to their mothers for warmth, quiet-time activities, and verbal stimulation, while they value their fathers as wonderful playmates who introduce them to the world at large. Both are important ... Father-play tends to be lively, unpredictable, imaginative and obviously exciting ... Not only are these differences normal, they are crucial to a child's development. Each parenting style teaches your child different things about the world. Mother's approach informs him that the world can be cuddly, safe, nurturing and supportive. Father's process lets him know that it can be all of those things but also jostling, unsettling, fun and surprising.

MITCH GOLANT and SUSAN GOLANT,
Finding Time for Fathering, New York: Ballantine Books,
Fawcett Columbine, 1992, pp. 45–46.

One of the great distorting idolatries of our day is the confusion between the standard of living and the quality of life. It is no wonder that so many books are being written about fatherhood at the moment, for it has rarely been the case that so many men who purport to believe in "family values" while in church are so absent from the home during the week. Many men leave home early in the morning, leave work late at night and even work at weekends. They may believe that men are the decision makers in the family, but it is their women who make the decisions. They may believe the man is the head of the household, but the household has to function without him. They may believe that the man should take the spiritual initiative, but they are too shattered to pray. Such men will improve the quality of their relationships only if they make more time for those relationships. In a world in which time is money, this means that they must accept a lower standard of living, less status and less power.

ROY McCLOUGHTY,
"The Yoke Of Masculinity," *On Being*, Vol. 20, No. 7, August 1993, pp. 17–18.

Fathers send subtle and not-so-subtle messages to both their sons and daughters about how men walk, talk, dress, relate to one another, and relate to women. These lessons are important. Without them, our children would have a void in their lives. Statistics show that boys who are reared without a father • have greater difficulty relating to other men • don't know how to treat women • have a higher rate of divorce • don't know how to raise their own sons.

Daughters who are raised without a father figure • have more difficulty relating to men • may turn to sexuality as their only means

137

of relating • have a harder time choosing a husband • and divorce those men at a higher rate than other women.

THOMAS WHITEMAN,
with Randy Petersen, *The Fresh Start Single Parenting Workbook*,
Nashville: Thomas Nelson Publishers, 1993, p. 166.

A man's personal relationship with God often mimics his relationship with his father.

The overall result of father wound on the religious life of most men is that they tend to be spiritually passive and inactive. They may come to church, but they are not really there. They may hear a sermon intellectually, but its message may never penetrate their hearts enough to make a difference in their lives. They may serve as ushers and shake people's hands before and after the service or as elders who make financial and policy decisions for the church, but they often cannot make themselves connect with what church is really about. They can't connect enough to be fully involved with heart, mind, and soul ...

Lacking a feeling connection in their relationship with God, most men feel inadequate to be the spiritual leaders they know they should be, so they feel shamed. They tend to withdraw from the church, leaving even less male leadership for the next generation ... If your church is like most churches, women either design or run a high percentage of its programs.

The fact is, today's church is primarily a feminine church. By saying this, I do not mean to imply that I am anti-feminine. However, I must ask, "Where are the men?" Where are the men who are spiritually alive? Who have a fire in their bellies – a passion to grow towards God, a passion to grow as men, and a passion to grow toward other men? Who are willing to take bold risks in their faith? Where are the men who will take action in sharing the gospel of Christ? Who will live out their faith through active involvement in the Christian church community?

The church desperately needs the involvement of such men, yet they are difficult to find. For generations, men have been wounded by the lack of male leadership and modeling of spiritual truth by older men. Consequently, men are greatly shamed when they realize that they should be spiritual leaders, teachers and models, yet have no idea how to assume those roles. Many men would rather abandon the church (either physically or emotionally) than deal with these feelings of shame and inadequacy.

EARL R. HENSLIN,
Man to Man, Nashville: Thomas Nelson Publishers, 1993, pp. 79, 80–81.

A Prayer for Fathers

Lord God, father of us all,
you have entrusted me with these little people,
and it's an awesome responsibility.

I am stretched beyond my limits:
I'm supposed to be
the provider of food and shelter and clothing
and of answers for school homework;
chauffeur, gardener/janitor, financier,
and fixer of everything.

I am supposed to model what it means to live and to love,
and to represent you as priest in my home.

They're big responsibilities.

Lord, I've found it's easier
for a father to have children
than for children to have a father.

The emotional demands of work,
financial pressures,
marriage,
and lots of other things
leave me with little left over for the kids.

Help me to compose myself before I reach home each day
so I'm available for my family.
Help me to be a growing person, so that out of the reservoir
of spiritual and emotional strength I'll have some energy
to give to my wife and children.

Help me to understand myself,
my past,
my strengths and my limits,
my masculine and my feminine traits,
my anger,
my fears,
my weaknesses.

What I say to my children may not be heard by the world,
but it will be heard by posterity.
These kids are like wax and are being formed into something
beautiful or terrible.
I carry a big responsibility for the outcome.
May they always know there is nothing or no one more
valuable to me than they are.

So, hear my confession of ignorance and failure;
cleanse me from all selfishness
and forgive my ignorance.
Help me to forgive my own father for his faults and failings:
I'm not responsible for them, but for me.
Help me to love my children's mother.
May I be a good priest in my home.

And when the Great Day comes and I stand before you,
my king and my judge,
I would like to hear you say,
"Well done, good and faithful father.
Your children have delighted in you,
and you are blessed." Amen.

A Benediction

May God the Father, Jesus our Friend, the Holy Spirit our counselor and teacher, empower you so that you may empower others. May the demands and the pain of fathering be for you a challenge rather than a burden. May your years with your children be the happiest in your life. Amen.

CAPSULE 8: Absent Fathers, Lost Children

As I look back on more than forty years of married life, I am astonished that the work of the ministry does not destroy ministers' marriages. The minister will have the best and biggest room in his house for his study. The minister sees less of his family than any member of his congregation does. He sees less of his children. He has to leave it to his wife to bring them up. Seldom can he have an evening out with his wife and, even when such an evening is arranged, something again and again comes to stop it. Demands to speak and to lecture take him constantly away from home and, when he does come home, he is so tired that he is the worst company in the world, and falls asleep in his chair. As I come near to the end of my days, the one thing that haunts me more than anything else is that I have been so unsatisfactory a husband and a father. As the Song of Solomon has it: "They made me keeper of the vineyards; but my own vineyard I have not kept." When the Pastoral Epistles are laying down the qualifications for the elder, the deacon and the bishop one of the unvarying demands is that "he must know how to manage his own household" – and for a minister that is the hardest thing in the world.

WILLIAM BARCLAY,
Testament of Faith, Oxford: Mowbrays, 1977, pp. 16–17.

We had a lot of good times together, but Mary [my wife] never got wrapped up in the corporate life. She didn't try to keep up with the Joneses. For both of us, the family was supreme. As for the responsibilities of the corporate wife, she did what was necessary, and she did it with a smile. But her values – and mine – were home and the hearth …

Your job takes up enough time without having to shortchange your family. The four of us used to take a lot of motor trips, especially when the kids were young. That's when we really got close as a family. No matter what else I did in those years, I know that two sevenths of my whole life – weekends, and a lot of evenings – was devoted to Mary and the kids. Some people think that the higher up you are in the corporation, the more you have to neglect your family.

Not at all! Actually, it's the guys at the top who have the freedom and the flexibility to spend enough time with their wives and kids. Still, I've seen a lot of executives who neglect their families, and it always makes me sad …

You can't let a corporation turn into a labor camp. Hard work is essential. But there's also a time for rest and relaxation, for going to see your kid in the school play or at the swim meet. And if you don't do those things while the kids are young, there's no way to make it up later on … Yes I've had a wonderful and successful career. But next to my family, it really hasn't mattered at all.

LEE IACOCCA,
Iacocca: An Autobiography, New York: Bantam Books, 1984, pp. 304–305.

A young man told me of a conversation he had in hospital with his father just before he died. The father, a perpetually busy man, had not spent much time with his children and the son expressed his regret that they had not shared more together. The father responded by reminding his son that he had worked long hours in order to put food on the table to feed the family. The son remained silent, but in his heart he was yearning to tell his father that he had never been as hungry for food as he had been for his father's presence.

RABBI NEIL KURSHAM.
Quoted in Mitch Golant and Susan Golant, *Finding Time For Fathering*,
New York: Ballantine Books, 1992, p. 60.

When the office work and the "information revolution" begin to dominate, the father–son bond disintegrates. If the father inhabits the house only for an hour or two in the evenings, then women's values, marvelous as they are, will be the only values in the house. One could say that the father now loses his son five minutes after birth …

The German psychologist Alexander Mitscherlich writes about this father–son crisis in his book called *Society Without the Father*. The gist of his idea is that if the son does not actually see what his father does during the day and through all the seasons of the year, a hole will appear in the son's psyche, and the hole will fill with demons who tell him that his father's work is evil and that the father is evil …

Not receiving any blessing from your father is an injury. Robert Moore said, "If you're a young man and you're not being admired by an older man, you're being hurt ... " Not seeing your father when you are small, never being with him, having a remote father, an absent father, a workaholic father, is an injury ...

Between twenty and thirty percent of American boys now live in a house with no father present, and the demons there have full permission to rage ...

When a father, absent during the day, returns home at six, his children receive only his temperament, not his teaching ... The father returns home ... usually irritable and remote ... [and] children do not receive the blessing of his teaching ... A father's remoteness may severely damage the daughter's ability to participate good-heartedly in later relationships with men. Much of the rage that some women direct to the patriarchy stems from a vast disappointment over this lack of teaching from their own fathers.

ROBERT BLY,
Iron John: A Book About Men, New York: Vintage Books, 1992, pp. 21, 31, 96, 97.

The men in my family are hardworking, good men, but most of them are disconnected from their feelings. That is the norm for upper midwestern farm families like ours. We value hard work and consider it noble to bear, in stoic silence, whatever physical or emotional pain comes our way. Our unspoken rule is "men do not feel." The men in our family know little about emotional expression. One rarely hears a hearty laugh or feels a warm hug from strong arms, or offers a spontaneous "I love you."

It is tragic that sons should suffer such loss and woundedness from fathers who truly love them, but it happens. I know my father loved me. I know he cared. He worked hard, sacrificed for his family, and was a good provider, but he did not know how to help me feel loved. I also know that my father did not feel loved by his father. He never received affirmation from his father, and I doubt that he ever felt the warmth and comfort of a loving hug from his father. My father was unable to give what he had never received himself. He didn't have a clue about how to reach out to me emotionally because no one had ever reached out to him ...

Every boy yearns to be sought out by his father. When a boy lacks this emotional connection, his natural response is to try to do something that will cause his father to demonstrate his love for him, something that will create an emotional bond between them. Different boys try different behaviors. One boy will become an over-achiever. "Maybe if I do well enough in school or make the basketball team," the boy reasons, "Dad will think I'm special." Another boy will cause trouble at home or at school until he gains his father's attention. Regardless of the outward behavior, the motivation is the same – to be emotionally connected or close to the father ...

There is no substitute for an intimate, emotional connection between father and son. This connection cannot be made by a father who is physically or emotionally absent. It cannot be made by a father who functions at home in the same way he functions in the workplace. It takes time and emotional involvement for a father to establish intimacy with his son.

EARL R. HENSLIN,
Man to Man, Nashville: Thomas Nelson Publishers, 1993, pp. 9–11, 41–42.

I was an overmothered son. At its simplest, overmothering means that the amount of time the mother devotes to the son is much greater – often hugely disproportionate – to the time the father spends with the son ... Here we see a pattern that has ensnared millions of men in passivity during this century: The father is absent, abusive, or unavailable, alienating the son and placing too heavy a burden on the mother ... Female traits can and should be encouraged in men. So many men are afraid to show tenderness and fear and hurt and other emotions that women can express more easily. Men need to be willing to nurture the female side of themselves, and mothers can be helpful in this process. But when it comes to a man's masculine traits, which include his perception of fatherhood and of mature manhood, these cannot be obtained through the mother, no matter how hard she tries or how pure her motives are.

VERNE BECKER,
The Real Man Inside: How Men Can Recover Their Identity and Why Women Can't Help,
Grand Rapids: Zondervan, 1992, pp. 68–70.

A man's relationship with his father has a tremendous bearing on his personal relationship with God. When a bond exists between father and son, the son will find it easier to trust his father's spirituality and to model his father's spiritual life. If a man's relationship with his earthly father has been marked by woundedness, he will find it difficult to know how to expect anything different in his relationship with God. In fact, a little boy's first image of God the Father reflects the image of his earthly father. A strong emotional connection between father and son makes it easier for the son to feel spiritually connected with God, but if no emotional bridge exists, the son may feel as though God is distant and disinterested.

Consider these common examples of how a man's relationship with God mirrors his relationship with his father: • If a man's father has been unpredictable or moody, made promises he did not keep, or failed to support him when he needed it, a man does not know what he can count on in his relationship with his Heavenly Father. • If a man's father has been critical, judgmental, difficult to please, or cruel, a man will tend to view God as a harsh taskmaster who is just waiting for an excuse to punish him. • If a man's father has been shaming or demanded perfection, a man will feel hopelessly inadequate before God, compelled to do as much as he can "for God," yet feeling guilty for never doing enough. • If a man's father has been passive when action was appropriate, a man will have a hard time trusting God to play an active role in his life. • If a man's father had a strong, macho personality, showed no compassion and denied or minimized pain, a man will find it hard to believe that God is compassionate and cares deeply about his pain, his struggles, or his fears.

Clearly, all of the emotions that are wrapped up in a man's relationship with his father are also wrapped up in his relationship with God. When healing for those issues begins to take place, a man will experience God differently and feel his presence more deeply.

EARL R. HENSLIN,
Man to Man, Nashville: Thomas Nelson Publishers, 1993, pp. 88–90.

A child arrived the other day
He came to the world in the usual way
But there were planes to catch and bills to pay
He learned to walk while I was away
And he was talkin' 'fore we knew it and as he grew
He said, "I'm gonna be like you, Dad,

You know I'm gonna be like you."
"When ya comin' home Dad?" "I don't know when
But we'll get together then, yeah,
We're gonna have a good time then …"

I've long since retired, and my son moved away
I called him up just the other day
Said, "I'd like to see you if you don't mind."
He said, "I'd love to, Dad, if I could find the time
But the new job's a hassle and the kid's got the flu
But it's been sure nice talking to you."
And as I hung up the phone it occurred to me
He'd grown up just like me
My boy was just like me.

HARRY CHAPIN,
"Cat's in the Cradle." Quoted in Edwin Louis Cole, *Maximized Manhood:
A Guide to Family Survival*, Springdale, Pa.: Whitaker House, 1982, pp. 58–59.

12 | Why God made mothers

Just as you do not know how the breath comes to the bones in the mother's womb, so you do not know the work of God, who makes everything (Ecclesiastes 11:5). Can a woman forget her nursing child, or show no compassion for the child of her womb? Even these may forget, yet I will not forget you (Isaiah 49:15). As a mother comforts her child, so I will comfort you; you shall be comforted in Jerusalem (Isaiah 66:13).

A capable wife who can find? She is far more precious than jewels. The heart of her husband trusts in her, and he will have no lack of gain. She does him good, and not harm, all the days of her life. She seeks wool and flax, and works with willing hands. She is like the ships of the merchant, she brings her food from far away. She rises while it is still night and provides food for her household and tasks for her servant girls. She considers a field and buys it; with the fruit of her hands she plants a vineyard. She girds herself with strength, and makes her arms strong. She perceives that her merchandise is profitable. Her lamp does not go out at night. She puts her hands to the distaff, and her hands hold the spindle. She opens her hand to the poor, and reaches out her hands to the needy. She is not afraid for her household when it snows, for all her household are clothed in crimson. She makes herself coverings; her clothing is fine linen and purple. Her husband is known in the city gates, taking his seat among the elders of the land. She makes linen garments and sells them; she supplies the merchant with sashes. Strength and dignity are her clothing, and she laughs at the time to come. She opens her mouth with wisdom, and the teaching of kindness is on her tongue. She looks well to the ways of her household, and does not eat the bread of idleness. Her children rise up and call her happy; her husband too, and he praises her: "Many women have done excellently, but you surpass them all." Charm is deceitful, and beauty is vain, but a woman who fears the Lord is to be praised. Give her a share in the fruit of her hands, and let her works praise her in the city gates (Proverbs 31:10–31).

Wives, in the same way, accept the authority of your husbands, so that, even if some of them do not obey the word, they may be won over without a word by their wives' conduct, when they see the purity and reverence of your lives. Do not adorn yourselves outwardly by braiding your hair, and by wearing gold ornaments or fine clothing; rather, let your adornment be the inner self with the lasting beauty of a gentle and quiet spirit, which is very precious in God's sight. It was in this way long ago that the holy women who hoped in God used to adorn themselves by accepting the authority of their husbands. Thus Sarah obeyed Abraham and called him lord. You have become her daughters as long as you do what is good and never let fears alarm you. Husbands, in the same way, show consideration for your wives in your life together, paying honor to the woman as the weaker sex, since they too are also heirs of the gracious gift of life – so that nothing may hinder your prayers (1 Peter 3:1–7). For the unbelieving husband is made holy through his wife, and the unbelieving wife is made holy through her husband. Otherwise, your children would be unclean, but as it is, they are holy (1 Corinthians 7:14).

Samuel was ministering before the Lord, a boy wearing a linen ephod. His mother used to make for him a little robe and take it to him each year, when she went up with her husband to offer the yearly sacrifice. Then Eli would bless Elkanah and his wife, and say, "May the Lord repay you with children by this woman for the gift that she made to the Lord"; and then they would return to their home. And the Lord took note of Hannah; she conceived and bore three sons and two daughters. And the boy Samuel grew up in the presence of the Lord (1 Samuel 2:18–21).

Then he went down with them and came to Nazareth, and was obedient to them. His mother treasured all these things in her heart (Luke 2:51). Meanwhile, standing near the cross of Jesus were his mother, and his mother's sister, Mary the wife of Clopas, and Mary Magdalene (John 19:25).

The women's movement in the 1960s was one of the most profound social revolutions humans have experienced. Women began to demand recognition, equality, and the right to choose their vocation – whether mothering or developing a career or a mix of both. This aggressive feminism mellowed in the 1970s, as most women affirmed that they were not anti-men, and allowed themselves to celebrate their femininity and softness as strengths, not weaknesses.

The challenge in the 1980s and '90s is for women and men to acknowledge their different biologies and psychologies, and to live with the idea of motherhood being a highly valued vocation for women. Until fairly recently, women had children soon after marrying, but now with more effective and safe contraception and easily-available abortion women are having fewer babies, and having them later, perhaps after five to ten years of pursuing other relational, financial and career goals. "We want our relationship and the mortgage to be manageable before we have children," is a comment I hear often. Sometimes the timing of the first baby is prompted by figuring out the parents' ages when the kids will be adolescents: "We thought we'd better start a family now, or we might not have the patience to cope with teenagers in our fifties."

Another factor is the woman's career: when is the optimum time to opt out, with the risk that the mother might not get her job back? Many people have to balance parenting with work outside the home, and no longer is it necessarily the case that a woman's career must suffer for the sake of motherhood. Our son Paul is a househusband and a splendid father to our grandson Jay; Paul's wife has a career. Jay is (of course!) a very well-adjusted little two-year-old.

Some mothers (a minority I believe) are comfortable with the idea of taking a few months' maternity leave, and entrusting their baby to a creche. Most women have very mixed feelings about daily child-care for their young: with good reason. The bonding of the child to both mother and father is best done if they are around more often than career-pressed strangers, even caring strangers, who will not be able to share in the richness of their baby's life. As I write Hillary Clinton, the wife of the United States President, has announced her intention to make child-care available to any mother who wants it: that would be a tragedy in many cases. There are too many children neglected by fathers; we don't need a generation of children neglected by mothers.

Noted British author Penelope Leach, in her new book *Children First*, elaborates at length on this theme. She writes: "It is clearly and certainly best for babies to have something close to full-time mother care for six months at least – conveniently linked with breast-feeding – and family care for a further year and better two. Using financial or career penalties to blackmail women into leaving infants who are scarcely settled into life outside wombs that are still bleeding is no less than barbarous."

Dr Leach goes on to ask us to imagine what it's like for a baby who tries to keep a "beloved adult" with them all the time while they are awake. But when they sleep, they can't prevent adults leaving them. The problem is when they wake, they wake up alone, and then sometimes or regularly find a strange adult coming to them. "If a baby is to accept that calmly – neither fighting to stay awake so as to prevent it, nor panicking when she awakens – she needs to know, from repeated experience, that she can get a parent or accepted substitute (not someone unexpected or strange) back again with a cry or call." And here's Leach's punchline: "All babies are physically helpless, but the babies who feel damagingly helpless in the longer term are the ones who cannot trust their special adults to be there and to respond to them" (quoted by Mary Helen Woods in the *Age*, Melbourne, April 14, 1994, p. 18).

Mothering, with all its heartaches and messiness, is the most strategic and rewarding vocation open to anyone. A God of love couldn't be everywhere, says an ancient Jewish proverb, so he created mothers. The Book of Proverbs (chapter 31) suggests a good wife and mother is a delight to her husband and children. My desk calendar recently cited a Spanish proverb: "An ounce of mother is worth a pound of clergy."

When I hear women talking about the positive aspects of mothering, they almost always mention sharing in the child's development, being needed and being loved.

But motherhood for many is not always a positive experience. Many mothers battle tiredness and depression. One of the best-put-together girls in our Teachers' College Christian group later married, had a baby, suffered post-natal depression, and threw herself under a train.

Researchers tell us that women with supportive partners are less likely to be depressed. Part of this support involves allowing the mum regular "time out" to be alone, or to enjoy the companionship of friends.

Mum, you are a VIP. Every child deserves to be wanted, accepted, and appreciated. Your love and care will help develop your children's feelings of self-respect. Your mothering style will be copied – for better or worse – by your daughters when they have children. (If your own mother was inadequate, and you see yourself copying her bad habits, get help: you can change!) And your sons will relate to their wives better if you do not "smother" them, particularly from their teenage years onwards.

And, ultimately, God is more likely to be viewed as a caring, accepting, and forgiving nurturer if you act like that towards your children!

I confess that one of the first questions I asked myself when courting my wife-to-be was, "I wonder what kind of mother she'll make?" I thought about that a lot before we got too "serious." When I met her mother, I felt reassured. Jan has been a superb mum to our kids, sometimes carrying a two-parent load when I was too busy.

My earliest memories are of my mother doing the housework in our Sydney home, singing hymns softly. I can still see that room, with sunbeams streaming through the window. She has prayed for me every day now for 58 years – from before conception! I once calculated that she prayed for me more than I pray for myself, and I felt very grateful.

Selected Quotations

There are exceptional women, there are exceptional men, who have other tasks to perform in addition to the task of motherhood and fatherhood, the task of providing for the home and of keeping it. But it is the tasks connected with the home that are the fundamental tasks of humanity ... if the mother does not do her duty, there will either be no next generation, or a next generation that is worse than none at all ...

THEODORE ROOSEVELT.
Quoted in James Dobson and Gary L. Bauer, *Children at Risk: Winning the Battle for the Hearts and Minds of Your Children*, Dallas: Word Publishing, 1990, p. 155.

Dictionaries define a mother as a female parent. Although that's true, we all know she is much, much more. A mother, a human being, a woman, a nurse, a counselor, a cook, a chauffeur, a philosopher, a teacher, a hostess, a cleaner, a homemaker, a listener, a talker, a social secretary and nutritionist – the list goes on and on.

In the eighties she probably has a full-time working position as well. Quite a job specification! All those duties without experience; one could say a starring role without a rehearsal. With almost no preparation, a new mother embarks on this huge role and, generally speaking, makes a success of it. Many excel.

MAREA STENMARK,
Mum's the Word, North Rocks, NSW: North Rocks Press, 1988, p. 41.

Children under fifteen add 132 minutes per day to household work for men and women in fulltime work. For women out of the workforce, the presence of children adds 135 minutes to their housework on average.

EVA COX,
co-convenor of the Women's Economic Think Tank, *Age*, January 7, 1994, p. 11.

Children have no real understanding (why should they?) of a mother's inner feelings or frustrations, for these have to be hidden for the sake of rearing happy, well-adjusted children. I know, after I had my own children, I felt quite differently about my parents. For the first time, I began to understand how much they had done for me. Children are never aware of work or sacrifice. In contrast, what I have observed in supermarkets, in the streets, in living rooms, is the mother consistently being in the position, not of being the loved parent, but the one who is constantly saying No. "No, you can't have that." "No, I can't afford that." "Keep still." "Keep quiet." "Don't shout at me like that."

As children grow older they not only see their mother as the disciplinarian, but someone to rebel against, to criticize, and even worse, as a figure of fun. Mums are fair game. Generally speaking, mothers spend most of their time building up their children's egos, not criticizing them, but older children regularly tease or "put down" their mothers. Mothers are expected to smile through this, as they smile through everything else.

JOYCE NICHOLSON,
The Heartache of Motherhood, Ringwood, Vic.: Penguin Books, 1983, p. 81.

Parents are amazed that they can go from relative calm to utter frustration in a few seconds. An uneaten egg or spilled juice at breakfast can turn a calm morning into a free-for-all. In spite of parents' best intentions, bedtime becomes wartime, meals end with children in tears and food barely touched, and car rides deteriorate into stress-filled shouting matches ... Whatever its source, we often experience parental anger as a horrifying encounter with our worst selves. I never even knew I had a temper until I had children. It was very frightening that these children I loved so much, for whom I had sacrificed so much, could arouse such intense feelings of rage in me, their mother, whose primary responsibility was to nurture and protect them.

NANCY SAMALIN,
Love and Anger: The Parental Dilemma, New York: Viking Penguin, 1991, p. 5.

The pace of living has become so frantic that we don't have time for our kids. That situation makes us willing to accept surrogate parenting uncritically from the "experts" who meander through our lives. Some parents resist the cultural mind-set, but the pressure to get out of the way and let various authorities take over for them can be quite severe.

I'm reminded of a mother who told me that she took her fourteen-year-old daughter to their pediatrician for a routine physical exam. The mother was aware that her daughter was beginning to develop physically and might be sensitive to her being in the examining room with her. She offered to remain in the waiting room, but the girl objected.

"I don't want to go in there by myself," she said. "Please come with me." After arguing with her daughter for a moment, the mother agreed to accompany her to the examining room.

When the exam was over, however, the doctor turned to the mother and criticized her for intruding. He said in front of the girl, "You know, you really had no business being in the examining room. It is time I related directly to your daughter. You should not even be aware of the care that I give her or the medication I prescribe. You shouldn't even know the things that are said between us. My care of your daughter should now be a private matter between her and me."

The girl had been going through a period of rebellion, and the mother felt her authority was weakened by the doctor's comments. It was as though he were saying, "Your day of supervision of your daughter has now passed. She should now make her own decisions." Fortunately, that mother was unwilling to do as she was told, and promptly found a new doctor. Good for her!

I have discussed this conversation with several pediatricians, and they have each agreed with the doctor in this case. They emphasized the importance of a youngster having someone to talk with in private. Perhaps. But I disagree with the autonomy demanded by the physician.

Fourteen-year-old boys and girls are not grown, and their parents are still the best people to care for them and oversee their development. It is appropriate for a physician to have some private moments with his young patient, but he should never forget to whom he is accountable!

JAMES DOBSON and GARY L. BAUER,
Children at Risk: Winning the Battle for the Hearts and Minds of Your Children,
Dallas: Word Publishing, 1990, pp. 76–77.

Here are the ten most common erroneous expectations of Type E women that form the cognitive bases of their stressful feelings and behaviours:

1. I have to do things perfectly.
2. I should be able to accomplish more in a day.
3. I should be able to do everything without feeling stressed or tired.
4. I have to please others by doing what they ask me to do.
5. I have to prove myself to everybody.
6. "Having it all" should make me happy.
7. I can't be happy until I "have it all."
8. I can't relax until I finish what I have to do.

9. If I make people need me because of everything I do for them, they'll value me.
10. I should be everything to everybody.

Each of the major areas of concern to Type E women ... is rampant with implicit or explicit erroneous expectations.

HARRIET B. BRAILNER,
Type E Women: How to Overcome the Stress of Being Everything to Everybody,
Sydney: Angus & Robertson, 1987, p. 151.

Do something for yourself every day, even if it's painting your toenails. Do something physical every day, even if it's only ten exercises. Spend some time alone every day. Most of all, avoid the conflict of your husband demanding your time when your kids are also demanding it. Openly discuss when your special time together is each day and stick to it, even if you all have mumps or all need attention. Organize your girlfriends to take your kids one Saturday or Sunday afternoon and then swap. At least you then have one glorious afternoon to enjoy together – don't do housework then.

Melbourne *Age* reader ROSA,
writing about being a working mum in Marriane Latham, *The Working Mother's Handbook,*
Blackburn, Vic.: Dove Communications, 1984, p. 123.

Our culture has paid attention in recent years, and rightly so, to men's physical incest with their daughters, which is hideous and revolting in its range and damage. And [there is] psychic incest as well between father and daughter. We are aware of the number of sons who report sexual abuse by mothers, as well as by fathers, uncles, and older brothers; but the culture still does not take very seriously the damage caused by psychic incest between mother and son.

Mari Sandoz in *These Were the Sioux* mentions that the young Sioux boy never – after the age of seven or so – looked his mother in the eyes. All requests were passed through his sister ...

Much sexual energy can be exchanged when the mother looks the son directly in the eyes and says, "Here is your new T-shirt, all washed."

Such precautions between mother and son seem absurd to us, unheard of, ridiculous, inhuman. And yet the Sioux men, once grown, were famous for their lack of fear when with women, their uninhibited conversations in the tepees, their ease in sexual talk with their wives. We recognize that the Sioux women were more aware of the possibilites of psychic incest between mother and son than we are …

American mothers sometimes confide details of their private lives to their small sons, details that might better go to adults their own age. Frank disclosure is often better than silence, but it becomes harmful if the son feels he has to do something about it. The boy in many a kitchen gets drawn to his mother's side, and he says in some form those terrible words: "Mama, when I'm grown up, I'm going to have a big house for you, and you'll never have to work again."

Twenty to thirty percent of boys now live in houses with no adult male present; and most speak these words, silently or openly. But psychic incest is by no means restricted to single-parent homes. The emphasis placed in recent decades on the inadequacy of men, and on the evil of the patriarchal system, encourages mothers to discount grown men.

ROBERT BLY,
Iron John: A Book About Men, New York: Vintage Books, 1992, pp. 185–186.

Far too many working parents find the weekdays so busy that they put off everything to the weekends. It's almost as if they only truly live on the weekends. They struggle through Monday to Friday figuring that Saturday and Sunday can make it all come out right. This is like having a seedling of a precious and beautiful plant and ignoring it five days of the week. Then, when it looks sad and wilted, you drown it with water and fertilizer. When a few weeds come up in the pot, the seedling is almost lost from sight. So you yank out the healthy weed and the sickly seedling gets uprooted too.

Parenting can be similar: days of ignoring family matters followed by overly intense attention and some bad decisions, and soon the main objective is lost from sight and family life becomes sickly and rootless. Like young plants, our children thrive on regular cultivation. A working parent can't afford to be just a weekend parent. I know, you are tired from your day at the office and you think you need "me-time." But you can feel refreshed as well by "us-time," good weekday moments with your child.

The weekend connection with your family will be much more productive if you nurture your togetherness during each weekday. I call these essential weekday times touch-base times. There are six of them:

1. At breakfast.
2. From the office by telephone.
3. Reunion at home.
4. At supper.
5. The special evening hour.
6. Bedtime.

CARYL WALLER KRUEGER,
Working Parent, Happy Child: You Can Balance Job and Family,
Nashville: Abingdon Press, 1990, pp. 22–23.

While the Good Lord was creating mothers He was into His sixth day of "overtime" when the angel appeared and said, "You're doing a lot of fiddling around on this one."

And the Lord said, "Have you read the spec on this order? She has to be completely washable, but not plastic. Have 180 moveable parts ... all replaceable. Run on black coffee and leftovers. Have a lap that disappears when she stands up. Have a kiss that can cure everything from a broken leg to a disappointed love affair. And have six pairs of hands."

The angel shook her head slowly and said, "Six pairs of hands ... not possible."

"It's not the hands that are causing me problems," said the Lord. "It's the three pairs of eyes that mothers have to have."

"That's on the standard model?" asked the angel.

The Lord nodded. "One pair that see through closed doors when she asks, 'What are you kids doing in there?' when she already knows. Another here, in the back of her head that see what she shouldn't, but what she has to know, and of course the ones here in front that can look at a child when he goofs up and reflect, 'I understand and I love you' without so much as uttering a word."

Said the Lord, "I'm so close to creating something so close to myself. Already I have one who heals herself when she is sick ... can feed a family of six on one pound of hamburger ... and can get a nine-year-old to stand under a shower."

The angel circled the model of The Mother very slowly. "It's too soft," she sighed.

"But tough," said the Lord excitedly. "You cannot imagine what this mother will do or endure."

"Can it think?"

"Not only think, but it can reason and compromise," said the creator.

Finally, the angel bent over and ran her fingers across the cheek. "There's a leak," she pronounced. "I told you you were trying to put too much into this model. You can't ignore the stress factor."

The Lord moved in for a closer look and gently lifted the drop of moisture to his finger where it glistened and sparkled in the light.

"It's not a leak," He said. "It's a tear."

"A tear?" asked the angel. "What's it for?"

"It's for joy, sadness, disappointment, compassion, pain, loneliness and pride."

"You are a genius," said the angel.

The Lord looked somber. "I didn't put it there."

ERMA BOMBECK,
Motherhood, the Second Oldest Profession, New York: McGraw-Hill, 1983, pp. 176–177.

There are many ... beautiful and uplifting accounts of ... inspirational mothers and children who overcome so much – stories of mothers who become better people for having endured difficulty, pain and distress because they help and are helped. In their common grief they draw together in mutual support, forming attachments which last and grow. They are givers and, therefore, they receive. The dispensers rather than the consumers in our society. I've heard it said "What I've gained is the joy – and it is a joy – of having my child really rely on me." We all know that suffering is an essential part of our human drama. We realise that it comes to every one of us in differing degrees. It is how we cope which is important.

MAREA STENMARK,
Mum's the Word, North Rocks, NSW: North Rocks Press, 1988, pp. 150–151.

A Prayer for Mothers

Dear Lord,
what sort of people am I teaching my children to be?
If I criticize them constantly, they will become critical.
If I undermine their worth-ness, they will become unworthy.
If I am impatient, I teach impatience.
Much of what they will become
is my doing …
or my undoing.

And I don't think of this, Lord.
I just try to blunder through today —
meeting today's deadlines,
tending to at least a portion of today's chores.
I'm not so much raising them
as just puttering about while they grow up.
And what an irretrievable waste of opportunity this is.

Lord, you know what I'd like them to be —
worthy adults,
real people
whose hands will bless, whose words will bless,
whose lives will bless those around them.

I want them to be the kind of people
who are at home in the universe.
Ah, so.
One hand in theirs, Lord,
the other hand in thine —
this is the only way I can lead them. Amen.

JO CARR and IMOGENE SORLEY,
Bless This Mess and Other Prayers, Nashville: Abingdon Press, 1969, p. 70.

A Benediction

Lord, bless every mother reading this. Give them humor to see the funny side of some disasters; give them joy as they do mundane chores for those they love; give them a sense of destiny as they shape the lives of those who will carry us all into the future. For your glory. Amen.

13

"Single and satisfied": is that possible?

Rejoice in the Lord always; again I will say, Rejoice. Let your gentleness be known to everyone. The Lord is near. Do not worry about anything, but in everything by prayer and supplication with thanksgiving let your requests be made known to God. And the peace of God, which surpasses all understanding, will guard your hearts and your minds in Christ Jesus (Philippians 4:4-7).

The unmarried man is anxious about the affairs of the Lord, how to please the Lord; but the married man is anxious about the affairs of the world, how to please his wife, and his interests are divided. And the unmarried woman and the virgin are anxious about the affairs of the Lord, so that they may be holy in body and spirit; but the married woman is anxious about the affairs of the world, how to please her husband. I say this for your own benefit, not to put any restraint upon you, but to promote good order and unhindered devotion to the Lord. If anyone thinks that he is not behaving properly toward his fiancée, if his passions are strong, and so it has to be, let him marry as he wishes; it is no sin. Let them marry. But if someone stands firm in his resolve, being under no necessity but having his own desire under control, and has determined in his own mind to keep her as his fiancée, he will do well. So then, he who marries his fiancée does well; and he who refrains from marriage will do better (1 Corinthians

7:32–38). Nevertheless, in the Lord woman is not independent of man or man independent of woman (1 Corinthians 11:11).

Finally, brothers and sisters, we ask and urge you in the Lord Jesus that, as you learned from us how you ought to live and to please God (as, in fact, you are doing), you should do so more and more. For you know what instructions we gave you through the Lord Jesus. For this is the will of God, your sanctification: that you abstain from fornication; that each one of you know how to control your own body in holiness and honor, not with lustful passion, like the Gentiles who do not know God; that no one wrong or exploit a brother or sister in this matter, because the Lord is an avenger in all these things, just as we have already told you beforehand and solemnly warned you. For God did not call us to impurity but in holiness. Therefore whoever rejects this rejects not human authority but God, who also gives his Holy Spirit to you (1 Thessalonians 4:1–8). You have heard that it was said, "You shall not commit adultery." But I say to you that everyone who looks at a woman with lust has already committed adultery with her in his heart (Matthew 5:27–28).

I appeal to you therefore, brothers and sisters, by the mercies of God, to present your bodies as a living sacrifice, holy and acceptable to God, which is your spiritual worship. Do not be conformed to this world, but be transformed by the renewing of your minds, so that you may discern what is the will of God – what is good and acceptable and perfect (Romans 12:1–2).

You are single, possibly through circumstance or chance rather than choice. First the good news: it is better to be unhappy single than unhappy married. And it is just as good being happy single as happy married, provided you're in some relationships of intimacy where you're loved when you are truly known and understood.

I'm not single: I've been happily married for thirty four years, and have four children (two of them single). So I really have only two qualifications to write about singleness. First, Jan and I have had a special ministry to adult singles, and we usually have one or two staying in our home as loving – and loved – members of our family. Second, many adult singles actually pay a fee to talk to me. About half of all the adults I counsel are single. And we talk about all aspects of their lives.

Single adults are forming a higher percentage of our population as each decade passes. In the United States, between 1975 and 1985 they grew from forty-seven million to sixty-eight million. Australians also are marrying later and divorcing more.

Singles comprised the majority of Jesus' close friends. That was no accident: because singles often suffer from feelings of marginal-ization, they were and are specially dear to him. And because he was single, he was ideally equipped to understand their special needs. Then, as now, single adults are freer in many ways to devote extra time and energy to the service of others.

However, most adult singles would prefer to be happily married. Most are lonely. Many, after their late twenties, find that their field of choice is alarmingly narrow: in the church, for example, single women over twenty-five outnumber single men by about two or three to one. A minority have deliberately chosen to live a "solo" lifestyle, and a few of these have made a choice or even taken a vow of lifelong celibacy. Some have a homosexual orientation and for them the idea of marriage to someone of the opposite sex may include feelings of fear or even repugnance.

Singleness is not easy. There's an awful aching loneliness in many singles who would love to be special for somebody. A single forty-year-old said to me recently, "If I didn't care about my mother, I'd have committed suicide last year. She's the only reason for my continuing to live."

But marriage and parenting are not easy either. For that matter, being a manager isn't easy; being a teenager isn't easy; being a Christian in our kind of world isn't easy. Accept the fact that you'll generally be in the minority, especially in Christian circles. It's O.K. to be different.

Singles have similar needs to other human beings. Their differ-ences from others are fewer than their "samenesses." Singles' groups are good; but it's also important to belong to mixed groups. A divorced woman told me: "Singles have essentially the same needs and struggles as do those who are married. All persons must find their own individual identity, must come to terms with themselves in their aloneness. They search for security, a place to belong, a home, a 'family' in which to love. They reach out for intimacy, closeness, touch, union with another. They strive for achievement – a sense of accomplishment, of mission – to give life meaning."

I've found that when adult singles talk to a counselor, seven topics emerge: acceptance, self-worth, combating loneliness, companionship, money, sexual concerns, and learning God's will for their lives. Let's look at each in turn.

1. *Acceptance.* This, of course, is a universal human need. The single person who feels a little "odd," who's lived with a dreadful label like "old maid," who feels left on the shelf, really has a hard time. The best remedy for anyone who has received negative messages from others is to know they're accepted – totally accepted – by God. Jesus accepted people who weren't accepted by others or themselves. Jesus is "the human face of God." He is "God's Christian name."

Singleness is a viable lifestyle for a Christian. Marriage is not the only way to live together in community. There are many reasons for singleness, and no person should be made to feel a second-class citizen – or Christian – on the basis of their marriage status. I'm sick and tired of "do-gooders" who say such things as "Why isn't a nice girl like you married?" or "She's an undiscovered jewel." Such phrases can be very hurtful; they touch a raw nerve. Such a woman may have just broken off a relationship or ended a tragic marriage, or may want to be married but isn't. I know a single lady who can't bear to watch TV commercials featuring happy families: she switches off.

There's no way God could love you any more than he loves you now. He wouldn't love you any more if you were married. He doesn't love you any less because you're single. If you feel that members of the "opposite gender" have ignored you, or haven't asked you out, please don't under-rate yourself because of that. You are "attractive." Societies are arbitrary in the way they define beauty. For example, in some African cultures a woman with a large bottom, or large lips, or elongated ear-lobes is a very appealing person to men. Everybody's beautiful in their own way.

However, all that said, when you feel miserable about yourself, you project that feeling when you're with others. I know some singles who might have won a partner except for one thing – the pout they wear!

2. *Self-worth.* You're unique. You're an unrepeatable miracle of God's creation. He's your "eternal parent," and you're a delight to him. You may not believe you were a delight to your biological father or mother, but you certainly are to God. When God made you he didn't make a mistake. He made someone who has infinite worth, someone he planned to create and love before anything else was made!

A sense of worth comes from realizing all this, and living in the enjoyment of one's aliveness. Keep growing, accept challenges, take risks. Self-worth is also a function of having some life-goals that involve the enrichment of others.

At this point let me suggest a few very practical things.

- Develop some skills in particular areas. This includes home-making. Whether you're male or female, why not become a gourmet cook? Or become very good at relating to children? Attend a course in something each year. Would you get a piano if you were married? Well, get one now!
- If you live alone, don't get sloppy with your meals. A meal, whether a cheese sandwich or a cheese soufflé, is an image of the eucharistic feast and ought to be treated as such. Entertaining people is a marvelous thing to do.
- You ought to become the very best in your profession or job. If you're a doctor, become a better diagnostician. If you're a cleaner, polish everything as if Jesus were visiting that place soon.

But be careful: some singles "sublimate" their loneliness in their career, and are "married to their jobs." God wants all your life to become integrated into a unity and to be balanced between work and play and rest, between solitude and company, between relating to various interests and relating to God and others. Having an over-developed career and under-developed (or non-existent) friendships is a lopsided way to live.

3. *Loneliness.* We're all made to live in community. That doesn't mean that family or community must live under the same roof as you do. But *you need others*, to talk with, laugh with, cry with, pray with, and check your thinking with.

Single people are the loneliest people I meet. Whereas there are pensioners' clubs, senior citizens' clubs, and lots of things for kids, it's sometimes hard to find a singles' group with which a single person can feel an affinity. Some tell me they are quite embarrassed in the groups they visit, and won't go back. Either they are blatantly propositioned by someone, or else the group is geared to a particular kind of person and they don't feel at home.

Now a tough word: *No one needs to be lonely!* And another: *Some people are lonely because they're selfish!* If you're a committed Christian, sincerely in love with God and serving others without any expectation of reward, you are less likely to be lonely. I'm not just talking about the helping professions here. It's possible to go into social work or nursing or child care or teaching – or into the pastoral ministry for that matter – and do your helping thing professionally. You can derive a lot of satisfaction from that. But what I'm saying is: outside the parameters of your professional life, do you *spontaneously* move towards others? For example, how many people do you briefly phone or write to, to cheer them up?

Many singles have only themselves to please, unless they have children or parents to care for. So join a few things. Get into a small group in your church. Get involved with the choir or a missionary society. Serve others (but without becoming their slave).

Avoid putting expectations on people. Some just don't know how to relate to singles – or anyone "different" for that matter. People who "don't know what to say" to a member of a particular group often aren't deliberately avoiding you; they just don't feel comfortable. This is especially so in cases of bereavement and separation or divorce.

4. *Companionship.* One of the most important things families can do is open their homes and love to singles, and thereby create "extended families." We all need other homes where we can drop in and be welcomed, whatever that family is doing. It's a fortunate single person who can eat a family meal with others regularly. Holiday times can be especially lonely for singles.

Adult singles also need a few children among their special friends. Some have no nieces or nephews and so look beyond their relatives for meaningful relationships with children. There are all sorts of reciprocal benefits here: you can take the kids out for special trips, or baby-sit and let a harried mother have some hours off. Sharing delightful happenings with kids is one of the richest experiences God allows anyone to have.

It's also important for the "never married" to have a few married people among their friends. Although many single adults feel terribly alone when everyone else is paired off, this is a situation you just can't avoid. And things which can't be changed have to be accepted with serenity, as the famous prayer has it.

A word of warning: for the single adult who's starved of love, there's a danger of "smothering" the person you're especially fond of. We have to learn to allow the other to have the dimensions of private space they uniquely need. You'll have to be open about how often you should be "around." On the other hand, sometimes singles over-react to an apparent "slight" by withdrawing, or even storming out of a friendship altogether. Happy is the person who can talk freely with their friends and know where companionship begins and ends. Total dependence on one person is not healthy – even after marriage one has to keep working at getting the right balance between the relationship and other areas of one's life. No one other person will satisfy all your needs.

It's important not to allow yourself to be panicked into a marriage that's wrong for you. The only thing worse than waiting is wishing you'd waited! While you "live in hope," the essence of mature living is the enjoyment of the present moment. Some singles who would like to be married can't find the balance between openness to that possibility and still making the most of their singleness.

The question "Should I actively look for a mate – or just wait for the right person to come along?" is not easily answered. *Don't let either choice become an obsession.* If it's God's will for you to marry later, that's O.K.: he's not bothered about age-limits and his timing is perfect. Treat living as an adventure in the meantime. Make the most of opportunities for work, fun, meeting new people, and serving others. (And by the way, it isn't true that it's harder to attract a partner when you're over forty or if you have children. All kinds of people find partners; your only limitations are your expectations!)

Many singles have lost confidence in themselves, so their appeal to a potential partner is lessened. This is where self-esteem comes in again. Work on it. Develop communication and assertiveness skills. Treat yourself well – every day. Set goals, attain them, then set others. Be the sort of person another would delight to live with. If you're aimless and unsatisfied, you won't be attractive to others.

Ask others for a date: the worst thing that can happen is that they will say "no" – and that's their privilege.

Learn skills about "breaking the ice" with a stranger. It doesn't really matter what words you use, so long as you have a friendly demeanor: "Hi, how are you?" "Been coming to this group long?" "What church do you stay away from – oops, go to?"

If you want friends, you've got to be friendly. And if you want *plenty* of friends, practice Philippians 2:4 ("Let each of you look not to your own interests, but to the interests of others")! Don't wait for others to invite you to their home: entertain them in yours. And don't keep a record of who doesn't invite you back!

How do I know if I've found the right person? Ask yourself: would I be prepared to make a life-long commitment to this person – no matter who I might meet later on? Make sure you agree on basic issues: who does what (role expectations), children, religious faith, and handling money.

To those in a singles' group who have become exclusive friends: be sensitive to others. In my view, in a group you should act as singles, not doubles. It's a sign of weakness, insecurity, and insensitivity to others to be obviously pairing off or cuddling while those around you are unattached. I personally don't worry about singles' groups being thought of as "dating bureaus." Having a special friend is a need of all of us, and we'd better frankly recognize that. Maturity means facing up to our needs and acknowledging them, then getting on with it.

5. *Money.* God loves a cheerful giver, and in these days of nearly-equal opportunities you'll (theoretically) have more money to give away than a wage-earner supporting a family. Generosity is a sign of an open heart, and your money and time and talents will be made available to others – in the church, in missionary societies, or to help the poor at home and overseas. And one of the most beautiful things anyone can do for others is to give gifts anonymously.

Many singles have difficulty managing money, investments, or tax returns. Don't be afraid to ask for help here. And that extends to practical jobs you find difficult. Some women I know need someone to change light globes; some older singles need help unscrewing lids. In these days of high unemployment there are many practical people out of work: give them odd jobs around your place and pay them to do them.

6. *Sex* is a big and exciting and dangerous subject. Single Christians who are unable to express their sexuality fully in a lifelong, monogamous, heterosexual relationship will face all sorts of challenges. Someone has summarized the Christian teaching about sex in four propositions: God's standards are right for us; God's standards are good for us; God's standards are difficult for us; and God's standards are possible for us. We will expand on this theme in chapter 19.

Although marriage might be God's normal intention, it's not his only one. Although God performed the first marriage ceremony in Eden, when he came among us he came as a single. If you say you're deprived sexually as a single, I guess my response is that married people are deprived in other ways (and more than you might imagine are deprived sexually too!). Whether single or married, you will never, in this life, always get what you want, when you want it.

7. *Gratefulness and the will of God.* God loves you and has a good plan for your life. His plan for Jesus and Paul and Mother Teresa and plenty of other beautiful and useful people is that they accept celibacy as a gift. If that is so for you too, be grateful.

You'll know God's will for you by staying close to him. Develop a rich devotional life. A single female Baptist minister I know spends a beautiful hour and a half with her Lord every morning. She is in love with him. She has a special place to meet him, lights a candle there to symbolize his presence, and employs many of the devotional aids available to us these days. In unhurried quiet (often a rare commodity for married people) she relates to him as an intimate friend. A single life can be rich and satisfying, fulfilled in the highest sense.

Selected Quotations
Single adults are forming a higher percentage of our population as each decade passes. Westerners are marrying later and divorcing more. Whilst it is God's will for most to marry, it's not his will for all to marry. But God doesn't elevate marriage over singleness: both

states are part of his calling for different people … Life is difficult – for the married and for singles. We have a simple choice: the pain of loving or the pain of not loving. The most important thing about being single is not that you're not married. It's that God loves and accepts you and you're special to him.

Singleness is like marriage: a happy marriage is the result of two people wanting to please the other, so the secret of a happy single life is to give yourself to others.

ROWLAND CROUCHER,
excerpts from "A Talk to Christian Singles," John Mark Ministries, 1991.

In Western society two out of every five adults are single. If present statistical trends continue, not long after the end of this century single adults will equal the married in number. A decade or so after that they may even exceed them. A significant proportion of adults will spend the major part of their lives living outside the framework of the traditional nuclear family.

For a variety of reasons many adults lead a single lifestyle. Some will have chosen to be single, others will have arrived there by chance, bereavement or matrimonial accident. Yet, their lives will be as full of challenge and will offer the same potential for joy or unhappiness as that of any other adult. They will, however, have lives that are significantly different to those of couples.

GAIL RATCLIFFE and HAMISH KEITH,
Being Single and Happy, Sydney: Simon & Schuster, 1992, p. 2.

Being single is not some social aberration or fearful fate. There can be enormous personal enjoyment and power and completeness in living as an unattached person. For the individual who totally accepts its challenge, a fuller and more balanced life than that of being half a couple is possible. Living a single life does not mean being alone or without love or even living without strongly defined relationships. However, it does mean accepting responsibility for and taking charge over your own life.

GAIL RATCLIFFE and HAMISH KEITH,
Being Single and Happy, Sydney: Simon & Schuster, 1992, p. 3.

First, an apology. By and large the church has failed to minister adequately to single adults. Only recently have books about the joys and frustrations of singleness been published – and some of them are, frankly, unrealistic. Some churches are particularly cruel to separated or divorced persons. Just when these hurting people need love and acceptance, they often get the "evangelical cold shoulder." Pharisees are still with us! Widows and widowers, in their loneliness, don't have an easy time in most churches either. And yet it's obvious that the church (and its missionary organizations) would fall apart without the faithful ministry of its singles.

ROWLAND CROUCHER,
"A Talk to Christian Singles," John Mark Ministries, 1991.

A week before I met my darlin' Arlyne I wrote a brilliant statement in my diary. Judge it for yourself: "If all the lonely people in the world would just get together … no one would ever be lonely again!"

Only after we got married would I realize how wrong my "brilliant statement" really was. The truth is, if all the lonely people in the world got together, there would simply be a lot of lonely people together …

Every unmarried person needs to understand what I hadn't understood when I wrote my "profound" statement about loneliness. The only thing worse than being SINGLE and lonely is being MARRIED and lonely!

RAY MOSSHOLDER,
Singles Plus: The Bible and Being Single, Lake Mary, Fla.: Creation House, 1991, pp. 17–18.

During every Singles Plus seminar I ask everyone to shout out the names of all the happily married couples in the New Testament. The result of this game shocks nearly everybody. After naming Joseph and Mary (Matthew 1:18ff.), Zacharias and Elizabeth (Luke 1:5ff.), Peter (1 Corinthians 9:5), Philip (Acts 21:8–9), and Priscilla and Aquila (Acts 18:1–3), they stop. I mean, who wants to mention the only other famous married couple of the New Testament: Ananias and Sapphira (Acts 5:1–10)?!

True, the Old Testament does name many more married couples, but nearly all those marriage relationships were dysfunctional, many polygamous.

Now, name every prominent single person who was a leader during New Testament times. Beginning with Jesus Christ, the list may include every writer of the New Testament except Peter. And then there are Timothy, Barnabas, Titus, Philemon, Onesimus, Epaphras, John the Baptist ... If any of these people were married, the Bible is silent about it. Isn't it strange that churches often want to consider only married pastors? Some have rules that stop singles from being elders. That means Jesus Christ couldn't have been an elder in their church! Granted, I've seen many married couples doing a powerful job of serving God together. But I've seen singles in the same places doing an equally powerful job.

RAY MOSSHOLDER,
Singles Plus: The Bible and Being Single, Lake Mary, Fla.: Creation House, 1991, p. 33.

Did you ever play hide and seek? Everyone else hides while the person who is "it" counts to ten. "Ready or not, here I come!" Then "it" dashes off in any direction, hunting down anyone to tag and make "it." That's no way to approach marriage. You don't want just any "it" for a lifetime partner – not if you have any desire for lasting happiness ... If we're pursuing marriage in our dating, we're pursuing the wrong thing. We start making up our own ideas of what love is. We don't allow the Lord to show us and teach us what love actually is through the relationships He gives us. "Pursue love," the Bible says, "not marriage." This is a simple principle, but it set me free in the past few months in my relationships with Christian sisters.

RAY MOSSHOLDER,
Singles Plus: The Bible and Being Single, Lake Mary, Fla.: Creation House, 1991, pp. 40–41.

There is one bottom-line reason to get married. If other factors don't rest on this base, stop. Ready to read it? Here goes: If the two of you can serve God better married to each other than the two of you could serve God singly, then, with all other reasons in total alignment with God's Word and both your hearts, you have a great reason to get married.

JOHN FISCHER and LIA FULLER O'NEILL,
Single Person's Identity, Palo Alto, Calif.: Discover Publishing, 1973, pp. 1–2.

As a single woman, I want to witness to a way of living that liberates me from inordinate attachment to the world of power, pleasure and possession so that I can serve the Lord as an instrument of transformation. My singleness frees me to see God's image in creation so that I can reverence the earth as his dwelling place, as the House of God. Living from this faith horizon, I am free to flow with God's will in the situation, free to travel lightly, unencumbered by the weight of self-will and its futile projects of salvation ...

Singleness is thus destined to generate a joyful spirituality that enables us to serve God in whatever walk of life he places us. The single soul is able to soar free and to experience moments of playful carelessness because of its being cared for by God. Such graced experiences transform us into grateful people who live in happy dependence upon the merciful kindness of our loving Lord. Our whole life is an exercise in gratitude as we try to reproduce his goodness in our own attitudes and actions. How sad that many associate singleness with long, gloomy faces and endless frustrations. The limits of this life open up exciting possibilities for meaning and creativity. The vocation to the single life offers opportunity for solitude and communion, for reflection and action, for an awareness of and a witness to the oneness each of us experiences in the heart of Christ.

SUSAN ANNETTE MUTO,
Celebrating the Single Life, New York: Crossroads, 1989, pp. 49, 5.

A Single Person's Prayer

Jesus, my friend, my companion in loneliness, my encourager in times of despair, my teacher and my Lord, I trust you with my whole life. I commit my memories to you: heal those that are painful, and may their long shadow dissipate to allow the sunshine of your loving providence to shine into my life. I commit my present situation to you: married or single, content or frustrated; my friends, my job, my community, my church, my leisure pursuits, and my thought-life. And I commit my future to you too: if you have ordained that I marry, give me patience to wait and certainty about the right choice of a mate. If it is your will that I remain unmarried, help me to be content, without making excuses or false comments about the advantages of the single life which I know are not true for me. On the other hand, give me a creative insight into the blessings of my present situation, and not simply to make the most of it, but the best of it.

Give me a magnificent goal in life: may my interactions with others make a difference to them. Give me a positive demeanor: when others are with me may they share, perhaps unconsciously, my joy. Give me a disciplined mind: may my thoughts be creative and constructive, pure and obedient to your will. And above all, I ask for a faith, hope, and love that will provide spiritual fuel for the journey.

I love you, Lord. Amen.

A Benediction

May God our Divine nurturer, Jesus our loyal friend, the Holy Spirit our teacher and advocate, be with us to guide us all through life's journey, until we enjoy life in all its fulness on the other side. Amen.

14

Divorce and
single parenting

The Lord ... said to me, "My grace is sufficient for you, for power is made perfect in weakness." So, I will boast all the more gladly of my weaknesses, so that the power of Christ may dwell in me. Therefore I am content with weaknesses, insults, hardships, persecutions, and calamities for the sake of Christ; for whenever I am weak, then I am strong (2 Corinthians 12:9–10).

Some Pharisees came, and to test him they asked, "Is it lawful for a man to divorce his wife?" He answered them, "What did Moses command you?" They said, "Moses allowed a man to write a certificate of dismissal and to divorce her." But Jesus said to them, "Because of your hardness of heart he wrote this commandment for you. But from the beginning of creation, 'God made them male and female.' 'For this reason a man shall leave his father and mother and be joined to his wife, and the two shall become one flesh.' So they are no longer two, but one flesh. Therefore what God has joined together, let no one separate." Then in the house the disciples asked him again about this matter. He said to them, "Whoever divorces his wife and marries another commits adultery against her; and if she divorces her husband and marries another, she commits adultery" (Mark 10:2–12).

Put away from you all bitterness and wrath and anger and wrangling and slander, together with all malice, and be kind to one another, tenderhearted, forgiving one another, as God in Christ has forgiven you (Ephesians 4:31–32). Do not judge, and you will not be judged; do not condemn, and you will not be condemned. Forgive, and you will be forgiven (Luke 6:37).

Father of orphans and protector of widows is God in his holy habitation (Psalm 68:5). Thus says the Lord of hosts, the God of Israel: Amend your ways and your doings, and let me dwell with you in this place … For if you truly amend your ways and your doings, if you truly act justly one with another, if you do not oppress the alien, the orphan, and the widow, or shed innocent blood in this place, and if you do not go after other gods to your own hurt, then I will dwell with you in this place, in the land that I gave of old to your ancestors forever and ever (Jeremiah 7:3–7).

We are afflicted in every way, but not crushed; perplexed, but not driven to despair; persecuted, but not forsaken; struck down, but not destroyed (2 Corinthians 4:8–9). The Lord is near to the broken-hearted, and saves the crushed in spirit (Psalm 34:18).

Therefore I tell you, do not worry about your life, what you will eat or what you will drink, or about your body, what you will wear. Is not life more than food, and the body more than clothing? Look at the birds of the air; they neither sow nor reap nor gather into barns, and yet your heavenly Father feeds them. Are you not of more value than they? And can any of you by worrying add a single hour to your span of life? And why do you worry about clothing? Consider the lilies of the field, how they grow; they neither toil nor spin, yet I tell you, even Solomon in all his glory was not clothed like one of these. But if God so clothes the grass of the field, which is alive today and tomorrow is thrown into the oven, will he not much more clothe you – you of little faith? (Matthew 6:25–30).

He will feed his flock like a shepherd; he will gather the lambs in his arms, and carry them in his bosom, and gently lead the mother sheep (Isaiah 40:11).

Marriage breakdown, separation, and divorce are some of the most painful of human experiences. All the symptoms of grief and bereavement are felt but without the finality of death (where the spouse is gone forever and won't be around to be vindictive). Some get over it and start afresh in a matter of months. For others, the pain lingers for years. Probably two years is about the average for a person to "recover" from a divorce. Some never do.

In my counseling practice I find there are many reasons people experience difficulties in their marriage and later divorce. One mate falls in love with someone else (which is hardly ever the real problem – the issues are deeper). Or the accumulated tensions associated with drug or alcohol dependency, sexual problems, gambling, or other addictive behaviors are all too much (again, there are deeper issues in these cases).

Sometimes in mid-life a husband begins to look for security rather than significance; but for his wife at mid-life the kids have grown up, she's back in the work force, and she's looking for significance. Her security as homemaker is being replaced by something else. So he and she have apparently incompatible life-agendas.

Sometimes there's the legacy of what used to be called the "shotgun wedding": they were too young and were pitchforked into a marriage for which they were inadequately prepared. Perhaps destructive baggage was brought into the marriage from his background or hers, or both, and they covered it up in the frenetic activity of raising children, but those old skeletons in the cupboard won't stop rattling. Sometimes he feels emotionally deprived and marries her to find a mother; she is a victim of abuse and marries him to find a sensitive, nurturing father; and it doesn't work out.

So most divorce is the culmination of a drawn-out process of growing disillusionment. They felt "conned." They didn't get what they expected – or what Hollywood taught them to expect!

The baby boomer "trade-it-in consumer mentality," plus easier no-fault divorce legislation, has enabled – some would say encouraged – many more people to divorce than would have done so a generation ago. To our parents, divorce was shameful. They would have toughed it out in a sick marriage, or stayed together "for the sake of the kids."

What do you do when your marriage is rocky? Begin by admitting there are problems. Hiding them won't help: relationship conflicts won't be swept under the carpet. Do both want the marriage? Are one or both prepared to work on their personal growth and the possibility of change? Is each partner willing to take some responsibility for their input into the marriage breakdown? Are both willing to get professional help? For most Christians and many others, there is the question of promise: did I say my vows back then with the genuinely real intention of keeping them? If the answer is "yes" to all or most of these, there is a better chance to work on the relationship. On the other hand, if there is a third party, there is a higher – though not an inevitable – chance of the marriage coming to an end.

If you decide to separate – and always make decisions like this with the help of a caring friend or counselor – work it through one day at a time. My strong suggestion is to regard separation/divorce as a last resort. Ask yourself: when I look back on this time, will I be satisfied that I made every endeavor to get our relationship fixed?

There will almost certainly be an experience of shock: is this really happening to me? The pain is dealt with by denial, perhaps retreating from friends, not getting help. Anger is the outcome of hopes built up then shattered. One's self-esteem takes a battering. But don't run from grief and bereavement; they are positive responses to loss. Work them through, externalize your feelings. If you don't, the negative process of self-pity will take over and begin, like a cancer, to rob you of emotional health.

Make the break as clean as possible. Yes, you can both stay friendly, if not "good friends." Don't feel you still have to solve the problems of your separated partner: some people learn faster when they are left alone and take responsibility for themselves. Forget about "getting even": just take it on the chin and get on with life.

There are three tested ways to recover from a difficult marriage: (1) Join a divorce support group of some sort where there is mutual support and accountability; (2) Get your spiritual and emotional life right; (3) Commit yourself to a twelve-step recovery program, like that for Alcoholics Anonymous. Create a new identity. Join one or two new groups. Learn new skills. Enjoy new experiences with new friends.

And now a word about parenting after divorce. It has been said, "Divorce is the process that turns whole parents into half parents." Someone else has said, "If divorce is like war, children are its orphans."

Remember your children are suffering their own grieving. Sometimes they wonder, "Is it my fault?" "Where will I live?" or "Where will I put my toys?" This may intimidate you: you are torn between your own surviving and the children's well-being. You must allow your children to grieve. And they have to learn to relate to both of you in this new, painful situation. By the way, don't ever, ever, speak a negative word about their other parent – even if they put garbage into the kids' heads about you!

In his excellent book, *Growing Through Divorce* (Eugene, Oreg.: Harvest House, 1986, p. 165) Jim Smoke lists these issues for single parents:

(1) "My circuits are on overload": the custodial parent has to make too many decisions without the help of a partner; the non-custodial parent suffers loneliness. (2) "Where are you when I need you?": in times of crisis in the lives of the children, the visiting parent is often accused (rightly or wrongly) of not taking their fair share of responsibility. (3) "I don't get any respect": children sometimes lose respect for their parents after the bitterness of divorce. (4) "Help, I'm a prisoner": single parents may overcompensate by allowing their parenting role to restrict their mobility.

He then offers these guidelines for single parents:

(1) Don't try to be both parents to your children: be what you are – a mother or father. (2) Don't force your children into playing the role of the departed parent: the nine-year-old can't be "daddy in the house now." (3) Be the parent you are: "Don't abdicate your parent position for that of a big brother, big sister, friend, buddy or pal." (4) Be honest with your children: tell them the truth about what is going on, but "speak the truth in love." (5) Don't put your ex-spouse down in front of your children: trying to convince your children the other parent is mostly to blame is a game nobody wins and everybody loses. (6) Don't make your children undercover agents who report on the other parent's current activities. (7) The children of divorce need both a mother and a father: don't deny them this right because of your anger, hostility, guilt, or vengeance. (8) Don't become a "Disneyland Daddy" or "Magic Mountain Mommy": tragically the single parent outside the home becomes the entertainer, because they can't think what

else to do. (9) Share your dating life and social interests with your children. (10) Help your children keep the good memories of your past marriage alive. (11) Work out a management and existence structure for your children with your ex-spouse. (12) If possible, try not to disrupt the many areas in your children's lives that offer them safety and security. (13) If your child does not resume normal development and growth in their life within a year of the divorce, they may need the special help of a counselor.

Smoke's summary: "Divorce – you can go through it or you can grow through it!"

You can begin again! We all fail, but never ever call yourself a failure. As one divorce workshop leader counsels, say to yourself: "I am divorced. I am single. I am O.K." You can trust God to help you and heal you and form a new person through the pain of divorce and recovery. You can ask him for a new attitude to life. Remember: your satisfaction as a single parent or ex-married is not based as much on your circumstances as on your attitude toward your circumstances.

Selected Quotations

Baby boomers think marriage is great, according to one observer. It is their partners they do not always like.

HANS FINZEL,
Help! I'm a Baby Boomer, Wheaton, Ill.: Victor Books, 1989, p. 115.

Every single parent or separated/divorced person has had, in reality, experiences in two families, and ought to find two others. They were born into a family without being consulted, and experienced the pains and pleasures of growing up with others. Then they married and/or had children, and made a new family of their own. If their experiences with their first family were mainly positive or negative, these will generally (though not invariably) be reflected in similar fashion in their second family.

The third family? Your children need other, perhaps surrogate parents for modeling and security. My suggestion: find the best-put-together families and invite yourself to do a few things with them (parties, outings, sleepovers, whatever). Many single parents are too timid to take an initiative here. Perhaps your pastors or elders could help.

And your fourth family? The family of God, the church. Find a strong, committed church with plenty of families who have kids your kids' age, and get right into it! Somewhere I came across this testimony:

I Came Searching

Out of my lonely place,
I came searching.
Out of my hidden fears,
I came searching.
Out of my need for friends,
I came searching.
Out of my quest for God,
I came searching.
And I found a people who care,
And a new love to share.

ROWLAND CROUCHER,
from an unpublished sermon.

Children go through the same basic stages of grieving as adults. Any time there is a loss of a significant relationship, either through death or divorce, we go through a process of grieving. This process usually lasts for at least two years and is distinguished by specific emotional stages.

In the first six months to a year children typically experience denial and anger ... Preschool children are usually too young to understand fully what's going on. They come by denial naturally ... School-age children [six to twelve] will often express denial by pretending nothing has happened ... Teenagers often deny by escaping. They will spend more time away from home ... Home reminds them of what they've lost, and they don't want to deal with that ...

Anger is the natural response when denial wears out ... Be cautious about anger that your children direct toward themselves. Watch for a preoccupation with guilt or self-destructive behavior ...

Eventually, children realize that anger doesn't work. They try ... bargaining ... Bargainers attempt simple solutions to complex problems and usually fail.

In the movie *Paradise*, the divorcing parents, played by Don Johnson and Melanie Griffith, are brought back together by their enterprising child. This is a classic bargaining fantasy. It is fun to watch because we want this to happen. But the truth is that children's attempts to manipulate their parents' decisions usually hurt more than help.

When a child realizes that there's little he or she can do to fix things, depression sets in ... Depression is basically a shutdown of emotions. Painful reality has finally penetrated to the core of one's being, and it hurts like crazy ...

Depression goes away, if you give it time. The wounds heal. Children regain self-confidence. They learn to forgive. They build new relationships and patch up old ones. They take risks again and accept responsibility ... When we reach the point of acceptance, we are able to deal with the world around us in healthy ways.

THOMAS WHITEMAN,
with Randy Petersen, *The Fresh Start Single Parenting Workbook*,
Nashville: Thomas Nelson Publishers, 1993, pp. 37–42.

I don't know of any other experience in life outside of divorce that can stretch a person's emotions and feelings from love to hate. Divorce can cause you to build walls in your life in place of bridges. You can start out by hating an ex-spouse, and end up by hating yourself and everyone around you. You can literally drown yourself in a sea of negative feelings towards others and yourself. This kind of emotional bath can keep you from growing and becoming a new person.

Time diminishes hate, but it does not heal it. Experiencing forgiveness gets the hate out of your life permanently ... When a person is caught in the heat of argument and emotional combat, forgiveness is usually the very last thing to come to mind. Be aware that forgiveness is not an instant thing, but a process you grow into ...

Forgiveness from God comes easiest and is the first step. Self-forgiveness is second, and is a little harder. Forgiveness in the ex-spouse realm is usually a long way down the recovery road and can only happen when the fires of divorce cool long enough to let sound thinking take over. A person asked me recently what to say to an ex-spouse in this area. You might start by saying, "I'm sorry. I ask your forgiveness for all my mistakes and whatever part I might have played in contributing to our divorce." Sounds hard, doesn't it? It is. But the personal sense of growth and well being that comes from doing it makes it worthwhile.

JIM SMOKE,
Growing Through Divorce, Eugene, Oreg.: Harvest House, 1986, pp. 96, 100–101.

How to Win with Stepchildren

No one can become an instant father or mother overnight. It is going to take time and adjustment on everyone's part. Many new parents simply expect stepchildren to welcome them with open arms and keep living as though nothing had happened. Few children make an easy adjustment, especially if their real parent is close by and in contact with them. The first rule of success as a stepparent is to give the new relationship time to grow and develop.

The second step would be to really work at building the relationship. Your new position in the home may grant you authority, but respect is something you earn. I feel that the responsibility is on the shoulders of the new parent to work at winning the respect and love of the stepchildren. A child may resent a new parent for showing love and affection for his mother or father when little of that love is shown to him. I have known stepparents who have literally ignored their stepchildren and left them entirely up to the natural parent. Few homes will survive this kind of cold treatment.

A third step in winning with stepchildren is to make them feel as important as your own natural children. A love that is shared equally will bring great returns. There are a million ways a stepparent can share and show love. Love always wins.

A fourth step is to realize that you are not a replacement for the other parent. Don't try to be. You are who you are and not a replica of the departed parent. Don't get trapped into playing the role and letting yourself be compared with the absent father or mother. Affirm your own individuality from the beginning and you will gain respect.

JIM SMOKE,
Growing Through Divorce, Eugene, Oreg.: Harvest House, 1986, pp. 118–119.

[In the United States in 1985] one-third of families run by persons under twenty-five years of age are single-parent households, and seventy-five percent of families maintained by a woman under twenty-five are living in poverty. Fifty percent of all Aid to Dependent Children expenditures went to families in which mothers were adolescents when their first child was born.

Presbyterians and Human Sexuality 1991, Louisville, Ky.: The Office of the General Assembly Presbyterian Church (USA), 1991, p. 45.

Ten Commandments for Formerly Marrieds
1. Thou shalt not live in thy past.
2. Thou shalt be responsible for thy present, and shalt not blame thy past for it.
3. Thou shalt not feel sorry for thyself indefinitely.
4. Thou shalt assume thine end of the blame for thy marriage dissolvement.
5. Thou shalt not try to reconcile thy past and reconstruct thy future by a quick, new marriage.
6. Thou shalt not make thy children the victims of thy past marriage.
7. Thou shalt not spend all thy time trying to convince thy children how terrible their departed parent is.
8. Thou shalt learn all thou can about being a one-parent family and get on with it.
9. Thou shalt ask others for help when thou shalt need it.
10. Thou shalt ask God for the wisdom to bury yesterday, create today, and plan for tomorrow.

JIM SMOKE,
Growing Through Divorce, Eugene, Oreg.: Harvest House, 1986, p. 168.

First ... no young couple should approach marriage as though it were a "trial" and divorce is easy if it does not work out. This is a perilous attitude as it psychologically gears them to prepare for a fragile and short-term relationship.

Second, many marriages go straight into the divorce court without any real attempt at settling differences. While it is good that ... the costs of divorce [are gradually being reduced], it may increase this rush to court without reference to the many marriage guidance and welfare clinics. Every marriage is worth saving, and the people involved will need humility and honesty to rescue it.

Third, the Christian church may have given the impression that divorce is the unforgivable sin, but in fact the Bible recognizes the human weaknesses that led to divorce, and provision was made for it. It is not God's ideal ... [but] divorcees should never be regarded in any way as second-class members of the church.

ALAN NICHOLS,
The Family, Sydney: The Anglican Information and Public Relations Office, 1973.

Factors that Contribute to Dysfunction

1. Years of fighting in front of the children before an eventual divorce.
2. A particularly messy divorce, including court battles and ongoing custody fights.
3. One or both parents being particularly manipulative or controlling.
4. Any type of physical, sexual, or emotional abuse of you or your children.
5. Any type of substance abuse (alcohol, drugs, etc.) by one or both parents.
6. Prolonged family disruptions when the children are in their formative years (ages one to ten).
7. One parent who is in and out of the children's lives with no regularity or consistent love.
8. Vastly different parenting styles and conflicting values being taught to the children.

THOMAS WHITEMAN,
with Randy Petersen, *The Fresh Start Single Parenting Workbook*,
Nashville: Thomas Nelson Publishers, 1993, p. 58.

Marriage breakdown is a significant trend in modern societies. Men and women are finding it increasingly difficult to maintain long-term stable relations when there are fewer social supports and when the function of the relationship is evaluated mainly in terms of emotional satisfaction to the individual.

Moreover, increasingly women are not remaining in marital relations which perpetuate male proprietal interests to the exclusion of any recognition of women's needs and rights, particularly when these are violently suppressed by their male partner.

> The Church … will need to recognise that marital breakdown is not caused by "feminism" but rather the accumulation of injustices. Women are simply exposing what was previously covered over.

ALAN NICHOLS, JOAN CLARKE, and TREVOR HOGAN,
Transforming Families and Communities: Christian Hope in a World of Change,
Sydney: AIO Press, 1987, pp. 42–43.

Marriage breakdown is a significant trend in modern societies. Men and women are finding it increasingly difficult to maintain long-term stable relations when there are fewer social supports and when the function of the relationship is evaluated mainly in terms of emotional satisfaction to the individual.

Moreover, increasingly women are not remaining in marital relations which perpetuate male proprietal interests to the exclusion of any recognition of women's needs and rights, particularly when these are violently suppressed by their male partner.

The Church … will need to recognise that marital breakdown is not caused by "feminism" but rather the accumulation of injustices. Women are simply exposing what was previously covered over.

ALAN NICHOLS, JOAN CLARKE, and TREVOR HOGAN,
Transforming Families and Communities: Christian Hope in a World of Change,
Sydney: AIO Press, 1987, pp. 42–43.

Robert Runcie, Archbishop of Canterbury, stated: "One of the reasons why failure in marriage is a particular problem today is its length. Two hundred years ago the average marriage would have lasted fifteen years, now it's more like fifty. It's a lot to ask young people to be faithful for that length of time, especially when by "faithful" we mean not just docile, well behaved, but romantic and companionable."

ANNE TOWNSEND,
Now and Forever: Christian Marriage Today, London: Fount Paperbacks, 1986, pp. 16–17.

Bill of Rights for Single Parents
1. You have the right to set aside time for yourself, your hobbies, your interests, and your social life.
2. You have the right to put the children to bed early so that you can have some time to yourself.

3. You have the right to attend a retreat or weekend away once in a while for your own mental health.
4. You have the right to say no to your children when they are too demanding or when they request unnecessary things.
5. You have the right to get baby-sitters for your children so that you can go out with your friends.
6. You have the right to insist that your ex-spouse maintain a regular and consistent visitation schedule.
7. You have the right to your own privacy.
8. You have the right to pursue your dream, whether it involves going back to school, changing careers, or saving for a special trip.

Adapted from *Better Homes and Gardens*, April 1992, p. 33.
Quoted in Thomas Whiteman, with Randy Petersen, *The Fresh Start Single Parenting Workbook*, Nashville: Thomas Nelson Publishers, 1993, p. 120.

Single mums probably have the most important job in society: raising the next generation. Therefore, they are lowly paid and constantly harassed by social security. Generally, they left school at sixteen and have to survive on the breadline. Yet they have the last laugh – they are the experts in the field of child raising, and quietly chuckle as they watch a married couple (he a Bachelor of Arts; she a Bachelor of Science Hons., combined income $100,000 p.a.) futilely trying to stop an eight-month-old completely humiliating them at the supermarket.

PAUL McDONALD,
She's Not Normally Like This, Milsons Point, NSW: Random House, 1991, pp. 127–128.

A Prayer for the Divorced
God, Master of Union and Disunion,
Teach me how I may now walk
Alone and strong.
Heal my wounds;
Let the scar tissue of your bounty
Cover these bruises and hurts
That I may again be a single person
Adjusted to new days.

Grant me a heart of wisdom,
Cleanse me of hostility, revenge, and rancor,
Make me know the laughter which is not giddy,
The affection which is not frightened.
Keep far from me thoughts of evil and despair.
May I realize that the past chapter of my life
Is closed and will not open again.
The anticipated theme of my life has changed,
The expected story end will not come.
Shall I moan at the turn of the plot?
Rather, remembering without anger's thrust,
Recalling without repetitive pain of regret,
Teach me again to write and read
That I may convert this unexpected epilogue
Into a new preface and a new poem.
Muddled gloom over,
Tension days passed,
Let bitterness of thought fade,
Harshness of memory attenuate,
Make me move on in love and kindness.

SOURCE UNKNOWN.

A Benediction

May God who heals the broken-hearted heal your broken heart. May the Savior who rescues us from our sins and our sorrows save you from despair or unnecessary depression. May the Holy Spirit, our comforter, comfort you in all your trials and testings. Amen.

15

How to parent teenagers and survive the experience

This is the story of the family of Jacob. Joseph, being seventeen years old, was shepherding the flock with his brothers; he was a helper to the sons of Bilhah and Zilpah, his father's wives; and Joseph brought a bad report of them to their father. Now Israel loved Joseph more than any other of his children, because he was the son of his old age; and he had made him a long robe with sleeves. But when his brothers saw that their father loved him more than all his brothers, they hated him, and could not speak peaceably to him. Once Joseph had a dream, and when he told it to his brothers, they hated him even more (Genesis 37:2–5).

Bear with one another and, if anyone has a complaint against another, forgive each other; just as the Lord has forgiven you, so you also must forgive (Colossians 3:13). How very good and pleasant it is when kindred live together in unity! (Psalm 133:1).

And when he was twelve years old, they went up as usual for the festival. When the festival was ended and they started to return, the boy Jesus stayed behind in Jerusalem, but his parents did not know it. Assuming that he was in the group of travelers, they went a day's journey. Then they started to look for him among their relatives and friends. When they did not find him, they returned to Jerusalem to search for him. After three days they found him in the temple, sitting among the teachers, listening to them and asking them questions. And all who heard him were amazed at his understanding and his answers. When his parents saw him they were astonished; and his mother said to him, "Child, why have you treated us like this? Look, your father and I have been searching for you in great anxiety." He said to them, "Why were you searching for me? Did you not know that I must be in my Father's house?" But they did not understand what he said to them (Luke 2:42–50).

Peace I leave with you; my peace I give to you. I do not give to you as the world gives. Do not let your hearts be troubled, and do not let them be afraid (John 14:27). May the God of steadfastness and encouragement grant you to live in harmony with one another, in accordance with Christ Jesus (Romans 15:5).

Then Jesus said, "There was a man who had two sons. The younger of them said to his father, 'Father, give me the share of the property that will belong to me.' So he divided his property between them. A few days later the younger son gathered all he had and traveled to a distant country, and there he squandered his property in dissolute living. When he had spent everything, a severe famine took place throughout that country, and he began to be in need. So he went and hired himself out to one of the citizens of that country, who sent him to his fields to feed the pigs. He would gladly have filled himself with the pods that the pigs were eating; and no one gave him anything. But when he came to himself he said, 'How many of my father's hired hands have bread enough and to spare, but here I am dying of hunger! I will get up and go to my father, and I will say to him, "Father, I have sinned against heaven and before you; I am no longer worthy to be called your son; treat me like one of your hired hands." 'So he set off and went to his father. But while he was still far off, his father saw him and was filled with compassion; he ran and put his arms around him and kissed him. Then the son said to him, 'Father, I have sinned against heaven and before you; I am no longer worthy to be called your son.' But the father said to his slaves, 'Quickly, bring out a robe – the best one – and put it on him; put a ring on his finger and sandals on his feet. And get the fatted calf and kill it, and let us eat and celebrate'" (Luke 15:11–23).

Love does no wrong to a neighbor; therefore, love is the fulfilling of the law (Romans 13:10). I hereby command you: Be strong and courageous; do not be frightened or dismayed, for the Lord your God is with you wherever you go (Joshua 1:9). If any of you is lacking in wisdom, ask God, who gives to all generously and ungrudgingly, and it will be given you (James 1:5).

Finally, all of you, have unity of spirit, sympathy, love for one another, a tender heart, and a humble mind. Do not repay evil for evil or abuse for abuse; but, on the contrary, repay with a blessing. It is for this that you were called – that you might inherit a blessing (1 Peter 3:8–9).

Bringing up teenagers is more complicated than getting an honors degree or managing a large business. Almost every other kind of person is, at least, fairly predictable! If a teenager feels that his or her sense of self-worth was not met during childhood, they embark on a search for status: and, like children of all ages, negative attention from bad behavior will be preferred to no attention at all! If the need for perceived competence has not been met, they will over- (or under-) emphasize performance. If the need for belonging has not been met, they will be angry. Their acting-up has the script: "I can't trust you: but no one else is going to reject me; I will reject them first." The heading on that page of the script is either guilt (I am bad) or hostility (you are bad). There are many devices to dull the pain of adolescence, one of which is "raging" with loud music, another drugs. Some teenagers begin running, or traveling to get away from it all.

If there was a problem with "belonging" in childhood, adolescents may become preoccupied with their appearance. If their natural mood-swings lead into prolonged depression, get help. Sometimes a teenager does not know how to deal with bottled-up anger, and may become suicidal, or have constant headaches or stomach aches, or develop body rashes. Again, get help. Unhappy teenagers sometimes drop out of school or form intense liaisons with a gang or a friend of the opposite sex. If a hasty teenage marriage results, it will have an eighty-five percent chance of dissolving within two years.

Deep down, most children and teenagers have felt they were guilty for their parents' not liking them. So they put themselves down. But later, if they get some indication that they were worth loving after all, they may become very angry.

As a parent of teenagers you may not feel confident much of the time, but if you try hard, with love and honesty, you'll reap some great rewards. Young people are likable, they're asking lots of questions, and they're responsive to adult interest.

It is vital for teenagers to receive adult input into their maturation during these formative years. The father is crucial here. As we saw in chapter 11, when a man's daughter starts developing into a woman, she is basically asking one key question: "Will I be attractive to guys?" The father (or another loving, safe older male) is the generic interpreter of masculine responses to her beauty. If she gets the message that some young man will be very fortunate to catch her one day, and if that message is sincere, it will do wonders for her self-esteem. Lots of surveys show that a woman's happiness, and even her sexual fulfilment in marriage, is correlated highly with how well her father loved her as a young teenager.

Similarly, the young male needs to be initiated into manhood. It hardly matters what they do together, so long as the boy feels he's important enough for Dad to spend time with. It can be serious discussion or adventuring. Above all, Dad needs to talk and to listen, very attentively.

I had a father who, from my memory of him, seemed not to be interested in my hobbies and school work (apart from my report card!), and seemed intimidated by his aggressively questioning son. I was not rude to him, but in my worst moments I despised him. I tended to be creative; he was a public servant with a boring job. I loved reading; he said "fiction" would do me no good. I wanted to excel in sport; he said I was at school to get good results to avoid a "dead-end job." Fortunately a Sunday school teacher rescued me and virtually initiated me into manhood – probably without his or my knowing it at the time. He listened to my dreams and affirmed me in the areas of my talents; he showed me how a car works and taught me to drive. I will be eternally grateful to that man for his interest and encouragement.

The danger for me, of course, has been that I would reproduce my father's behavior with my own children. After I wrote the last paragraph, our remaining teenager came and told me she felt drained and needed to externalize it all. I could have said, "Later, Lindy, I'm busy working." Instead we went for a long walk and prayed. The hour was very precious, and later she would say that the problems burdening her had lifted in that hour.

Friends of ours were going to buy a house they didn't like, but it was near a railway station. I asked, "Why there?" Their response: "So we won't have to drive our kids everywhere." "Why don't you want to drive your teenagers around?" I asked. "They won't be home much longer and you'll wish you'd spent more time chauffeuring." They ended up buying a house a full kilometre from the station.

Between our two sets of teenagers I read Ross Campbell's immensely useful book, *How to Really Love Your Teenager* (Wheaton, Ill.: Victor Books, 1987). Some of his suggestions are still vivid:

- Adolescents need more family time, not less;
- Find time regularly to spend alone with each of your children;
- With teenagers becoming more independent, parents are liable to make the mistake of using their greater free time to meet their own pleasure needs: every teenager interprets this as rejection;
- Take your teenager to a restaurant regularly (choose the one with the slowest service);
- Make eye contact with your teenager: if a father does not look into the eyes of his daughter she'll wonder why she is not attractive to him;
- "Focused attention" is emotionally draining for you, but it is the only way for a teenager's "emotional tank" to stay full;
- Don't force your teenager to talk about anything in particular: let them choose the subject-matter and the timing (which, if it's important, will sometimes be at the last few minutes of a car drive before you arrive home – that's a safety "escape" if it's embarrassing or difficult).

One thing teenagers need more than anything else is unconditional love. The father of the prodigal son is our model here. Whatever happens, your teenager needs to hear you say, "You will always be loved by us. We may tell you when your behavior is not what we would desire, but you, as our son/daughter, will always be special to us whatever you do, whatever you look like, however well you perform."

I like this wisdom from James Dobson in *Discipline While You Can* (Eastbourne, E. Sussex: Kingsway, 1987, pp. 202–203) about parenting adolescents: "Our objective as parents, then, is to do *nothing* for boys and girls which they can profit from doing for themselves." He suggests three phrases to guide us: • "Hold on with an open hand" (they must accept the consequences of their choices). • "Hold them close and let them go" (the tendency is to retain control in order to avoid hearing the wrong reply to the question "Did I train them properly?"). • "If you love something, set it free. If it comes back to you, then it's yours. If it doesn't return, then it never was yours in the first place."

The teenage years, I believe, are God's time for building on or breaking up the foundations. Teenagers begin to realize that they must make choices their parents cannot now make for them. More people make serious commitments to Christ in this period than any other. So hang in there: your modeling of patient love, even in the midst of sometimes severe provocation, will be an example your teenage children will never forget.

Selected Quotations

As our children go and take on their own identities, painfully banging them together little piece by little piece, just as we did before, the process repeating from generation to generation, those identities may be in conflict with ours. "I am not the mother of a fifteen-year-old who wears one black sneaker and one white," says a parent, incredulously, or "That kid with the one earring clearly can't be mine. There's got to be an emotional problem. Got to get him to see somebody." Or conversely, the new "straight" kid who says, "Hey, Dad, you dress like a hippie, you know that? You're out of it!" We adults sometimes feel as if our identities, our very reasons for being, are under siege …

Growing up also means growing away, becoming someone separate from parents in meaningful ways. The conflict between parent and child is often over *which* meaningful ways. It gives truth to the expression, "You can't win for losing." The house as haven begins to lose meaning on one level, for the child is preparing, bit by bit, to leave the nest. On another, the aspect of haven becomes terribly important, for it is the one place where you may go to rest, to go forth again to take up battle for the self. Alas, the house itself becomes a battleground as we parents feel challenged, threatened, not wishing to give up our hold on "our" children. Thus, control becomes ... [an] issue. Another irony: Children control us with their behavior, while we attempt to control them with our words. Who's in charge here, indeed?

JEFFREY and CAROL RUBIN,
When Families Fight, New York: William Morrow & Co., 1989, pp. 184–185.

Teenagers can be so darned superior and, with the first tingling of adulthood, hurtful and even insolent, especially to parents. "I wish you were dead!" is a favourite exclamation when things are not going their way, or "Ahhh, the Great Man speaks!" when a father chides his son for something. We would be loth to accept without reprisal such insults from people of our own age, but we should not become upset now. We must quell our pride and remember that this is a passing phase. Liken it, if you like, to bedwetting, cuts and bruises, picking the nose, squinting, and other problems which came and went when the children were small. One day they may recall their rudeness and be sorry, but probably not until they have had kids of their own and faced a similar barrage.

It is hard to remain silent when adolescents mouth that old bit about "the rotten world we will inherit from the older generation," a myth spread by adults who should have known better ...

Of course, not all parents have problems with their teenage sons and daughters. I have been told of families in which the children's transition from childhood to young manhood or womanhood proceeded without a ripple ... Somehow, such families seem rather dull. In fact, I admire young people with firm opinions on things, even if they know little about them; at least they don't bottle it up.

KEITH SMITH,
How to Get Closer to Your Children, Surry Hills, NSW: Waratah Press, 1985, pp. 164–165.

The job of parents is to encourage their teenager's own sense of responsibility. In "parents win" families teenagers have little opportunity to develop self-responsibility. In "teenager wins" families what happens is usually what the teenager wants. The parent may have an idea of what should happen and try to persuade the teenager to adopt it. But the teenager – usually operating from an "I win" style – has his own ideas. He tries to persuade the parent to adopt those. If that persuasion fails, then the teenager uses his power – and teenagers can be just as powerful as parents. Teenagers may use emotional blackmail, threats of violence, tantrums, they may storm out … The problem with such a situation is that teenagers may develop strong feelings of insecurity about their parents' feelings for them. For the parents' attitude may become dominated both by feelings of resentment at being dominated and guilt at failing as a parent …

In turn, the teenagers learn very self-centered, controlling ways of behaving. They do not learn to respect other people's needs and may have difficulty in forming relationships with friends as equals, based on mutual respect. They come to believe that their own wants and needs are always the most important. They may find it very difficult when they have to cope with institutions like school and work where some adults may be working in the "I win" styles. For, above all, they learn that the "I win" style works for them – at least at home.

Being a parent of a teenager in such a "teenager wins" family is seldom fun. By definition, parents do not find that their needs as people count for much. They get little satisfaction as parents and may feel a failure for reasons they cannot fathom, and once the pattern is set, cannot change.

CLIFF SCHIMMELS,
Surviving the Terrible Teenage Years, Illinois: LifeJourney Books, 1991, p. 21.

Classic descriptions of the factors in family life which contribute to young people's individual development include –
- Provision of stable bonds, serving as a basis for the individual's growing circle of relationships outside the family.
- Provision of models to follow by imitation or identification.
- Degree to which parents establish a set of attitudes which the individual may follow or rebel against.
- Degree to which the family acts as a secure base from which an individual can test new ways of exploring and responding to the environment.

L. OWEN,
"Some Observations on the Themes of I.Y.Y. 1985 – Part 2,"
Australian Child and Family Welfare, Spring 1985, p. 14.

I, for one, cannot feel love for my teenagers all the time. But I will give myself credit for trying to arrive at that wonderful goal of loving them unconditionally. I help myself by constantly keeping in mind that:

- Teenagers are children.
- Teenagers will tend to act like teenagers.
- Much of teenage behavior is unpleasant.
- If I do my part as a parent and love them despite their unpleasant behavior, they will be able to mature and give up their immature ways.
- If I love them only when they please me (conditional love), and convey my love to them only during those times, they will not feel genuinely loved. This in turn will make them feel insecure, damage their self-image, and actually prevent them from developing more mature behavior. Therefore their behavior development is as much my responsibility as theirs.
- If I love them unconditionally, they will feel good about themselves and be comfortable with themselves. They will be able to control their anxiety and, in turn, their behavior, as they grow into adulthood.

ROSS CAMPBELL,
How to Really Love Your Teenager, Wheaton, Ill.: Victor Books, 1987, p. 25.

Could alcohol be a part of the life of a teenager close to you? Materials from the U.S. Department of Health and Human Services describe some of the early warning signs:
- Abrupt changes in mood or attitude
- Sudden decline in attendance or performance at work or school
- Sudden resistance to discipline at home or school
- Impaired relationship with family or friends
- Ignoring curfews
- Unusual temper flare-ups
- Increased borrowing of money, possibly stealing from home, school, or employer
- Increased secrecy about possessions, actions, and use of money
- Associating with a new group of friends who use booze and other drugs
  Could alcohol be a big part of your life?

JERRY JOHNSON,
It's Killing Our Kids, Dallas: Word Publishing, 1991, p. 41.

"U.S. News & World Report," September 11, 1989, reports that it is a rare case, indeed, when an illegal drug user does not start with tobacco, alcohol, or marijuana, and well over ninety-five percent of marijuana users learn to inhale by starting with tobacco. The entrance drugs for illegal drugs are "legal" drugs. Over one hundred times as many lives are lost each year because of tobacco and alcohol as are lost because of illegal drugs (*Dallas Morning News*, October 9, 1989).

NOTE: We lost 106,000 men and women in World War II. We lose 390,000 each YEAR to tobacco and 150,000 to alcohol.

JERRY JOHNSON,
It's Killing Our Kids, Dallas: Word Publishing, 1991, p. 205.

Perhaps the best help a parent can offer ... is to help the junior higher see beyond the present ... Spend some time with your child reflecting about what life is going to be. Talk of adult things such as work, marriage, and family. Give her some adultlike responsibility.

If you promise not to tell, I'll share my secret weapon, which I save for my children when they are struggling through these critical periods of reidentification. I find a vacant parking lot somewhere, and I teach them how to drive. You would be amazed at how much thirty minutes at the wheel in an isolated parking lot can do for a thirteen-year-old's morale!

CLIFF SCHIMMELS,
Surviving the Terrible Teenage Years, Illinois: LifeJourney Books, 1991, p. 21.

The principle of letting the punishment fit the crime is sound. Perhaps the following guidelines will help:

- If the issue is more serious and requires some form of punishment, talk over the problem with your partner and decide on a suitable consequence.
- The most effective punishment is one that is completed quickly; ones that extend over weeks will lose their impact and lead to resentment.
- Teenagers will respond to parents who are seen to be fair and just.
- Avoid drawing comparisons with others whose behaviour is more desirable.
- Target the behaviour and not the person. It is important to differentiate between saying "You're cheap," and "That makes you seem cheap."

- Select a punishment that will have an impact. It is pointless to deny them TV when they never watch anyway.
- The punishment should be seen as wiping the slate clean again. It is very destructive to build up a case record against them, that is used whenever the need arises, as this leads to a "can't win" mentality in the teenager: "My record is so bad, I've got nothing to lose."
- When the punishment is concluded, parents should be able to show that there are no residual grudges.
- Try and be creative with the punishment as this is more likely to appeal to their sense of justice; remember that fairness and justice are big issues for teenagers and, while they may be angry at being punished, they will also see its rightness.
- Try to retain a sense of humour through it all, then it will be seen as good parenting, not retribution.

TERRY COLLING and JANET VICKERS,
Teenagers: A Guide to Understanding Them,
Moorebank, NSW: Bantam Books, 1988, pp. 28–29.

Less than a generation ago children grew up in the family home, and stayed on as young adults until they got married. Our fledgling adults are now flying earlier and often further away. Some leave because they can no longer endure the emotional fall-out from warring parents. Most are seeking independence, a chance to run their own lives, to be accepted as adults.

But the transition will be a tougher challenge than expected for the young person. They will need new disciplines, and will experience new loneliness.

And the parents will feel rejection; some will refuse to cooperate and may distance themselves from their children, perhaps for ever. If letting go is done with love and respect your child will always come back – whether he or she actually lives at home or not.

The following guidelines (suggested by Patrick Farrell, Director of the Marriage and Family Counseling section of the Cairnmillar Institute in Melbourne) may help:

- Recognize that your child's wish for independence indicates the success of your parenting rather than any failure on your part.
- See this as a turning-point in your relationship with your child,

the transition from parent–child to adult–adult. If you handle it right you may lose your child but you'll have gained a friend and kept your son/daughter.

- Participate in the move, as far as you are permitted, to show your child that you are supporting this move into adulthood, not abandoning him/her. Suggest a shared set-up: most young adults are rarely able to cope with the unaccustomed loneliness of living alone. Some furnishings should be taken from the child's room, but some should also be left behind. And if renting for the first time there might need to be some warnings about unscrupulous landlords. Offer your advice as a friend, not as an examiner.

- Be available for advice and encouragement, but don't force it. It's not your life you are organizing. Wait till your young adult is ready before you visit the new "digs." And don't poke around or criticize.

- Recognize the time your child grows up and moves out of the family home as the re-establishment of the relationship of parents as a couple. You'll miss your child, but don't brood on your loss. With more time together you and your spouse can concentrate on each other, plan a new life together unhindered by the day-to-day responsibilities of caring for another adult around the place.

- Because, rightly or wrongly (depending on the age and maturity of the girl), we feel a daughter is more vulnerable than a son outside the security of the family home, many parents tend to overreact when their daughter expresses the desire to leave. This overreaction can take the form of outrage or anger. If this is your initial reaction, explain to your daughter that it is caused by your concern and your love for her. Then discuss the pros and cons of the proposed move. You will still have to let her go (eventually), but she won't have to make a major statement about her need for independence by moving out prematurely, matching her anger to yours.

GLENDA BANKS,
Your Guide to Successful Family Living,
Blackburn, Vic.: Dove Communications, 1985, abridged from pp. 142–147.

A Prayer for Parents of Teenagers

Lord God, I'm needing you right now, especially now. I didn't get an instruction manual telling me how to bring up teenagers. Life didn't seem so complicated when I was young. (But, as I reflect on it, I wasn't too happy – or good – all the time back then either.)

Help me to realize that becoming separate is not just an issue for the teenage years but starts from birth. May I not forget that the process we are struggling with is one of which we already have some experience.

Also, themes of freedom, responsibility, trust, discipline, mutual respect, and having one's own opinions run through childhood as well as adolescence. Sometimes I forget that the child is not overnight changed into a teenager. Give me the patience and genuine interest when my child needs to be able to air her views. My child needs to have her own opinions and I want to respect those opinions as I have asked her to respect mine. May I not be threatened when a desire for freedom is expressed by my teenager. It does not matter, provided she grows up to be responsible.

Help me to understand the external pressures my teenager faces from peers, the internal pressures from biology, and the incorporated messages of parents and society about what is desirable and "right." The adolescent's job is to become somebody in these years, despite the stresses. When I'm tempted to say, "It's about time you grew up," give me an awareness that it doesn't happen just like that, like magic.

May I pray faithfully for my child, my teenager, my soon-to-become an independent adult. May I develop a relationship that will blossom into a good friendship as we grow together, learn together, and, hopefully, trust you together.

Through Jesus Christ our Lord. Amen.

A Benediction

May the eternal God, who has helped others before you in similar – and sometimes worse – predicaments and challenges, give you a firm assurance of his love and wisdom and patience. May God, who out of defeat and frustration always brings new hope and new alternatives, continually give you new strength, and when you need them, new ideas. Amen.

16

Adolescence is tough but you can mature through it!

Remember your creator in the days of your youth, before the days of trouble come, and the years draw near when you will say, "I have no pleasure in them" (Ecclesiastes 12:1).

Listen to your father who begot you, and do not despise your mother when she is old (Proverbs 23:22). Do not speak harshly to an older man, but speak to him as to a father, to younger men as brothers, to older women as mothers, to younger women as sisters – with absolute purity (1 Timothy 5:1–2).

I adjure you, O daughters of Jerusalem, do not stir up or awaken love until it is ready! (Song of Solomon 8:4).

May you be made strong with all the strength that comes from his glorious power, and may you be prepared to endure everything with patience (Colossians 1:11).

While your obedience is known to all, so that I rejoice over you, I want you to be wise in what is good and guileless in what is evil (Romans 16:19). The fruit of the Spirit is love, joy, peace, patience, kindness, generosity, faithfulness, gentleness, and self-control. There is no law against such things (Galatians 5:22–23).

Jesus increased in wisdom and in stature, and in divine and human favor (Luke 2:52). Let no one despise your youth, but set the believers an example in speech and conduct, in love, in faith, in purity (1 Timothy 4:12).

We have had four marvelous teenagers: the youngest is in her last year of this wonderfully complicated era. On their thirteenth birthdays, at the beginning of this hazardous journey, I would make a little speech, which they took with good grace (I think!): "Now listen. The next few years are going to be all mixed-up, both for you and for us. Your chemistry will go berserk, you'll have mood-swings like you've never experienced, and there'll be phases when you won't know whether you're a child or an adult or what. As I said, these mood-swings are going to be hard for you and for us, and I have just one request: please make 'em quick!"

Adolescence is when the Big Questions about a person's identity and significance come hurtling in upon them. They want the security they experienced as children but also the independence they see adults enjoying. In most teenagers there's a tendency to be lazy: they want the benefits of a disciplined life without the effort (which is not possible).

Their changing bodies are a source of embarrassment; they don't seem to develop in the right places evenly. And adults expect them to be more mature than they are. Teenagers ask themselves questions about how they "come across" to others; at no time in life is a person's self-consciousness as much an issue as in these years. They often put themselves down, and don't seem to fit into situations as easily as before. Teenagers are easily embarrassed, and therefore often teased – though teasers often lack confidence themselves. There is a constant preoccupation with clothes and how they look (researchers tell us teenagers look into shop mirrors more than anyone else).

A few pointers about bringing up parents. Let's take the difficult curfew issue as an example. The excellent book by Clayton Barbeau, *How to Raise Parents: A Teenager's Survival Guide* (Blackburn, Vic.: Collins Dove, 1988, pp. 180–181), describes the following typical scenario: Sally rushes out of the door while "Lunkhead" is outside leaning on the horn. She asks Dad if she can stay out an hour later tonight. Dad looks out of the window at Lunkhead, still leaning on the horn, and immediately thinks "Sex!" "No," he yells in panic. So there's an argument. The problem is, Sally's talking about time, Dad about sex. She should have negotiated earlier, been explicit about where she was going, and why she needed the extra hour. Parents, believe it or not, have had more experience with the Lunkheads of this world, and they have good reason to be worried. It's not for nothing that bumper stickers ask: "It's 10 o'clock. Do you know where your children are?" Sally: after a track-record of responsibility keeping prearranged curfew hours, you'll be in an excellent position to negotiate a new time.

In Western countries we are ready for "making babies" and parenthood about ten years before we marry. Most movies dangle sexual enjoyment before us, and so it requires a lot of maturity not to give ourselves away in this area before we're ready for a serious commitment. A suggestion: always be a little skeptical about the moral messages you're getting on TV and in the movies. Such messages, if not viewed critically, can bring about subtle and cumulative changes in our perceptions of our surroundings, which are particularly potent for adolescents who are going through a difficult and formative phase of life.

The best wisdom about the "mating game" may be summarized as follows. Assume that decision-making about complex moral and other issues is not easy until you are into your twenties. Find a partner you'd be happy to put up with when he or she is in a bad mood. Would this one be O.K. as mother/father of your children? What kinds of traumas did they suffer in their childhood? (The things sown in the past you'll harvest later: almost all girls who were sexually abused, for example, have problems in their married sex lives.) If you start "going steady," be steady on all fronts: mental, emotional, physical, and spiritual. Don't let one of these areas get ahead of the rest.

Back to relating to imperfect parents. I remember doing two things as a teenager. First, I sounded off about my parents to a friend. I realize now I was getting a lot of frustration out of my system. And second, when I was about fifteen I said to myself, "My parents are narrow, square, and uninteresting, but I'm not going to let their view of the world affect me." So I got on with life, taking the best from my parents' culture and religious faith and adding it into a new mix of my own. I'm very glad I approached it like that. Some older people – even into their thirties and forties – have not forgiven their parents for being human. It's one of the key marks of a mature person to do that – hopefully before you've finished being a teenager.

Teenagers: you can create a hell in your home. Don't. If you've got problems, find a sensitive adult to talk to. Perhaps you could phone them up and say something like this: "I read in this book that I should talk to someone about my problems with my parents. Can I talk to you?" Go on, do it.

A final word about peer pressure. Teenagers aren't the only group suffering from the tyranny of friends' expectations; look at business-men and politicians, for example: they all dress and behave the same as their peers. But as a teenager you're not as sure of yourself as you will be when older, and peer culture is replacing adult authority in some kids' lives because it offers intimacy and belonging. It can be tyrannical, but unlike the family it has no responsibility for conse-quences, and is more concerned for "now" rather than longer-term effects. And it can be reactive: adults are down on drugs, so your peer group will tell you drugs are O.K. and parents just don't want you to have a good time. I hope you give that kind of nonsense the treat-ment it deserves.

I forget who said it, but the following is the best wisdom I've read on all this: "The so-called 'generation gap' doesn't have to get in the way of your relationship with your parents if you don't want it to. You can develop a mutual understanding with your parents, different from the one you have with your friends, but just as good if not better. Keep the lines of communication open and use them."

Selected Quotations

It's unusual for families with teenagers to eat together, much less pray together. Families these days tend to graze. If the teenager comes home from school and parents are still out at work, they'll raid the fridge. Mum isn't there to tell them not to eat because it will spoil their dinner.

Kids have more freedom, we all know that. But so has everybody else. The nine-to-five working routine is going. Kids have more things they can do, more movies they can watch, more television. They have more money, and more freedom to get around.

The old disciplines are going. Kids have more options. And yet they are both more responsible and irresponsible, in some ways. They drop more litter than previous generations (partly because they have more wrappers to dispose of), but they also have some good opinions about nuclear power, whales, and the biosphere.

One study found that most Australian young people, when asked the ideal characteristics in a partner, said they looked for honesty, caring, trust, intimacy, stability, and the ability to communicate. Physical attractiveness was mentioned by ten percent of women and thirty percent of men.

This same study found that basic values haven't changed very much. Young people prize family values. They don't want the family to die.

ROWLAND CROUCHER,
from an unpublished talk.

Does life get easier as you get older? Yes. Adolescence and puberty is a very stressful period. You are like a continent being formed by volcanic eruptions and fires. There are calm periods and then more eruptions. But despite all the stress, a continent truly is being formed.

You face the stresses of your body changing and of trying to identify who you are and what you want to be. You face the stresses of learning to relate to the opposite sex and of handling peer pressures about drugs, booze and sex. And all the while you have pressures in school.

Later, of course, you will encounter different stresses, because there's no such thing as life without stress. But you'll be able to cope more maturely. You'll be more realistic about yourself and the world.

But even so, it takes most people about forty years to discover the map is not the territory. Aristotle, for example, said it takes forty years to be a philosopher. Thomas Aquinas, one of the great thinkers of the Middle Ages, agreed.

What they meant was that as we gain experience dealing with life and all kinds of people (not just the narrow world of our family and friends), we learn to accept responsibility for ourselves. At that point – about age forty – we begin to take another look at our values. We begin to see that reality may not be what we thought it was when we were eighteen. Then, finally, we let go some of the baggage. We learn grudges are useless and only harm us, that holding onto anger gives us ulcers. We learn how to love more unselfishly ...

Just as once it was difficult for you to tie your shoes but today it's a snap, by the time you're forty you'll automatically be doing loving things for your family or friends – things that you were too self-conscious to do when you were sixteen or seventeen.

As you mature, you learn how your parents influenced who you are. You begin to see how wise they were in some things. Mark Twain said that when he was seventeen his father was the stupidest man on earth; when he reached twenty-three, he was astonished how much his father had learned in six years.

CLAYTON BARBEAU,
How to Raise Parents: A Teenager's Survival Guide,
Blackburn, Vic.: Collins Dove, 1988, pp. 218–219.

Some people confuse *adolescence* and *puberty*, as if these terms mean the same thing. They don't. Puberty begins between the ages of nine and eleven, depending on whether you are a boy or a girl, and ends around sixteen to eighteen. It's basically a physical and hormonal process.

Your soft baby skin becomes thicker and more oily. That's why about seventy per cent of young people will have skin problems. Your baby jaw will be moving forward to take its adult shape, and this may temporarily affect your eardrums – and that means the stereo gets played louder. Parents will yell, "Are you deaf?" and the answer, in puberty, is "Yes, partially."

Hair is thickening and growing in strange places. The word *puberty* comes from the Latin *pubescere*, which means "to get hairy." In fact, puberty is a very hairy time. At least seven powerful hormones are being shot through your body, chiefly testosterone in boys and estrogen in girls. These chemicals cause dramatic emotional shifts – real highs and real lows. Suicidal depression can be followed by a wonderfully exhilarating mood. That's one reason it is particularly stupid to take drugs at this time: your body is producing all of its own mood-altering chemicals. Pubescents have natural highs.

KEITH SMITH,
How to Get Closer to Your Children, Surry Hills, NSW: Waratah Press, 1985, pp. 164–165.

Adults and young people can feel as if they live in different worlds from time to time. Society is changing so fast that the life experience of one generation can be very different from the next. Rock music, invented on washboards and acoustic guitars, is now a sophisticated electronic production. Work that once took a clerical worker's day now takes a few seconds on a micro-computer.

Adults and young people are sometimes hostile to each other because each feels threatened by the other. The enthusiasm many young people have for challenging things adults take for granted can be unsettling for those adults. It can appear to be attacking the very things that make those adults secure. By contrast, the young feel that they are powerless. That they are surrounded by adults telling them what to do, how things are, and generally getting in the way of young people's freedom.

There is some truth in both these attitudes. But there are also many things adults and young people have in common. Adults' freedom and power to direct the course of their own lives is not great in many cases. Young people's attitudes are rarely as rash as some adults fear. Young and old discover this as soon as they begin talking with each other.

JULIE WARREN,
How to Handle Your Parents, Edinburgh: Macdonald Publishers, 1983, p. 51.

The transmission of [the media's] message isn't magical or mysterious: the power of the entertainment industry to influence our actions flows from its ability to redefine what constitutes normal behavior in this society. The popular culture now consumes such a huge proportion of our time and attention that it has assumed a dominant role in establishing social conventions. The fantasy figures who entertain us on our TV and movie screens, or who croon to us constantly from our radios and CD players, take the lead in determining what is considered hip, and what will be viewed as hopelessly weird. In every society, ordinary folk have been able to cultivate a sense of style by aping the airs of the aristocracy; in this stubbornly democratic culture, the only aristocracy that counts for anything is the world of "celebrities" who appear on the tube and in the tabloids.

MICHAEL MEDVED,
Hollywood vs. America, New York: HarperCollins, 1992, p. 261.

A Melbourne current affairs show recently reported on a new "fad" sweeping some teen circles: chastity. According to the report, virginity and abstinence until marriage is becoming a new "trend." Imagine that: chastity is now up there on a par with hula hoops and glue-sniffing. Modern society is certainly progressing ...

The Journal of Child Psychology and Psychiatry (34, 1993) reports that when compared to peers from intact families, adolescent children of divorced parents show higher rates of problem behaviours, psychological distress, and academic underachievement. Also, according to the study done by a Medical School in London, parental remarriage does little to alleviate these problems ...

Teens are much less likely to leave home for life on the streets if their parents' marriage is intact than if their parents are divorced or never married. According to a Canadian University study, a life of crime on the streets was more likely if teens came from broken homes.

Australian Family Association, *Family Update*, Vol. 9, No. 5, Sept.–Oct. 1993, p. 8.

God is a God of love who comes to us, offering us the gift of a new and meaningful life through Jesus Christ. This bold declaration of faith is good news to a generation of young people caught in a crossfire of mixed messages about their sexuality:

From the clergy: "Do not have sex until you are married."

Parents: "Do not have sex until you are really ready – preferably not until you are married."

Educators: "Delay sex or consider abstinence, but if you do have sex, use protection."

Researchers: "Most young people have sex by the time they enter college ... average age of intercourse ... fifteen."

Peers: "What do you mean you slept with him! You're crazy!" or "What do you mean you are still a virgin?"

Magazine ads: "If you wear these jeans, you can have your pick of sexual partners."

TV: "If you are rich, you can have sex whenever and with whomever you want."

Movies: "If you just relax and enjoy being swept off your feet, you will have great sex and live happily ever after."

Fairy tales: "The knight-in-shining-armor will swoop into your life – no matter how bad your life seems now – and carry you off to a castle in fairyland and you will live happily ever after."

Presbyterians and Human Sexuality 1991,
Louisville, Ky.: The Office of the General Assembly Presbyterian Church (USA), p. 43.

Having to report to your parents on your day's encounters can be a bit of a trial. The more your parents want to know, the less you want to tell them. And so the plot thickens. If you have this sort of problem with your parents, ask yourself this question. "Could it be that my parents are actually genuinely interested in my life?" As the question–answer routine has built up it may seem that the questions are more important than your answers. Your parents may appear only to want to pry into your affairs, or control your movements.

Usually, however, parents have more to do with their time than to make idle enquiries of what you do with yours. They ask because they are concerned that you do not come to harm as you explore the world about you, just as they've always been. This concern extends to being interested in what you find there and how it affects you. They can see you growing and developing and want to keep in touch. For all these reasons, and the simple fact that they are responsible for you, your parents have a right to know where you are when you're not at home and who you're with. What you tell them is important. Try avoiding your parents' irritating questions by getting in first with the information. For example, "I'm going to see so-and-so tonight, we're planning to go to such-and-such a place. Do you know it? What time would you like me home?" The questions at the end actually invite your parents to share a bit in your plans without necessarily restricting them.

JULIE WARREN,
How to Handle Your Parents, Edinburgh: MacDonald Publishers, 1983, pp. 16–17.

A Prayer for Teenagers

Jesus, I don't pray much, perhaps, but now I'm needing to talk to you. About me.

Jesus, I'm confused. I sometimes really don't know who I am. Some of my relationships aren't working out. I'm trying to figure out what kind of lifestyle I'm to follow and there are so many alternatives.

Life is pretty difficult. I can't understand my parents sometimes, school is hard, friends come and go, I don't like myself very much, and I'm scared about the future. I know unless I work hard I won't make it, but it seems a long grind.

I want to be independent, but I also want to respect my parents and I want my parents to respect me. If I make mistakes help me learn from them, and if my parents are critical of some things, help me remember they're mainly trying to protect me and warn me because they care about me.

I don't know very much about how to be a Christian, but I want to learn more. I want my questions answered. There are big moral issues – smoking, drinking, drugs, sex – and I'm torn between finding the truth, and having a good time and keeping my friends. If something's right, I want to do that, rather than wearing a mask and being a phony just to be popular.

If I really choose to follow you, it's going to be hard at school. Other kids don't easily accept people who are different.

Jesus, when it's tough, help me make a stand, see me through another day.

I give my life to you: take me as I am, and make me into a worthwhile person. Forgive me for living without you. You have a great plan for my life – help me to find it. I want to make a difference in the world. Help me to live so that, when the time comes to die, I will have lived well. Amen.

A Benediction

May the God who made everything make you into a beautiful and useful person. May Jesus, who was the special friend of people who were confused, be your special friend too. And may his Spirit live in your life and through your life so that other people in our messed-up world can find the way. Amen.

17 | A chapter for children (of all ages)

You shall love the Lord your God with all your heart, and with all your soul, and with all your mind, and with all your strength (Mark 12:30).

It was you who formed my inward parts; you knit me together in my mother's womb. I praise you, for I am fearfully and wonderfully made. Wonderful are your works; that I know very well. My frame was not hidden from you, when I was being made in secret, intricately woven in the depths of the earth (Psalm 139:13–15).

When the chief priests and the scribes saw the amazing things that he did, and heard the children crying out in the temple, "Hosanna to the Son of David," they became angry and said to him, "Do you hear what these are saying?" Jesus said to them, "Yes; have you never read, 'Out of the mouths of infants and nursing babies you have prepared praise for yourself'?" (Matthew 21:15–16).

Honor your father and your mother, so that your days may be long in the land that the Lord your God is giving you (Exodus 20:12). My child, keep your father's commandment, and do not forsake your mother's teaching (Proverbs 6:20). Children, obey your parents in the Lord, for this is right. "Honor your father and mother" – this is the first commandment with a promise: "so that it may be well with you and you may live long on the earth" (Ephesians 6:1–3).

People were bringing even infants to him that he might touch them; and when the disciples saw it, they sternly ordered them not to do it. But Jesus called for them and said, "Let the little children come to me, and do not stop them; for it is to such as these that the kingdom of God belongs. Truly I tell you, whoever does not receive the kingdom of God as a little child will never enter it" (Luke 18:15–17).

Unless the Lord builds the house, those who build it labor in vain (Psalm 127:1).

Why does everyone (or almost everyone) love children? Partly because little ones remind us of the pure innocence we once experienced, but have left behind as we grew up. Just today, our "granddaughter" Cathy, aged two, was handed back to her parents after a four-day "holiday" with us. She taught us so many things this Easter weekend. She noticed birds and colors and sounds we had taken for granted. She was full of spontaneous aliveness. Looking into her face as she wondered, about the stars or the story I read to her, was to look into the face of the divine …

No one ever really stops being a child. The adult simply suppresses the child that is deep within the reality of their psyche with layers of sophisticated complexity and seriousness.

Every child's history begins in the creative mind and heart of God. God knew you were coming into the world before anything else was made. He knew exactly what you would be like: "In your book were written all the days that were formed for me, when none of them as yet existed" (Psalm 139:16).

Then, from the security of the womb, you were thrust into a frightening world. From earliest years the child needs to experience belonging. "You are to whom you belong": if a child hears loving parents communicate "You belong to us and we love you," he or she is saved from becoming a psychopath – a person who felt they never belonged to anyone. Belonging is also communicated through touch: you may have heard of hospitals years ago where children's wards emptied when people cuddled and touched them.

The story is told of a man in New York who joined twenty-six golf clubs but never really belonged to any of them. Why? He never felt he belonged anywhere as he grew up.

Children need a regular, daily diet of human love and praise. These should be given in a fully-focused way, not from behind the ironing or a newspaper. Rats, we all know, prefer electric shocks to nothing at all. Children, too, if they have to choose between being ignored or scolded, will be naughty to get the latter.

Professor Selma H. Fraiberg in *The Magic Years* describes how human disasters have resulted in children being emotionally deprived. Children orphaned by war early in life generally are unable later to bond themselves with other people or experience tenderness, grief, or shame. They become slow learners, apathetic, a prey to many kinds of mental illness.

From age two a key question dominates: Do I have worth? If you do not have a sense of worth, it's because you received messages from significant others that you're "not O.K." I'm not what I think I am, I'm not what you think I am, I'm what I think you think I am. The self is a series of reflected appraisals.

The two-year-old also begins to learn the meaning of a little word formed from the middle two letters of the alphabet: "NO." Parental discipline helps the child figure out the difference between what is right and wrong, what is safe and what is not.

My own father had a "military belt" for what he regarded as serious offences committed by his three sons. (There was a church-going father in England who had a motto under his belt: "I need thee every hour.") My father used to quote from the Authorized Version: "Foolishness is bound in the heart of a child, but the rod of correction will drive it far from him" (Proverbs 22:15).

Discipline is necessary to teach the child what is harmful. But the child must know that the behavior is being attacked, not the self. Otherwise children get the idea they are only loved when they are good. Or clever. So reject the behavior, not the child. The child should not believe "I am only accepted when I please Mum or Dad." All children (of any age, including adults!) ought to know they are loved for who they are, not for what they do or don't do. One of the worst things you can say to a child is "God will not love you if you're naughty!" God loves us as we are, naughty or good. Of course, he loves us too much to be happy with us staying the way we are. One of the tragedies of our day is that children are not taught more about the God Jesus described.

Child psychologist Dr Maurice Balson has the view that most problems in a child's behavior stem from those children having doubts about whether their parents respect them. Respect is the happy mean between ignoring the child on the one hand (remember when we were to be "seen and not heard"?) and pampering them, so that the child does not learn to solve problems on their own. Respect means asking the child to help you make some decisions – when shopping, for example ("Should we buy pears or apples today?"). Respect means never ridiculing a child's opinions or making them feel foolish. When discipline is related to respect, the child gets the feeling that he or she is not living up to the parents' high opinion of them. So smacking or yelling is rarely, if ever, necessary. I like the "time out" or "thinking spot" idea, where children who have mis-behaved are given an opportunity to think about the consequences of their behavior before they can join in another activity.

So what makes a happy childhood? Feminist Germaine Greer (who wrote a book with the haunting title, *Daddy, We Hardly Knew You*) said, "Children come up just the same, brought or not." That's too simplistic. But so is behaviorist J.B. Watson's view that depending on early conditioning the child could become either a violent criminal or a genius.

I like noted child psychologist Bruno Bettelheim's concept of the "good enough parent." What kinds of childhood experiences cause an adult to look back and say they were well pleased with the way they were raised? As a parent you may occasionally become irrationally fed-up with your child, and spank him or her too hard in your anger. But if there is a genuine love and affection, and it is communicated to the child in loving ways, they'll be O.K.

A parent is the architect who designs the rooms of the temple in which the child will live for the rest of his or her life. We learn to relate to other people by how our parents and others relate to us. But no parent perfectly satisfies all the deep needs of the child's soul. All parents, in a sense, sin against their children. Later the child in the adult wants to blame their parents for who they have become. One of the best maturity-producing "aha!" moments a child will ever have is when they realize the horrifying truth that some of their needs will not be met by their parents.

Some psychologists talk about "the too precious child": the idea
in some parents' minds that a single negative event may ruin the
"fragile ego" for life. This is a heavy responsibility to have on one's
conscience. However, that is not to say that painful experiences in
childhood do not discolor one's life, even one's whole life. Just this
week a man told me of a humiliating thing his father said after he felt
good about something he had done, then showed his dad: he still
shrivels a little inside, he told me, when he thinks about his father's
sarcastic reaction. And women who have been sexually molested
don't easily get over it.

In the 1980s we took up the idea of "quality time" with our
children. This is a good notion, provided it doesn't mean scheduling
time away from leisure or chores because the kids need you and you'd
better pay attention to them. Perhaps for some this was really
"leftover time."

Don't be too negative or scolding. Communicate in positive ways
("How was school today?") rather than nagging all the time ("Why
aren't you dressed?" "Have you cleaned your teeth?") Some child
psychologists are telling us that Anglo-Saxon parents are not good at
being positive in parenting. One of the most positive things you can
do is praise your children. Praise tells them they have competence:
that they can do something well. Every one of us has been created by
God to experience significance: not necessarily being more clever
than others, but with a strategic goal for our lives. In effect we say to
every child, "Congratulations, you're gifted!" Effective parents will
tease out what a child does best and encourage the child in those
areas. And if parents always finish projects their child starts, those
children may eventually opt out or become workaholics. Children
want to join their parents in the work they do: to identify with father
and mother, before later moving away from them.

Recently I was told, "Bill has had a breakdown." "Why?" I asked.
"Oh, he was made redundant." Later in the conversation I had to say,
"That was not the real reason he broke down. Somewhere back in his
formation he believed what he was worth was defined by what he did,
and how well others appreciated what he did. His self-esteem was
geared to positive or negative feedback about his performance."

So when what we perceive as needs are not met, we experience
pain. Each of us has "moments of existential despair." We live in a
terrifying world where we cannot get everything we want or need.

This is where God comes in, I believe. You are designed to enjoy a relationship with God. As Tolstoy said, the soul is a God-shaped blank: only God can fit into it. But within us there is a stubborn desire for independence. That which Adam and Eve experienced is our experience too. There is in all of us a clenched fist saying, "I will survive without God." Shirley Bassey has a song "This is My Life!" Frank Sinatra sings "I did it my way!" Hell, wrote Dorothy Sayers, is the enjoyment of one's own way forever.

At some stage the mature person moves beyond dependence (my self-worth is a function of what you do or say to me) through independence (I'm going to make it on my own) to interdependence (I need you and you need me, but we don't have to be victims of each other's feedback). The stubborn commitment to independence, if it continues too far into adulthood, is manifested in too much self-sufficiency (I'll manage my own life without anyone else's interference), self-protection (I won't get close to people who are likely to hurt me), or an exaggerated selfishness (I will put myself first, and pursue only those things which enhance my own well-being). Rather a mature person is able to grow through experiences of helplessness, vulnerability, and humility.

To paraphrase a couplet of James Russell Lowell: Children, of all ages, are God's apostles, day by day sent forth to preach of love, and hope, and peace.

Selected Quotations
All children everywhere have these rights:
1. To enjoy special protection;
2. To be given opportunities and facilities to enable them to develop in a healthy and normal manner and in conditions of freedom and dignity;
3. To have a name and a nationality from their birth;
4. To enjoy the benefits of social security, including adequate nutrition, housing, recreation and medical services;
5. To receive special treatment, education and care of any handicap;
6. To grow up in an atmosphere of affection and security, wherever possible in the care and under the responsibility of their own parents;
7. To receive education;

8. To be the first to receive protection and relief in times of disaster;
9. To be protected against all forms of neglect, cruelty and exploitation;
10. To be protected from practices which may foster any form of discrimination.

Declaration of the Rights of the Child, United Nations, 1959, reaffirmed in 1979.

Children have never been very good at listening to their elders, but they have never failed to imitate them.

JAMES BALDWIN,
in Robert I. Fitzhenry (ed.), *Chambers Book of Quotations*,
Edinburgh: W&R Chambers Ltd., 1986, p. 76.

It seems children grow on praise ... The more children receive praise from their parents, the better they are able to achieve.

Many parents fear that if they praise their children, the children will get a swollen head and will not strive any further. It seems this fear is misplaced. Children are more likely to stop striving if they feel too anxious or depressed about their failures and faults. One mother said, "You should praise your children often, then they will be able to withstand the criticisms of others." Most studies report on praise for genuine achievement. Praise given indiscriminately is probably not associated with achievement ...

Studies of well-functioning families find a constant stream of praise and affirmation of other family members running through the conversation.

MOIRA EASTMAN,
The Magical Power of Family, Blackburn, Vic.: Collins Dove, 1991, pp. 23–24.

1. Regardless of the ambitions you have for your children, your children have a mind of their own. 2. Allow your children to feel comfortable expressing their feelings and even sharing their secrets. 3. Mentally prepare yourself to be patient and persistent. 4. It isn't money or social status which leads to family well-being. 5. Have faith in children so they may believe in themselves. 6. Don't withhold love. 7. Behaviour which is acknowledged or praised tends to be repeated.

PATRICIA C. BERNARD and MICHAEL E. BERNARD,
The You Can Do It Little Book for Parents, Blackburn, Vic.: Collins Dove, 1993, pp. 1–2.

God does things quite differently from us. When there is trouble, we send a policeman, a soldier or a diplomat. He sent a baby! ... The American preacher, Halford Luccock, said that whenever the ordering of society is discussed, whether for nations or small groups, the first question is "Who is the greatest?" "For about thirty centuries," he said, "people have discussed that question" ... Jesus took a small child, placed him in the midst of them, put his arms around him, and said, "Whoever wants to be first, must place himself last. Unless you reverse your attitude and become like this little child, you will never enter the Kingdom of heaven" ... In Jewish society that was an incredible thing to do. In Gentile society of the period, it was unthinkable. The worth of a child was seriously questioned.

NEIL ADCOCK,
"Child in the Midst," *NSW Baptist*, Nov./Dec. 1993, p. 25.

Recently I wrote and recorded a series of sound cassettes for use by children in primary schools. A number of teachers listened to the tapes and ... put forward some good ideas to improve them. This was "teacher" domain and I respected it. However, I was told that one narration would have to be changed because it "put children down" and was "patronising." The reason given was that it suggested I knew more than the children and that I was less awkward than them. In reply, I explained that what really puts children down is assuming that they will be offended by being told the simple truth that an adult knows more than they do. Children are more intelligent than that; more charitable, too, in accepting such facts with goodwill. I went on to say that if I had been talking to the children in a class I would have explained the difference between us this way: "You don't know as much as me, not because I'm smarter but because I'm older and have been around more. You are clumsier than me in some ways – don't know how to use your limbs as smoothly perhaps – because I've been using mine for years longer than you. It's like learning the piano. Somebody who has been at it for ten years must be better at it than somebody who took it up last week. Right?" This is the kind of talk which presents facts to children in a way they understand.

KEITH SMITH,
How to Get Closer to Your Children, Surry Hills, NSW: Waratah Press, 1985, pp. 58–59.

We need love's tender lessons taught

As only weakness can;

God hath his small interpreters;

The child must teach the man.

JOHN GREENLEAF WHITTIER,
Child-Songs. Quoted in Carol Tannenhauser and Cheryl Moch (eds),
In Celebration of Babies, New York: Ballantine Books, Fawcett Columbine, 1987, p. 57.

Your children are not your children. They are the sons and daughters of life's longing for itself. They come through you but not from you, and though they are with you yet they belong not to you.

You may give them your love but not your thoughts, for they have their own thoughts. You may house their bodies, but not their souls, for their souls dwell in the house of tomorrow, which you cannot visit, not even in your dreams. You may strive to be like them, but seek not to make them like you. For life goes not backward nor tarries with yesterday. You are the bow from which your children as living arrows are sent forth. The archer sees the mark upon the path of the infinite, and he bends you with his might that his arrows may go swift and far. Let your bending in the archer's hand be for gladness; for even as he loves the arrow that flies, so he loves also the bow that is stable.

KAHLIL GIBRAN,
The Prophet, London: Heinemann, 1926 (reprinted 1974), pp. 20, 23.

Syndicated columnist Mike Royko spoke for many when he recently declared, "I enjoy TV trash as much as the next slob. But the quality of truly trashy trash has declined." ... One reflection of viewer restlessness is the tendency toward "grazing" in their nightly viewing – using remote controls to switch stations in the middle of a program. According to a major survey for *Channels* magazine in 1988, 48.5 percent of all viewers regularly change programs during a show – and nearly sixty percent of viewers in the crucial eighteen-to-thirty-four age group. "Grazing is by definition a sign of dissatisfaction," explained James Webster, professor of communications of Northwestern University.

MICHAEL MEDVED,
Hollywood vs. America, New York: HarperCollins, 1993 pp. 5–6.

The illusions of childhood are necessary experiences. A child should not be denied a balloon because an adult knows sooner or later it will burst.

MARCELENE COX,
Ladies' Home Journal. Quoted in Carol Tannenhauser and Cheryl Moch (eds),
In Celebration of Babies, New York: Ballantine Books, Fawcett Columbine, 1987, p. 139.

Kids are not the "adults of the future." I wince when I hear some church elders use this expression. To say this is to deny kids any status or value in the present. They exist now as persons in a specific developmental stage. They may be in another developmental stage in six months' time. Sometimes kids are aware of this rate of change. Sometimes they find it frightening. What they need is to be valued, loved and discipled right now. It is not healthy to infer that they will be valued at some later stage (when given adult status).

TED ENDACOTT,
"Discipling Kids," in *On Being*, Vol. 20, No. 5, June 1993, p. 31.

Is it fair to be stuck to a painful past? Is it fair to be walloped again and again by the same old hurt? Vengeance is having a videotape planted in your soul that cannot be turned off. It plays the painful scene over and over again inside your mind. It hooks you into its instant replays. And each time it replays, you feel the clap of pain again. Is it fair?

Forgiving turns off the videotape of pained memory. Forgiving sets you free. Forgiving is the only way to stop the cycle of unfair pain turning in your memory.

LEWIS B. SMEDES,
"Forgiveness: The Power to Change the Past," *Christianity Today*, January 7, 1983, p. 26.

Why do children seem to love teachers who are the strongest disciplinarians? [This] statement is only partially true. No one likes a mean old grouch, even if he does maintain strict order. [But] children are drawn to the teacher who can control a class without sacrificing an attitude of love and pleasantness. And that is a highly developed art which most topnotch teachers have discovered. Children love good disciplinarians primarily because they are afraid of each other and want the security of a leader who can provide a safe atmosphere. *Anything* can happen in the absence of adult leadership.

JAMES DOBSON,
Discipline While You Can, Eastbourne, E. Sussex: Kingsway, 1987, p. 85.

Prayers

Lord, bless our children, and bless them through us. Help us to be genuinely interested in what they are doing. Remind us that children can read feelings very well, and quickly recognize insincerity. Give us an ability to adjust to the quick shifts of a child's mind. Our children use actions rather than words in expressing feelings or problems: give us humor and understanding in relating to them at these difficult times.

May our children know, without a shadow of doubt, that they are loved, and respected, that they belong, they are worthy of praise, and are special and unique.

Lord, keep the child alive within us all. Help us to enjoy play and fun and stories, to delight in wondrous things and the world of the imagination, to listen to the sounds and see the colours around us, to be trusting and unafraid, because our trust is in you.

So may our children learn to love and trust you because they have experienced your love and trust in our lives with them. May they increasingly experience hope and purpose, knowing that you are their special Parent, loving and guiding them always. Amen.

Father, look kindly on your children who put their trust in you; bless them and keep them from all harm; strengthen them against the attacks of the devil. May they never offend you but seek to love you in all they do. We ask this through Christ our Lord.

Daily Mass Book, Brisbane: The Liturgical Commission, 1990, p. 38.

A Benediction

May your home be a foretaste of the joys of heaven. May your laughter and fun be a reminder of the joy of the Lord. May you have faith and hope and courage and wisdom in times of hardship and difficulty. May the living God, Father, Son, and Holy Spirit, bless you always. Amen.

18

"Romantic" and "realistic" love are not the same

"You shall love the Lord your God with all your heart, and with all your soul, and with all your mind." This is the greatest and first commandment. And a second is like it: "You shall love your neighbor as yourself." On these two commandments hang all the law and the prophets (Matthew 22:37–39).

Beloved, let us love one another, because love is from God; everyone who loves is born of God and knows God (1 John 4:7). Therefore encourage one another and build up each other, as indeed you are doing (1 Thessalonians 5:11). Love one another with mutual affection; outdo one another in showing honor. Do not lag in zeal, be ardent in spirit, serve the Lord. Rejoice in hope, be patient in suffering, persevere in prayer (Romans 12:10–12).

If I speak in the tongues of mortals and of angels, but do not have love, I am a noisy gong or a clanging cymbal. And if I have prophetic powers, and understand all mysteries and all knowledge, and if I have all faith, so as to remove mountains, but do not have love, I am nothing. If I give away all my possessions, and if I hand over my body so that I may boast, but do not have love, I gain nothing. Love is patient; love is kind; love is not envious or boastful or arrogant or rude. It does not insist on its own way; it is not irritable or resentful; it does not rejoice in wrongdoing, but rejoices in the truth. It bears all things, believes all things, hopes all things, endures all things. Love never ends … And now faith, hope, and love abide, these three; and the greatest of these is love (1 Corinthians 13:1–8, 13).

Finally, all of you, have unity of spirit, sympathy, love for one another, a tender heart, and a humble mind (1 Peter 3:8).

Remember the song, "What the world needs now is love, sweet love"? It does. But it all depends what you mean by "love."

I am using the term "romantic love" to refer to psycho-sexual attraction. "Realistic love," on the other hand, is the strong desire to act towards another for their well-being. Romantic love has a selfish component; realistic love is unselfish. Romantic love is subjective; realistic love is objective. Romantic love is driven by feelings (which is why we "fall in love"); realistic love is a choice of the will. Romantic love is love responding to worth; realistic love is love before or love apart from worth. Romantic love is "circle love" – it presumes a reciprocal loving; true "realistic love" is "arc love" – it is love which creates worth in the object, even if the love is not returned. Romance can be addictive; there are self-help groups around the world for "romance addicts." Realistic love is a choice of one's will. Romantic love happens when a need in me corresponds with a response "out there." Realistic love is a gift.

In romantic love I respond to what the other is for me. In realistic love I grant the other autonomy and respect – indeed, I see them as made in the image of God, and because God loves that person so do I. In romantic love I relate to the other for the good I will derive from the relationship. In realistic love I relate to the other for the good he or she will derive from the loving.

Romantic love is not – repeat not – the basis of a good marriage. It's nice to have a pretty-colored car (ask my wife or daughters) but a car is much, much more than its color. Romantic love is primarily an emotional experience. It can cause irrational behavior and can immobilize its "victim." One form of romantic love is called "infatuation," a name which comes from the Latin *infatuare*, meaning "to make a fool of."

How does one graduate (yes, that's the best word) from "romantic love" to "realistic love" in a marriage? First, there must be a commitment by one's will that the marriage vows were taken seriously: not grudgingly but joyfully. There must be a resolve to act lovingly, to forgive, even when you feel justified in withholding your love. During courtship, romantic love steered the relationship: holding hands, kissing, sharing your life story and your hopes and dreams – a succession of delightful experiences. Now, in "realistic love," romance may still play a part (ask: if I were courting him/her now what would we enjoy doing?). But strong, enduring relationships are not forged by romantic love. Experts say you can expect romantic love to last about three years ...

Lyle came for counseling reluctantly. His wife, Christine, had been seeing me, after she discovered Lyle's infidelity. Lyle was a Christian, he said, worshiped every Sunday, taught a Sunday School class, but, yes, he had been seeing another woman. "I just fell out of love with Christine. We had a good relationship, but somewhere it lost its zip. After the kids came along she was preoccupied, and I got to know a very caring lady at work. She listened to me (Christine was too busy to do much of that), and gradually, well, you know, we found we were very special to each other. I love Fiona, but I respect Christine. I don't want to leave Christine, but I guess she can't cope with two women fulfilling different needs in me. I can't help it if I fall out of love with one woman and into love with another!"

Really? I asked Lyle to tell me his "story of love" from his childhood. It was really a story of lack of love. His parents were stern, unemotional members of a Christian sect. He entered adulthood with a lot of maturing to do, and at first the relationship with Christine was "fantastic." She "met his needs" for emotional warmth, sex, and companionship. But mothering moved her attention away from him, and he couldn't cope with that. Christine's version in summary was that really Lyle was a little boy in a man's body who married her to find a nurturing mother. He had to grow up and take responsibility for himself. "I'm sick of playing games just to pamper this little boy I married," she said.

Romantic love is a primal instinct for boundary-less intimacy. The Song of Solomon is a beautiful poetic celebration of sexual, romantic love. Such love involves an evocative use of voice, touch, gestures, and vision, especially the vision of the beloved's body.

When you're "in love" you see the other not as just another creature, but as a very special, very beautiful person.

However, you can't build a successful marriage on romantic or erotic love alone. So how does one learn to love in a more mature way?

In Christian terms, the one loving must be sure of being loved – by others and also by God. This process begins with physical and emotional nurturing by a mother who dedicates herself to the care and well-being of the baby. Reliable, trustworthy parental love provides the context for the child to develop an inner security and confidence and the internalized belief that he or she is lovable. So love for others grows out of a healthy self-esteem.

What if one's upbringing did not provide this kind of nurturance? Can one's reservoir of self-love be filled some other way? The answer is yes, in two ways: through work and through faith. We can receive love from significant others who are not parents or family: this process involves someone relating to us with integrity, so that eventually we gain the impression that we are indeed lovable after all. Ultimately, however, love like God's love is a gift, which we receive from him by faith. All the Christian saints attest to that. Selfless "gift-love" is not something we learn in a self-improvement course. Rather it is gained through prayer, and then through practice.

Selected Quotations

When we date, we have the freedom to say, at any time, "This isn't working out," and to end the relationship. The other person has the same freedom.

What does this mean for the person whose boundaries have been injured? Often, she brings immature, undeveloped aspects of her character to an adult romantic situation. In an arena of low commitment and high risk, she seeks the safety, bonding, and consistency that her wounds need. She entrusts herself too quickly to someone whom she is dating because her needs are so intense. And she will be devastated when things "don't work out."

This is a little like sending a three-year-old to the front lines of battle. Dating is a way for adults to find out about the other's suitability for marriage; it's not a place for young, injured souls to find healing. This healing can best be found in nonromantic arenas, such as support groups, church groups, therapy, and same-sex friendships.

HENRY CLOUD and JOHN TOWNSEND,
Boundaries: When to Say Yes, When to Say No, to Take Control of Your Life,
Grand Rapids: Zondervan, 1992, p. 147.

Our sexually immature and hypereroticized society dictates that we withdraw our physical demonstrations of our love from our children and teenagers at just that time in their young lives when they need that energy, the powers of reconciliatory love, the most ... The ability to show love, to talk of love and shared life energy, has become a casualty of a sexual revolution that has guaranteed only our freedom to "make" love, not to experience and share loving. Touching, talking gently and sweetly, hugging, and kissing have become casualties in the de-sacredization process of our society.

Romantic physical contact is now seen almost exclusively as prelude to genital interaction, rather than an intimate and profound way of connection with those we love the most and the longest. We have only succeeded in limiting our romantic capacity to sexual encounters rather than broadening it to tenderness with those we love as family. The sexual revolution has resulted in the involution of loving, a narrowing of our ability to show our caring ...

Somewhere between "incest" and being "in love" is the path of mature family loving that allows intense embracing and closeness without eroticizing our tenderness.

PAUL E. PEARSALL,
The Power of the Family, Garden City, New York: Doubleday, 1990, p. 212.

Courtship is a form of honoring and delighting the other person, with the hope of winning a loving, accepting response in return. A man and a woman may show their care and concern for each other in many ways; by dutifulness, by faithfulness, by offering comfort. Courtship is simply finding words, gestures, and tokens to make explicit what those other forms of caring imply.

Thus, courtship often leads to marriage. The tragedy is that it too often ends there. If one chief purpose of marriage is to "build up communion between persons ... and confirm to them the fact that they are truly loved," then clearly courtship has as much place within marriage as before it. The forms that courtship takes, like the forms of sexual expression which are regarded as permissible, will vary according to their cultural setting. But Christians are more concerned with the love that is conveyed than with the forms of expression which convey it.

In exquisite theological poetry the Song of Solomon proclaims that the fiery flashes of love are as a raging flame – in some translations, a most vehement flame of God. Energized by the divine eros, human beings were created by God with the fiery flame of God's own passion, to love each other as God has loved us. Our impulse to love each other in right relationship may include relationships of sexual intimacy, but goes well beyond them to include a passionate caring for all creation. Instead of fearing our deep calling to love and be loved, Christians are invited to embrace eros – embodied in both women and men – and influence all of our relationships with the deepest feeling and care.

Presbyterians and Human Sexuality 1991, Louisville, Ky.: The Office of the General Assembly Presbyterian Church (USA), pp. 30, 33.

Some ways to develop love in a marriage:
1. "Count the ways" you appreciate your partner. List the good qualities you appreciate. Recite them often. Regularly begin a prayer with "Lord, thanks so much for …. Thank you for his/her …."
2. Be sensitive to your partner's vulnerable areas. Self-esteem problem? Weight/diet/sleeping/sex problem? Think of creative ways to encourage in these areas.
3. Every day commend your partner for something: either what they've done, or simply who they are. Put your appreciation into words.
4. Treat your spouse with courtesy and respect. How would you honor the person you most admire? Well, do that for your partner, who is the most significant VIP in your life!
5. Don't ever nourish the thought that you could be happier with someone else. As Billy Graham used to preach: "If I felt I was falling out of love with my wife, I'd get down on my knees and stay there until God gave me love for her again!"

6. Listen to your partner's ideas, feelings, frustrations, opinions. Try to accommodate to them. If there is an impasse and the issue is very important, talk to a trusted counselor.

7. Smile at your spouse more than you smile at anyone else. Gently touch and caress (at times when sexual foreplay is not on the agenda!). Look into each other's eyes. Get as physical in terms of holding hands when walking etc. as you are each comfortable with.

8. Occasionally buy a surprise gift – something he or she likes.

9. A little love-note on your spouse's pillow, or in his or her luggage when traveling away from you, is nice.

10. Remember important birthdays and anniversaries, and plan something special together for those days.

ROWLAND CROUCHER

A Jules Feiffer cartoon shows a couple talking about their relationship. "You have contempt for me," the woman complains. "You treat me as if I'm stupid. You have no interest in my opinions. When my friends are around you behave as if I'm invisible."

When the man protests that he loves her, the woman asks, "Then why do you act as if you don't like me?"

"Who said I liked you?" the man responds, "I just love you."

The insightful cartoonist has identified part of the confusion that many ... encounter in their relationships. Sometimes couples take the time to know and to like each other before they make love sexually, but often they love first, like later, and leave relationship building to the end. Is it surprising that [those] marriages are so often shaky and confusing?

LEONARD CARGAN,
Marriages and Families, New York: HarperCollins, 1991, p. 107.

The *feeling* that people call love is not what the Bible means by love at all. According to Scripture, love is not a feeling; *love is a way of acting.* True love, as God's Word tells us, is *a way of treating other people.* Love involves two aspects: *doing* and *enduring.* We can understand this better by looking at Jesus Christ. The life of Christ can be divided into two parts: *his active obedience* and *his passive obedience. The active obedience* of Jesus was everything he did: Jesus went about doing good.

He healed the sick; he fed the hungry; he forgave the sinner; he comforted the mourner. Christ's *passive obedience* (from which we get the word passion) involves the things he *endured*: mockery, insults, betrayal, injustice, emotional turmoil, sorrow, physical pain, separation from his heavenly Father. Jesus Christ was the perfect embodiment of love. Doing good and enduring evil – that is what love is all about.

JAMES KENNEDY,
Learning to Live with the People You Love, Springdale, Pa.: Whitaker House, 1987, pp. 11, 13.

Aristotle's famous view that if children did not love their parents and family members, they would love no one but themselves, is one of the most important statements ever made about the relation between family and society.

The family permits an individual to develop love and security – and most important, the capacity to trust others ... In the words of the German ethologist Eibl-Eibesfeldt, "The human community is based on love and trust: and both are evolved through the family" ...

Emile Durkheim was one classical social theorist who has argued that, at its core, every human society is a moral community; conversely ... in the absence of shared moral values, a society must begin to disintegrate ... The reason for this is simple: In the absence of moral consensus, coercion remains the only instrument for the maintenance of even minimal social integration.

BRIGITTE and PETER BERGER,
The War Over the Family, New York: Anchor Press, 1983.
Quoted in *The Australian Family*, Vol. 13, No. 1, March 1992, pp. 3, 5.

Up until 1937 I was stateless ... up to the age of fifteen life had been very hard, we had no common roof and I was at boarding school which was rough and violent. All the members of my family lived in different corners of Paris. It was only when I was about fourteen that we all gathered under a common roof and that was real happiness and bliss – it is odd to think that in a suburban house in Paris one could discover perfect happiness but it was so. This was the first time that we had had a home since the revolution. But before that I ought to say that I had met something which puzzled me a great deal. I was sent to a boy's summer camp when I was about eleven years old and there I met a priest who must have been about thirty. Something about him struck me – he had love to spare for everyone and his love wasn't conditioned by whether we were good and it never changed when we were bad. It was an unconditional ability to love. I had never met this in my life before. I had been loved at home, but I found it natural. I had friends too and that was natural, but I had never met this kind of love. At the time I didn't trace it to anything, I just found this man extremely puzzling and extremely lovable. Only years later, when I had already discovered the Gospel, did it occur to me that he loved with a love that was beyond him. He shared out divine love to us, or if you prefer, his human love was of such depth, and had such scope and scale that he could include all of us, either through joy or pain, but still within one love. This experience I think was the first deep spiritual experience I had.

ARCHBISHOP ANTHONY BLOOM,
School for Prayer, London: Darton, Longman & Todd Ltd., 1971, pp. x–xi.

A Prayer

Lord, you do not love us because you find us wonderfully attractive. You do not love us because we are beautiful or kind or religious. You love us because "God is love."

Jesus, when you died on the cross, in some mysterious way you "paid the price" to demonstrate your love for us, and to save us from lovelessness. No one can have any greater love than to lay down their life for another. So yours is a love that pays a costly price, that is sacrificial. You loved me and gave yourself for me. You still love me and give yourself to me.

So, Lord, help us to love one another like this. Amen.

A Benediction

May the loving God work his will in your heart so that you may become more like him, drawing a circle that includes others rather than excludes them, loving those you like and those you do not like, appreciating the image of God in every person in your family and in the human family. Amen.

19

The mating game: sex is exciting and beautiful and dangerous

Everything created by God is good, and nothing is to be rejected, provided it is received with thanksgiving (1 Timothy 4:4).

You are altogether beautiful, my love; there is no flaw in you … Let him kiss me with the kisses of his mouth! For your love is better than wine … How beautiful you are, my love, how very beautiful! Your eyes are doves behind your veil. Your hair is like a flock of goats, moving down the slopes of Gilead. Your teeth are like a flock of shorn ewes that have come up from the washing, all of which bear twins, and not one among them is bereaved. Your lips are like a crimson thread, and your mouth is lovely. Your cheeks are like halves of a pomegranate behind your veil. Your neck is like the tower of David, built in courses; on it hang a thousand bucklers, all of them shields of warriors. Your two breasts are like two fawns, twins of a gazelle, that feed among the lilies (Song of Solomon 4:7, 1:2, 4:1–5).

My beloved is all radiant and ruddy, distinguished among ten thousand. His head is the finest gold; his locks are wavy, black as a raven. His eyes are like doves beside springs of water, bathed in milk, fitly set. His cheeks are like beds of spices, yielding fragrance. His lips are lilies, distilling liquid myrrh. His arms are rounded gold, set with jewels. His body is ivory work, encrusted with sapphires. His legs are alabaster columns, set upon bases of gold. His appearance is like Lebanon, choice as the cedars. His speech is most sweet, and he is altogether desirable. This is my beloved and this is my friend, O daughters of Jerusalem (Song of Solomon 5:10–16).

When a man is newly married, he shall not go out with the army or be charged with any related duty. He shall be free at home one year, to be happy with the wife whom he has married (Deuteronomy 24:5). Enjoy life with the wife whom you love, all the days of your vain life that are given you under the sun, because that is your portion in life and in your toil at which you toil under the sun (Ecclesiastes 9:9). Husbands should love their wives as they do their own bodies. He who loves his wife loves himself ... Each of you, however, should love his wife as himself, and a wife should respect her husband (Ephesians 5:28, 33).

The husband should give to his wife her conjugal rights, and likewise the wife to her husband. For the wife does not have authority over her own body, but the husband does; likewise the husband does not have authority over his own body, but the wife does. Do not deprive one another except perhaps by agreement for a set time, to devote yourselves to prayer, and then come together again, so that Satan may not tempt you because of your lack of self-control (1 Corinthians 7:3–5).

For this is the will of God, your sanctification: that you abstain from fornication; that each one of you know how to control your own body in holiness and honor, not with lustful passion, like the Gentiles who do not know God; that no one wrong or exploit a brother or sister in this matter, because the Lord is an avenger in all these things, just as we have already told you beforehand and solemnly warned you. For God did not call us to impurity but in holiness (1 Thessalonians 4:3–7).

So, whether you eat or drink, or whatever you do, do everything for the glory of God (1 Corinthians 10:31).

Sex is a dynamic force in our lives and in our culture. Young people are under great sexual pressure – from peers ("You haven't done it yet?") and from the media ("Do what comes naturally." "If it feels good, why not?"). Today sex is no longer taboo; the entertainment and advertising industries are sex-saturated. And popular sexual mores have moved well away from Judeo-Christian ethics: someone calculated that ninety percent of TV references to sexual intercourse depict out-of-marriage experiences.

In the old days there were three fears which inhibited sex before or outside marriage – the fears of detection, infection, and conception. Except for the second, with the prevalence of AIDS, those fears have been neutralized with greater modern mobility and access to contraception.

Our society is obsessed with sex, but there is gross ignorance about "good sex."

The Bible is clear that chastity outside marriage and fidelity inside marriage are God's intention for us. Selfish or unhealthy sex is a distortion of God's will for us, destroying intimacy and sometimes becoming addictive. The biblical writers are unanimously against fornication (sexual relations between an unmarried person with someone of the opposite sex), adultery (sexual relations with some- one other than one's spouse), and homosexual practice.

Now Christians have differing views on what all this means for us today. An American Presbyterian Church report, for example, asserts that because sexual gratification is a human need and right, it ought not be limited to heterosexual spouses or bound by "conventional" morality. A couple of decades ago, a British Quaker report said something similar: sexual behavior ought not to be governed by rules or laws. Those who espouse so-called "new morality" ethics say "nothing is prescribed except love."

That's at one end of the spectrum. At the other end of the spectrum are the "Pharisees" who are utterly prescriptive and highly selective in their indignation against sins of the flesh rather than sins of the spirit. Jesus got very angry with this sort of hypocrisy in his day.

Chastity and fidelity are prescribed in the Old Testament, and it's interesting that our Lord (a celibate single) made it even tougher: we are to keep to these not just in deed, but also in thought. When the tempting thought is nourished into covetous desire, adulterous transgression is at work, just as it is at the end of that road in actual genital intercourse. That's frankly pretty hard, with the sort of films we see and the freedom single adults have these days.

But God is no wowser. He's made us as sexual beings. Nowhere does the Bible say "sex is sinful." The very first commandment God gave said, "Be fruitful and multiply" – that is, "Have sex" (Genesis 1:28)! God's in favor of sex. He doesn't make laws to spoil our fun but to protect us from our worst selves and our potential for self-destruction, and to provide stable, loving homes in which children can be secure and grow into emotionally healthy adults.

These biblical standards are difficult for us. But in the ministry of Jesus we hear him saying to a woman caught in the act of adultery: "Neither do I condemn you. Go your way, and from now on do not sin again" (John 8:11). Moralistic wowsers – then and now – either cannot say with conviction "Neither do I condemn you," or they reverse the order: "When you repent and behave yourself we'll stop condemning you." Be like Jesus: have a clear understanding about what God wants, but also a strong love for all who have sinned. Avoid the disease of "moralism" like the plague! The Samaritan woman had had five husbands, and the man she was living with was not legally married to her, but although Jesus knew this and told the woman he knew it, she stayed and talked with him. Prostitutes knew Jesus loved them. He didn't approve of their lifestyle, but he honored them as people. It would be good if Christians followed his example.

So our sexuality must be held in tension between law and love. Law is to love what railway tracks are to the train: the tracks give direction, but all the propulsive power is in the train.

When we come to the question, "Well, what part does a physical/sexual relationship play in a friendship between unmarried people?" my response is that of Walter Trobisch in several of his books. If you are committed Christians and heading for marriage all aspects of your relationship – spiritual, emotional, and physical – should be synchronised. *If one gets ahead of the rest the relationship is awry.* Each couple should talk freely and frankly about all this, and realize that, sexually, the woman will usually have her foot somewhere near the brake if he's got his on the accelerator!

To be more specific, as a father giving guidance to our two teenage daughters, I've made this suggestion: "His hand shouldn't reach beneath your bikini unless and until you're firmly committed to one another and definitely planning marriage. And keep full sexual intercourse for the honeymoon." Old-fashioned? Perhaps. But I've found that Christians who practice this sort of discipline have higher self-respect and are more healthily disciplined in other areas of their lives.

Walter Trobisch (*I Married You*, London: Inter-Varsity Press, 1971, pp. 89–92) suggests six tests of "true love": • The sharing test (the desire to give to the other). • The strength test (experiences together help each to have greater spiritual and psychological energy). • The respect test (not respect for the other's giftedness, but for their personhood). • The habit test (accepting the other with their habits, rather than wanting to change them). • The quarrel test (the most important premarital experience is the ability to forgive and be reconciled). • The time test (time to see the other at work and play, in stress and calm, groomed and untidy etc.). Notice *sex is no test of love*.

So the issue of sex and the single adult is a complex one. I believe sexual satisfaction is not a basic life need. It's a modern myth that the sexual appetite must be satisfied. It doesn't. A commitment to celibacy is O.K. Abstinence won't kill you.

There are some dangers in stress-related sexual behaviors. I've known missionaries who have engaged in homosexual or lesbian activity and later regretted it, but they were lonely in the early years of adjusting to a strange culture. An initial decision to avoid homosexual practice is an anchor in times of pressure. Make a deliberate decision to abstain from homosexual activity, or heterosexual intercourse outside marriage; such a decision can be a great strength when the test comes. Many who say "It can't happen to me!" are later disillusioned. When you are lonely or stressed, sexual temptations can be overpowering.

Masturbation is another problem area. Dr Marjorie Foyle, a doctor who counsels missionaries, has this to say: "Masturbation … is in my view often no more than a pressure cooker blowing off steam. Usually some life adjustment resolves the problem … [in times of tension] the pressure cooker blows: in anger, in masturbation, or in other ways" ("Overcoming Stress in Singleness," *Evangelical Missions Quarterly*, April 1985, pp. 141–142). If a habit like masturbation becomes compulsive, get professional advice.

How about non-sexual touch between unmarried males and females? Great – and good – but I frankly think there isn't any such thing between heterosexuals as "non-sexual touch." That said, we all need physical touch, but we have to be careful. Even the church at one stage had to define exactly what a "holy kiss" was! Some people are not "huggers," so let's be careful and sensitive to one another's feelings on this score. Some guys I know think they're God's gift to women and go around greeting them with a hug or kiss when it's entirely inappropriate. Some girls need to know that when a fellow cuddles them, it may be more of a "sexual" act for him than for them. Be aware of that possibility.

What about married sex? Here are some cases from my recent counseling (the names and some details have been changed to preserve confidentiality):

- Jill and Andrew: Married for about five years, Jill and Andrew had just had a blazing row. His mother-in-law suggested they see me. We talked about their histories, the psychological "baggage" they had brought into their marriage, and their apparently incompatible expectations about some things. When we came to talking about sex he said, "She's not usually creative, but it's not just the "headache" excuse – she must have about 100 reasons or combinations of reasons why we can't have sex tonight. Eventually I get cranky and she gives in grudgingly, and I feel I'm making love to a piece of meat. Why is she like that?" We soon discovered some complex reasons why she was like that: a mix of bad experiences in her childhood and her failure to resolve her guilt and pain, plus his insensitivity and an inability to understand each other's expectations in this complex area.

- Lurline, aged about thirty: "We have different reasons for not enjoying sex: he comes home tired from work and just dozes off. I'm emotionally drained after caring for our three pre-schoolers, and at night I don't need another demand on my body. What can we do?"

- Tom is about forty five, with a bad back, and has just lost his job: "Our sex-life is almost zero. I can't get an erection and she puts impossible demands on me, so I just give up."

- Jane, a pastor's wife in her fifties: "I masturbate most Thursdays: that's the day I spend by myself. We enjoy occasional sex but for some reason I need to comfort myself. Why do I do this?"

My estimate would be that only about one in five married couples have what they would regard as a highly satisfactory sexual relationship.

Reasons? Probably the most common are emotional rather than physical causes. If there is unresolved anger or conflict, or one partner feels "used," or some other needs are not met, or there are lifestyle changes (working late, for example, or tiredness from getting up to the kids at night), spouses find themselves creating distance from each other. Often women tell me their man "wants to experiment" sexually in what to them are repugnant ways, and they react by withholding sex. Physically she may be putting on weight and is less "attractive," so he ogles other women or comments on the shape of Elle Macpherson, and his wife is further demeaned. Now I believe a husband and wife should do their best to stay healthy and attractive for one another: and if it's a self-esteem problem that's causing the over-eating or the lack of exercise, see a counselor. If we don't find intimacy with our spouse, we are vulnerable if another person comes along and "understands my needs."

To be honest, Christians throughout history have found sex to be a problem. A *US News and World Report* article on sex and Christianity began: "The history of western religion is a dramatic chronicle of conflict between the sexual and spiritual sides of human nature" ("The Gospel on Sex," June 10, 1991, p. 59). Some of the early church fathers (like Augustine) believed that sex and conception transmitted original sin, so sex was at best a necessary evil, permitted for procreation, not for pleasure.

But the Bible has a different emphasis. We were created by God with bodies. (When God wanted to communicate with us he came in the person of Jesus, with a human body.) When God made us this way he pronounced his creation "good." We were made for intimacy, and the trust and self-disclosure involved in a sexual embrace enhances intimacy. Then, as C.S. Lewis observed somewhere, sexual attraction acts as the essential spark that gets the engine of marriage going in the first place, even though it is a quieter, steadier "agapic" love that fuels it for the long run. Eros is an important kind of loving (though dangerous without agape). Sex is a good gift – both for procreation and to enhance the intimacy of the man–woman relationship.

What are the ingredients for terrific sex?

1. The couple is committed exclusively to one another (in my view for life, within a legally-recognized marriage).

2. Sex is more than the "rub and tickle" of two bodies. A wife told me: "I wish he knew that foreplay begins in the morning." The husband's response: "I reckon sex brings us closer together; she believes it works the other way around – if we felt closer, sex would be better."

3. Sex is more, much more than romance, but romance "colors" sex. Soft lighting, quiet mood music, allowing enough time, mutual massaging and stimulation, nice perfumes and after-shaves are all nice touches for "coloring" sex.

4. Talk to one another about what pleases you. You have not inherited an intuitive knowledge about the other sex's body: you have to learn. So don't be bashful about giving information. Read a book every second year about sex and talk about it.

5. If possible, be uninterruptible. Shut the door and lock it. If necessary, get an intercom to hear the baby, and switch on the telephone-answering machine. John said to me: "We went on holidays and she wouldn't make love." Jenny responded: "It was because the other couple were in the next room, and they would hear everything!" There are some creative ways around that one.

Selected Quotations

Sexuality is a figure or symbol of our ultimate destiny with God, because it is a search for the other. We feel that it is not good for us to be alone. We feel mysteriously incomplete, so all our life is a searching for a remembered unity we have never yet known. Sexuality is one of the modes of our search; it is both a symptom of our incompleteness and a sign of our fulfilment. For the Christian, therefore, there are two ingredients in sexual experience. One is clearly a participation in the joy of God. We need not be afraid to rejoice in the pleasures of our bodily nature, but we must remember that these pleasures are the sign and seal of unity, relatedness, bondedness. For the Christian, sex should be a part of a covenant between two persons, because it is a reflection or earthly representation of the Godhead, and it is a reflection or earthly representation of the covenant or marriage between God and his people and Christ and his

Church. Sex is the outward and visible sign of the mutual commitment that is achieved in a true relationship.

RICHARD HOLLOWAY,
Anger, Sex, Doubt and Death, London: SPCK, 1992, pp. 34–35.

Most people have owned a cheap bomb of a car at least once in their
life. My second car, an old Ford station-wagon, fitted that description
admirably. Because it wasn't worth that much, I'd lend it to my
friends as often as they wanted to use it. But if I owned a brand new
Porsche, there's no way I'd lend it out to just anyone. In fact, I'd
probably be scared to drive it myself. But I'd certainly have particular
guidelines for using something so precious. The media is selling us a
cheap old-Ford view of sex. Lend it out whenever, to whomever – it's
not worth that much. In contrast, God has a very high view of sex. It
is so special and wonderful to him that there are guidelines for its use,
so it isn't cheapened and demeaning. For Christians, our sexuality
goes well beyond physical gratification. It is intrinsically tied to our
being.

ANGUS McLEAY,
"Let's Talk About Sex," in *On Being*, Vol., 19, No. 4, May 1992, p. 17.

In spite of the claims made by sexual utopians in the 1960s, sex is
never value-free, never without its human and emotional consequences. Sex may be fun, but it is unpredictable and mysterious fun.
Mary Calderone put it well when she said, "The girl plays at sex, for
which she is not ready, because fundamentally what she wants is love;
and the boy plays at love, for which he is not ready, because what he
wants is sex." Sex is not just about sex. That is why all societies and
religious systems have sought some kind of control and ordering of
the thing.

RICHARD HOLLOWAY,
Anger, Sex, Doubt and Death, London: SPCK, 1992, p. 53.

The sexual revolution has exacted a heavy price – particularly from
women. Nearly half of the women entering an abortion clinic have
had prior abortions. In most cases they are driven to this traumatic
"solution" because the men in their lives have abandoned them and
have run from their responsiblilities. Rates of pelvic inflammatory

disease among women, a leading cause of sterility, have soared in recent years.

As arresting as the numbers are, they give only a hint of the emotional damage. Margaret Liu McConnell, writing in *Commentary*, referred to the impact of the new sexual ethic on women as a "demeaning and rather lonely treadmill" of meaningless sexual encounters, unintended pregnancies, and abortions. "Having pre-marital sex," one girl wrote, "was the most horrifying experience in my life. It wasn't at all emotionally satisfying or the casually taken experience the world perceives it to be. I felt as if my insides were being exposed, and my heart left unattended."

JOSH McDOWELL and DICK DAY,
Why Wait? What You Need to Know about the Teen Sexuality Crisis,
San Bernadino, Calif.: Here's Life Publishers, 1987, p. 15.

In a broken-down world, sex invites two extremes: avoidance or worship. The first has to do with fear; the second, lust. In *The End of Sex*, George Leonard maintains that sexuality, with its powder kegs of guilt and disillusionment, is simply not worth the trouble. Add on top of that the fear of disease, a broken heart, and a failed marriage or two, and sex simply makes people too vulnerable.

The other extreme is excess. The attitude toward sex today is often one of worship. The thirst for intimacy and transcendence, lacking better options, gets routed into the closest thing many can come to a miracle: sex.

When intimacy and community disappear from a culture, sexuality is often pushed past its limits. It is like a starving man who, finding no real food, eats a handful of dirt because, if nothing else, it temporarily fills his stomach. Because such sex is mostly disconnected – from values, partners, and the movement of life – it often leads to promiscuity. It is the act of sex that matters. Promiscuity of this kind is a modern mutation of the classic idolatry, a commitment of spirit to something that cannot bear its weight.

PHILIP YANCEY,
"Not Naked Enough," *Christianity Today*, February 19, 1990, p. 48.

Sexual dreams don't always become reality. Many people have unrealistic expectations about sex:

- Sex will bring joy, passion, and unending ecstasy to my life.
- Sex will solve my problems or depression.
- Sex will make me feel constantly bonded with my husband.
- Sex will stop me from masturbating.
- Sex will make life all seem like a fairy tale, complete with a happy ending.

Let me tell you, sex is not the cure-all for our problems; moreover, it takes work, discipline, spiritual maturity, and honesty to provide the environment for our sexual competency to mature. We will often fail. Good sex, the kind that outlives infatuation and expresses oneness of souls, rarely comes easily. Most couples have the scars to prove it.

BILL HYBELS and ROB WILKINS,
Tender Love, Chicago: Moody Press, 1993, p. 83.

SEX OUTSIDE MARRIAGE DISCONNECTS A PERSON FROM HIMSELF OR HERSELF. In psychological terms, this phenomenon is known as shame, alienation, and fragmentation. It is impossible to walk away from sex unchanged, for sex is, by definition, the giving of the essence of oneself to another person. In sex outside marriage, you leave part of yourself with that sexual partner ...

SEX OUTSIDE MARRIAGE DISCONNECTS A PERSON FROM GOD. In theological terms, this is known as guilt. And sin, as we know, separates a person from God. But sexual sin has an incalculable power to make people feel alone, stained, and incapable of connecting with God ... For Christians, the guilt of falling to sexual sin is often overwhelming ...

SEX OUTSIDE MARRIAGE DISCONNECTS A PERSON FROM HIS/HER FUTURE SPOUSE. Time and again, I have counseled with couples whose story goes something like this. Female: "I don't feel I'm connecting with my spouse in sexual intercourse. It feels like only a fraction of him is present." Male: "I just can't seem to get my former sexual encounters out of my mind" ...

SEX OUTSIDE MARRIAGE WARPS GOD-GIVEN DESIRES. When sex occurs outside God's design, it is always reduced. When we buy into such a reduction, we often risk trading love for lust, a longing for intimacy for an obsession with pleasure, and a lifelong fulfillment for a series of thrills ... the reduction of sex also leads to the distortion of values. Pornography, addiction, perversion and abuse are natural outcomes of disconnected sex.

BILL HYBELS and ROB WILKINS,
Tender Love, Chicago: Moody Press, 1993, pp. 75–76.

Love is of God, and true love is always giving. God's love desires to satisfy the object of his love. "For God so loved that he gave … " God is love. Love gives. But lust wants to get. It is basically selfish. Love gives – lust gets … When a man or woman is lusting they desire to satisfy themselves at the expense of others … When they are loving, they desire to satisfy the loved one at the expense of themselves.

A man may be married but lust for his wife sexually when he only cares about satisfying himself, and leaves her unfulfilled and unsatisfied. It's obvious that the young man professing love for the girl is only lusting when he satisfies himself sexually, and leaves her to face pregnancy alone and fearful.

EDWIN LOUIS COLE,
Maximized Manhood: A Guide to Family Survival,
Springdale, Pa.: Whitacker House, 1982, pp. 18–19.

Rape … is a violent act of power, anger, and control, rather than an expression of uncontrollable sexual passion. The confession of a convicted rapist confirms this new awareness:

"It was one of the most satisfying experiences I have ever had. I got more pleasure out of being aggressive, having power over her, her actions, her life. It gave me pleasure knowing there was nothing she could do. My feelings were a mixture of sex and anger. I wanted pleasure, but I had to prove something, that I could dominate a woman. The sex part wasn't very good at all."

MARIE MARSHALL FORTUNE,
Sexual Violence: The Unmentionable Sin, New York: Pilgrim Press, 1983, p. 9.

There are many Christian ministries that attempt to provide opportunities for growth and healing for the homosexual. Many of these groups are represented by the umbrella Exodus International organization or use the 12-Step methods of Homosexuals Anonymous. These groups offer a variety of approaches, but generally agree that change from homosexuality is a difficult and painful process of renouncing sinful practices and attitudes and reaching out to grasp the promise of God's help. These groups suggest that struggling with homosexual attraction is a life-long task, but that the person who takes on that struggle can expect gradual change. Some aim for conversion to heterosexuality; others aim at freedom from overpowering homosexual impulses and increasing capacity to experience life fully as would be desired for any Christian single person.

Presbyterians and Human Sexuality 1991, Louisville, Ky.: The Office of the General Assembly Presbyterian Church (USA), pp. 116–117.

According to the Westminster *Dictionary of Christian Ethics* there are four broad attitudes to homosexuality among Christians. First of all, there are the punitive rejectors who would treat it as both a crime and a sin and punish it, though it is doubtful if many of them would actually insist upon the implementation of the Levitical purity code in sentencing to death homosexuals caught in flagrante delicto. Next there are the non-punitive objectors who would always treat homosexual relations as sinful, but not as criminal. An apt parallel would be adultery, which is no longer a statutory offence in this country, though the Christian Church and most public opinion holds it to be a sin. The third group are qualified acceptors who would probably seek to apply the norm of monogamous sexuality to gay people, as well as to heterosexuals. And they would claim that by this acceptance or permission, many gay people have established stable relationships that have rescued them from loneliness and the promiscuity that has often characterized their search for love and companionship. Finally, there is a group, probably a small group, of total acceptors, who believe that gay people should create their own norm and not be dictated to by a section of the population that can have no real inner knowledge of their condition.

RICHARD HOLLOWAY, *Anger, Sex, Doubt and Death*, London: SPCK, 1992, pp. 47.

AIDS brings together in one potent package the two greatest fears of our culture: sex and death. Now they have been united. Because of these deep fears, because of the already marginalized character of the disease's major victims, because of the ways in which this illness has been moralized, because of the extraordinarily complicated public policy issues – for all these reasons, in addition to the concrete suffering of countless people, AIDS is a major new challenge for us. And particularly for men, for we men have had great difficulties with sex and death.

JAMES B. NELSON,
The Intimate Connection: Male Sexuality, Masculine Spirituality,
Philadelphia: The Westminster Press, 1988, p. 81.

When all is said and done ... the struggle for Christian freedom is not between men and women, nor even between feminists and traditionalists. The struggle is within each one of us, male or female, between the old person and the new person, between the flesh and the Spirit, between the impulse to be the first among all and the call to become the servant of many. Debates about sex and gender will be around for a long time to come, both in the community of the church and the community of social science. But long after our current questions have been settled or forgotten the radical words of Jesus to his followers, both women and men, will ring down through history from the Gospel of John: "Unless a grain of wheat falls to the ground and dies, it cannot bear fruit." And this is a saying which will rightly continue to offend us all.

MARY STEWART van LEEUWEN,
Gender and Grace: Women and Men in a Changing World,
Leicester: Inter-Varsity Press (UK), 1990, p. 250.

A Prayer

Creator God,
Thank you for the gift of sex;
for maleness and for femaleness;
for making man and woman sexual as part of your good creation.

Thank you for my own sexuality:
for its beauty and its usefulness,
for its ecstasy and intensity and intimacy,
for love and care and pleasure and fulfilment.

Thank you for marriage, when a woman and a man leave parents,
cleave to one another
and become one flesh.

Lord, keep me faithful to you and to your will for me.
Keep me faithful to the one I promised to love and cherish
all our lives.

So that our pure loving may reflect
just a little
your love for your people,
and Christ's love for the church. Amen.

A Benediction

May God, who created us as sexual beings, and designed marriage and community for our wholeness and the well-being of children, loved ones, and friends, make your home a colony of heaven. May his peace rule in your hearts; may his grace enable you to accept one another as you have been accepted; may his love empower you to serve and forgive others; may his Spirit give you a disciplined will to obey his Word. For Christ's glory and our wholeness. Amen.

CAPSULE 9: Childhood Sexual Abuse

Between the ages of five and nine "Jane" was looked after by an uncle when her parents were sometimes away, working on a distant farming property. This man used to bath her, play with her sexually, and sometimes have full sexual intercourse with her. He would rationalize what he was doing ("lots of people enjoy tickling each other like this"), but he would threaten her with dire consequences if she told anyone ("this is our little secret"). She became very fearful, but couldn't scream when it was happening. The parents were so pre-occupied with their work they didn't take any action when their daughter became depressed ("she'll grow out of it").

Now aged thirty-eight, Jane has terrible nightmares every night, with dark monsters coming at her with knives and other fearful objects. She "puts up with" the sexual side of her marriage, but uses all kinds of excuses to avoid sex if possible. She has been hospital-ized regularly for severe depression. She feels "cheap and nasty," and very angry with the uncle who abused her.

Except for a high school girlfriend, she had never told anyone else about these events until her doctor referred her to me. She remem-bered everything, she thinks, but it took three or four sessions before she could talk with some freedom about what happened. On one occasion I suggested she pretend her uncle was sitting in a chair across the room and tell him precisely how she felt. She spoke to a large cushion we have, and after ten minutes of pouring out her pain and anger, she turned to where I was seated and even more angrily cried out, "And where were you, God, when this little girl was being raped? Did you care?"

Recently I received a letter from Jane. Here are some excerpts:

"For the past few weeks I have been praying that God will bring to the surface all the painful things that happened to me as a child. I have suppressed so much of my past. I want everything to come out because I know that if it doesn't it will destroy me and I will never be free to leave the past where it belongs. The nightmares won't go until I bring everything out ...

"[As I talk] more things are coming out about the sexual abuse. I have held so much in out of fear and guilt. I feel so unclean and hate myself for what has happened. I know my anger should be released and redirected towards the one who did it all to me, but I find it so hard to do. It seems easier to punish myself. I can't scream because I'm still afraid. I feel choked and nothing comes out. Yet I long to scream to let everything out … This past week all I seem to have done is cry and have panic attacks. The memories are so painful. I keep on getting hurt. My uncle hurt me so badly … There are no excuses for my uncle sexually abusing me. He should have been there to protect me. Sorry for rambling on. I can't even write this letter without stopping and crying. Thanks again for listening …"

What can we say to Jane and the many others like her?

- You are not dirty, cheap, "damaged," or to blame if you were abused as a young child. The abuser was to blame; you did not deserve it.

- Small children feel they're responsible for what was done to them: that is what the abuser tells them. The child is afraid because they are usually threatened with dire consequences if they tell anyone. You were also fearful because you were weak and helpless through the process.

- Victims of abuse tend to have low self-esteem, so you are not unusual there either. Periods of your childhood may be totally forgotten. Abused children are very angry but generally direct their anger inward. They get depressed, experience severe mood swings, and suffer from one or more phobias. They usually have severe sleep disturbances and often have terrible nightmares. They have an inability to trust others along with problems figuring out their various roles. Addictions (eating, drugs, alcohol, spending) are common.

- Until they are healed, sex is unpleasant (to choose the softest word). They have problems becoming aroused and find some forms of sexual activity repugnant, or emotionally and even physically painful. Adults who were abused as children may become promiscuous or addicted to pornography or other forms of aberrant sexual behavior.

- Every victim of child abuse I have counseled has been suicidal, or at least prone to self-destructive behaviors.

- How then can you, as one of these sinned-against people, be healed? First, affirm you were not to blame. Then face what happened squarely. Talk it out with a counselor. Write letters to the one you are angry with – even if you don't post them. When and if you're ready, face the abuser with another person. The abuser will generally deny everything, but the benefit in this process is for you, not the abuser.

- At some stage (for many it takes years) you might go through a process of forgiving the one who violated you, and about the same time pursue a "ritual of release and healing" where you say good-bye to every aspect of the hurt and trauma. Perhaps you can imagine Jesus accompanying you on a journey through the events of your past, cleansing you of guilt and healing you of pain. Then prepare for a new identity. Shed the old self. Devise a plan for dealing with more negative and destructive thoughts and behavior. Write down half a dozen encouraging Scripture passages and say them aloud to yourself when you are tempted to "cave in" to feeling sorry for yourself (for example, Philippians 4:13, Jeremiah 33:3, and Jeremiah 29:11). Live a day at a time, and perhaps before you go to sleep tell yourself how you went that day – emphasizing particularly the positive aspects.

- Why do people do this to defenceless little children? Put simply, incest is a destructive example of love gone wrong. The adult is emotionally immature, unable to develop a true love and closeness with other family members without genitalizing that loving. As one psychologist put it, "Sexually abusive persons do in the family what millions of persons do outside the family; they 'use' someone for the 'act' of love in a misdirected and desperate search for a sense of true loving and for safety from their fear of true intimacy." The person wants to connect and share with another, but doesn't know to do it responsibly. The most frequent form of incest is between brother and sister, then between father and daughter or male family members and younger girls and women. The least frequent form of incest is between an older female and a female child. Because male-initiated incest is more common, this means that sexism, power, and control are behind these corrupt interactions.

- "Where was God when I needed him?" is a common question. There is no simple answer, but one thing I'm sure of: he suffered too. The abuser did it, not God. That's the kind of evil world we live in.

- "But that person messed up my life." True and false. Certainly your childhood was spoiled, but you can be healed.
- "How long does it take to be healed?" Usually two or three years of solid work. But weigh that against the alternative: what will you still be like in a few years if you don't work on the problem?
- Write down something like this and repeat it to yourself every day: "I was sexually/emotionally abused, but I was not to blame. I will therefore not carry the responsibility for this violation of my personhood. The abuser will have to answer to God and their conscience for this atrocity. Although I was the victim, I am not going to let those events cause me to live in the 'victim-mode' now. I will not allow the past to govern how I feel in the present or the future. I am going to get on with my life, and with the help of God become a whole person."

20 | Grandparents are very special people!

Do not cast me off in the time of old age;
do not forsake me when my strength is spent (Psalm 71:9).

Gray hair is a crown of glory;
it is gained in a righteous life (Proverbs 16:31).

Even to your old age I am he, even when you turn gray I will carry you. I have made, and I will bear; I will carry and will save (Isaiah 46:4). The Lord bless you from Zion. May you see the prosperity of Jerusalem all the days of your life. May you see your children's children. Peace be upon Israel! (Psalm 128:5–6).

I am reminded of your sincere faith, a faith that lived first in your grandmother Lois and your mother Eunice and now, I am sure, lives in you (2 Timothy 1:5). Thus says the Lord of hosts: Old men and old women shall again sit in the streets of Jerusalem, each with staff in hand because of their great age. And the streets of the city shall be full of boys and girls playing in its streets (Zechariah 8:4–5). Grandchildren are the crown of the aged, and the glory of children is their parents (Proverbs 17:6).

Tell the older men to be temperate, serious, prudent, and sound in faith, in love, and in endurance. Likewise, tell the older women to be reverent in behavior, not to be slanderers or slaves to drink; they are to teach what is good, so that they may encourage the young women to love their husbands, to love their children, to be self-controlled, chaste, good managers of the household, kind, being submissive to their husbands, so that the word of God may not be discredited (Titus 2:2–5).

Suffering produces endurance, and endurance produces character, and character produces hope, and hope does not disappoint us, because God's love has been poured into our hearts through the Holy Spirit that has been given to us (Romans 5:3-5).

In New York I was once given a guided tour of Harlem by a local Presbyterian minister. He told me the kids never say "Our Father" in the Lord's Prayer because most of their fathers were alcoholic or absent. The person who most represented God to them was grand-mother …

I know two high-profile brothers who have different political orientations. When I asked one of them how this came to be, he said, "We related to different grandparents."

One of my grandmothers loved God and loved the Bible: I was most impressed by her faith. And we ourselves have three gorgeous grandchildren – Abbie, Coralie, and Jay, aged thirteen, eleven, and eighteen months respectively. Photos of each of them are prominent in our home, and we have a "brag book" of drawings and other precious things about each of them. We see them most weeks, and we love taking home-baked chocolate-chip cookies and other surprises or gifts to them. Sometimes Abbie and Coralie bring their parents for dinner, and afterwards we play our version of cricket together. Before our meal we have a little ritual, singing the "Johnny Appleseed" song ("Oh, the Lord is good to me / And so I thank the Lord / For giving me the things I need / The sun and the rain and the appleseed / The Lord is good to me, Johnny Appleseed. Amen"). They love it!

Tonight, as I type this, Abbie and Coralie are sleeping in our spare room while their parents have a night out together. It's a delight and a privilege to have them visit us.

In traditional societies, older people – who may have the status of "patriarchs" or "matriarchs" – are respected partly because they are repositories of the wisdom of the group. But in Western cultures this is not entirely so. As anthropologist Margaret Mead used to say, older people are now strangers in the world of the young, and while our seniors ought to be respected and honored, they do not necessarily have all the know-how needed in a world that has changed dramatically since their day. Today grandparents are invited to give support rather than knowledge to their married children. Sometimes older people presume they can offer advice about all sorts of complicated modern problems, and they may become a nuisance. The best thing we can offer our grandchildren is friendship.

In previous generations, grandparents often lived with their married children's families; they helped wipe runny noses, change diapers, cook, and clean – and therefore earned the right to participate more directly in advice-giving. But these days many grandparents won't settle for a baby-sitting role in exchange for a small room in the house. Some of them won't babysit at all.

It's a pity that today's grandparents live further away than previously, so there may often be less contact with their grandchildren. However, we have telephones and cars – and remember, grandparents often died in the past before many children ever knew them.

The best thing we can do for our married children is simply to "be there." They should know without a shadow of doubt that we are always available and, no matter what disasters may occur, they are not alone. Support, encouragement, a roof, and food are always available to them.

And while it's common for grandparents to say they enjoy both having the grandchildren and handing them back to their parents, let's not underestimate the powerful effects our company and our love have on those children. Grandchildren all over the world love to hear about how it was long ago when we were young. "What did you do when you didn't have TV, Grandpa?", they ask, and you tell them of games in the street when cars were rare (and how it was interesting to stop the game to watch the car go by) – games the kids still play like "hide 'n' seek" and "tag." It's important to widen our grandchildren's view of reality to encompass a past, and for them to experience the continuity of generations of loved ones who also enjoyed adventures, had fun, and coped with problems. It's a sheer joy to share in the beginning of their long journey and to be near enough to them to observe it.

We grandparents communicate to our loved ones that growing older is O.K. Above all, Christian grandparents model for their grandchildren how to live lives of faith, hope, and love. They provide some stability and security in a world of rapid change and bewildering complexities – including, hopefully, the security of believing that a good marriage can last a long time and be interrupted only by death; and the knowledge that as that inevitable day draws near, they do not need to fear.

Selected Quotations

In view of all the millions of pages that have celebrated young love and married love and illicit love and parental love, it really seems strange that so little has been said about grandparental love ... Some of its quality is undoubtedly conveyed by the old cliché, "all the pleasure and none of the responsibility"... Being a parent involves a staggering amount of work. The days are crammed, and in the early months no night yields unbroken sleep ... The typical grandparent is a little smug in his reflection that he has served his turn at all the messy chores, back-breaking lifting, unremitting watchfulness, broken sleep, noise and confusion. All such matters are for parents, he thinks ...

I was prepared to enjoy my spectator status, for everybody talks about that. But nobody told me how my eyes would swim when I first saw the baby at her mother's breast and noticed the expression on my child's face had become maternal. Nobody told me how excited I would be at each new small accomplishment or what swelling delight I would feel when a toothless grin announced that I was recognized. Nor was I prepared for the fun it would be to converse with budding minds that seemed to enjoy my stories of "how it was."

AVIS D. CARLSON,
In the Fullness of Time, Chicago: Henry Regnery Co., 1977, pp. 96–98.

No matter how many grandchildren we have, our love encompasses them all, as if it were from a bottomless pit. Every time a grandchild is born, there is a wonderful sense of achievement, of having started something that is flowing through to future generations. The tiny baby is bonded to us, and one of the greatest pleasures in life is watching them grow. Grandparents are usually the first ones recognized by the baby other than its own parents and siblings. Even those grandparents who for various reasons do not want to achieve that status at that stage of their lives are transformed into devoted slaves by that first smile.

LEILA FREIDMAN,
Why Can't I Sleep at Nana's Anymore?, South Melbourne:
Matchbooks, Magistra Publishing Co., 1990, p. 17.

Becoming a grandparent for the first time is a big emotional experience, usually first met in middle age. But if we had more than one child and they married at different times, the appearance of new grandchildren and, eventually, great-grandchildren is an experience covering many years. Welcoming in a new generation is, take it from me, an almost dizzying experience. As I walked out of the hospital that morning of the first grandchild, I knew at last what the word "giddy" means. My feet seemed not quite to touch the ground!

We don't need to become self-conscious or hide our feelings just because the not-yet-old regard them as comic. Grandmother jokes are almost as ubiquitous as Scotchman or psychiatrist jokes. Grandfathers do not figure so largely in folk humor, but they are equally and sometimes more absurd. Almost all that can be said for us is that most of us know that we are absurd and couldn't care less.

AVIS D. CARLSON,
In the Fullness of Time, Chicago: Henry Regnery Co., 1977, p. 95.

Possibly the highlight of being a grandparent is to love having the children to care for and mind them and then, at the end of the day, holiday, etc. blissfully hand them back.

It is an aspect you should consider in retirement plans – housing, garden, furniture, as well as financial provisions. Everyone's views are different on what grandparenting involvements they desire. I have heard many regrets. These range from being involved far more than they desire or can cope with, to finding, in their new choice of home, no space or facilities for young children.

[Unfortunately] some grandparents are indeed unloving, uncaring, sometimes absolute tyrants, while at the same time being a regular and potent force in the extended family situation. How many bitter quarrels erupt over this well-meaning but interfering couple. Their expectations can be impossible to fulfil and their standards of behaviour unheard of by today's young generation, while their reminiscences about the old days "when we were your age" reduce the young parents and children to the depths of frustration and irritation.

I consider grandparenting an art to be studied and observed in the context of whatever the family situation, with emphasis on "how not to interfere."

GARY MATTHEWS,
Retirement: Make it Easy, Ringwood, Vic.: Penguin Books, 1988, pp. 73–74.

It is wonderful separating your grandchild, or grandchildren, from their parents for a while, but with the experience comes a surprising discovery: the time you are capable of spending with them without going berserk is much shorter than it was when your own children were little … If you want … clues to your success or otherwise as a parent, take a look at your grown sons and daughters, then answer these questions: Do they seem to be living life to the full or are they travelling at half-speed, neither satisfied nor dissatisfied, just drifting along? Are they good communicators? Do they talk interestingly, with confidence and enthusiasm? Do they have a lively sense of humour? Are they willing to drop everything, however serious, for the sake of a good laugh, occasionally? Are they as sensitive to their children as you were when they were young, or are they apt to whack out or bark at them instead of taking a softer course, diverting them or reasoning with them? If they were not your children, would you want them as friends?

The answers should tell you whether or not you have been a successful parent.

KEITH SMITH,
Get Closer to Your Children, Surry Hills, NSW: Waratah Press, 1985, pp. 180–181.

If you are lucky enough to be able to see your grandchildren on a fairly regular basis, that's wonderful. Children need someone to listen to them, to pay attention to them. The main thing all grandparents must learn and practice is to mind their own business. Not interfering seems to be the most difficult aspect of grandparenthood. You may know positively that certain methods your daughter or son is using to raise children are wrong. At the very least, you know a better way. You absolutely must keep your opinions to yourself. Look the other way; don't say one word. Even if it nearly kills you. It's extremely difficult, I know. You have been through all the things they are going through, and you have learned so much by actual experience that it hurts to see them making mistakes. Stay out of it. This kind of meddling is the worst thing you can do ...

E. JANE MALL,
And God Created Wrinkles, New York: Ballantine Books, 1988, pp. 145–147.

Grandpa tell me 'bout the good old days
Sometimes it feels like this world's gone crazy
Grandpa take me back to yesterday
When the line between right and wrong didn't seem so hazy
Lovers really fall in love to stay
Stand beside each other come what may
Promise really something people kept
Not just something they would say
Families really bowed their heads to pray
Daddies really never go away
Grandpa tell me 'bout the good old days.

"Grandpa (tell me 'bout the good old days)" by Jamie O'Hara. Copyright 1985 Cross Keys Publishing Co. All rights administered by Sony Music Publishing, Nashville, Tenn.

Of all the little rituals that are part of day-to-day family life, the bedtime story may be the most delightful. In many homes, ours included, these important moments alone with your children at the end of a long day can be the most satisfying moments you spend ... Reading is a great way, before prayers, to prepare a child for bedtime ... When I was very young, my grandmother spent hours reading to me. I was fascinated by the childhood stories she shared, and the little asides she would add, to make those stories even more vivid and alive. After my grandmother's death, my mother did most of the reading. My father preferred to sit at the side of my bed in the evening and tell me stories he knew by memory. Together, all of them instilled in me a love for books. And that love of books helped me to overcome the odds and get through college and law school.

GARY BAUER,
Our Journey Home: What Parents Are Doing to Preserve Family Values,
Dallas: Word Publishing, 1992, pp. 177–178.

Adopt a Granny

Is there an older person in your neighbourhood or church who lives alone? Make attempts to get to know her and potentially adopt her into your family. How to begin?

Drop in to visit this person and introduce yourself or get further acquainted. (Go without the children on your first visit.)

Invite her to family tea some evening to meet the rest of the family.

Bake biscuits and send one of the children to deliver them and visit her.

Include her in family holiday celebrations if she has no family nearby.

Offer to mow her grass or do odd jobs for her.

Ask her to babysit after you have established a solid friendship.

Take her with you to run errands when she needs a ride.

Have the children include her on their handmade Christmas card and Valentine lists.

Give her a subscription to a magazine she would enjoy.

After you are well acquainted, instinct will take over. You won't need my suggestions any more. And everyone will benefit from the friendship.

KATHY BENCE,
Turn Off the TV: Let's Have Fun Instead!, London: Marshall Pickering, 1990, p. 58.

My grandmother was a very devout Christian. During my early childhood her influence on me was profound. God was real to her, and somehow that was all the proof for the existence of God that I needed. She would read Scripture to us, pray, and sing hymns with us. And it was always happy singing; her faith was a joyful faith.

My grandparents lived about one hundred twenty miles from our home city in a small rural community … My brother and I spent every school holiday with my grandparents. We loved being on that farm! Not only was it a change from city life, but it was also a relief from the tensions of home ... There were three sources of help for my healing [after my parents divorced]: my grandparents, my Sunday school teacher, and – believe it or not – my mother's new husband.

Grandparents and other concerned adults such as family friends and teachers can help tremendously in bridging the divorce gap and in providing a stabilizing force in the tempestuous life of a divorced child ... My grandparents' love and acceptance was comforting and reassuring to me. They never pushed me to talk about the problems at home, yet were always good listeners if I said something. They provided distraction from the emotional pain I was suffering and, above all, they restored my faith in God. I came to see that God transcended the paltry problems of human existence. God was there, despite what my parents were doing. His presence could not be destroyed by human suffering, and he offered dependable help in the midst of that suffering.

ARCHIBALD D. HART,
Children and Divorce, Dallas: Word Publishing, 1982, pp. 19–21, 139.

Every boy has a place in his soul that only a grandfather can fill. The grandfather is usually the first man (other than the father, of course) to whom a boy becomes connected. When an older man speaks, he speaks from the well of a lifetime of experience ... A grandfather who has lived a rich and passionate life automatically seems to command respect from his family. He imparts a stability and wisdom that only he can give ... I'm not envisioning a man who walks on water, but I want to emphasize the solid, masculine influence a grandfather can have on a boy who is maturing into manhood. All men need an infusion of the strength, fullness, and depth that sharing in the life of an older man can provide.

For many boys, such a wonderful relationship has been lost. Many grandfathers, for example, do not understand that God designed children with a deep need to share intimate experiences with their grandparents. A grandfather may not realize that his grandson hungers for such a relationship. This relationship should include more than holiday visits, although those gatherings of the generations certainly are significant.

Grandfathers must realize that, just as fathers need to build an emotional bridge to their sons, grandfathers need to build an emotional bridge to their grandsons. That emotional bridge does not exist on its own. Grandfathers must take steps to build it by being involved in their grandsons" lives. Perhaps the greatest gift a grandfather can give to his grandson is time – time to share a walk, time to help him bait a hook, time to freely share confidences, time to teach his grandson how to pound in a nail, time to listen. Where distances or finances make regular interaction of this type difficult, the relationship between grandfather and grandson can be encouraged through phone calls and letters.

It means so much when a grandfather consistently and purposefully maintains his deep emotional and spiritual relationship with his grandson throughout his childhood, teenage years and adulthood. A grandfather can influence a growing boy in ways that a father cannot. A young man will often take advice from his grandfather that he would not even consider if it came from his father. In today's world, when one in two marriages ends in divorce, the stability of a relationship with a grandfather does much to comfort and strengthen a boy or young man whose life is in turmoil.

EARL R. HENSLIN,
Man to Man, Nashville: Thomas Nelson Publishers, 1993, pp. 100–101.

The grandmother still has to make her own life, create her own happiness, keep herself occupied and in good health. If she expects or demands too much from her children, they come to resent it and there is then little pleasure in it … I know families who are tremendously supportive of each other, and where a strong bond exists between them all. I know women who love caring for their grandchildren. I am quite convinced that when a marriage and a family group works and is really happy, particularly if it exists in an extended family circle, then there is no better way of living, no better basis on which to enjoy the good things and face the bad things in life, certainly no better way to rear children.

JOYCE NICHOLSON,
The Heartache of Motherhood, Ringwood, Vic.: Penguin Books, 1983, p. 80.

Older is wiser, but not necessarily smarter. Every family at one time in its life has had the parents ask the question "Isn't there any respect for age anymore?" Many family arguments center around control and individual family member's rights to individuality. Attempts to make and enforce rules can result in rebellion and testing of the family laws. I ask the families to allow some deference just based on age alone. I ask them to allow more tolerance, more time, more listening to the older members of the family, simply because they are older ... Such deference does not imply that the older family members, a parent or older brother or sister, know more, or are likely to be more rational than a younger member ... the older person may, just may, have learned something through experience. Of course, experience can just be doing the same thing incorrectly over and over again, but the idea that older people get listened to a little more seems to help just a little.

PAUL E. PEARSALL,
The Power of the Family, New York: Doubleday, 1990, p. 103.

I believe the one undiluted pleasure being a mother has brought me is my three grandchildren. They are beautiful, sturdy, amusing, loving, intelligent, appreciative, and absolutely no trouble to me. People say grandchildren are so much pleasure because you can "hand them back." I feel the reason is that I feel absolutely none of the guilt that went with my own children. If they are naughty, it is not my fault. If they won't eat, it is not my worry. If they do badly at school, no blame lies at my door. I guess I will not escape entirely. If they experience unhappiness in the future, as they most assuredly will, I will suffer with them. But at the moment they, and my daughter-in-law, bring me much happiness.

JOYCE NICHOLSON,
The Heartache of Motherhood, Ringwood, Vic.: Penguin Books, 1983, p. 82.

A Grandparent's Prayer

Lord, I'm getting older, but may I never believe I'm getting useless.
I am wiser through the learnings of the years, but may I
never stop growing.
I am weaker and more frail, but may my spirit stay strong.

Thank you for your faithfulness during my whole life,
for your comfort in times of difficulty,
for courage to face trials of all kinds,
and for the gift of joy at all times.

Lord, I have many gifts to give – of friendship and love,
encouragement and instruction, solace and praise.
Help me not to interfere in the lives of others
but to give these gifts with humility
when the time is appropriate.

Keep my faith, hope, and love strong, so that from the
overflow of these rich spiritual resources
others may see the light and feel the life of your healing presence.

Through Jesus Christ my Lord. Amen.

A Benediction

Now to him who is able to keep you from falling, and to make you stand without
blemish in the presence of his glory with rejoicing, to the only God our Savior,
through Jesus Christ our Lord, be glory, majesty, power, and authority, before all
time and now and forever. Amen. (Jude 24–25)

CAPSULE 10: Caring For Your Aging Parents

An important question you may have to resolve is whether one or more of your parents will live with you in your family, or in a self-contained facility, or in a nursing home? Here is the wisdom of others on this issue:

- Check with your brothers/sisters and get their feelings and wisdom about the possibilities. Check also with parents' doctor.
- What kind of personal help do they need? Does your family have the emotional and physical resources to provide this? Don't be afraid to ask for special help from others if necessary. What is "Plan B" if one or both parents need more specialized help and "Plan A" proves inadequate? Until that point give them as much independence as they can cope with.
- Financial considerations. Will pension, superannuation, or social welfare cover costs? Has a will been made? Where are important personal papers kept?
- Remember your parents have the qualities and irritable habits they've always had. And if their physical and mental health deteriorates, the transition may be difficult to adjust to. You can't "fix" old age: most of the adjusting will be by you to them! Old age is hard work – for everyone. So there's not much to be gained by criticizing or correcting older people. However, they can be manipulative, wanting you to do things for them they could do for themselves. Don't fall for too much of that. And if they are critical of your spouse or children, respond by affirming some of the positive qualities of the latter.
- If one or both parents are to live in your home, ask these questions: Do they get along with everyone (including pets)? Are they independent or semi-independent? Discuss frankly how short or long term the arrangement will be. Will there be company for them? Are there possibilities for them to visit others, or to join in district or church seniors' activities? To share chores? What physical arrangements are necessary – special features in the bathroom, for example? What furniture is needed? Do they eat your food? Will it be possible to have family and spouse time without the parents feeling "left out"? If your family is away, can the parents be adequately cared for?

- Wherever your parents live they need you to contact them regularly. Of course, the conversation may repeat itself almost exactly each time: it's the loving concern rather than interesting ideas that is transmitted in this process!

- Live one day at a time. Remember you'll eventually be old and will need the support and care of others yourself – another good reason to build loving relationships with your own children.

21

Communication and fun: how to enjoy being with others

If a house is divided against itself, that house will not be able to stand (Mark 3:25).

One given to anger stirs up strife, and the hothead causes much transgression (Proverbs 29:22). Keep your tongue from evil, and your lips from speaking deceit (Psalm 34:13). To make an apt answer is a joy to anyone, and a word in season, how good it is! (Proverbs 15:23). Therefore you have no excuse, whoever you are, when you judge others; for in passing judgment on another you condemn yourself, because you, the judge, are doing the very same things. You say, "We know that God's judgment on those who do such things is in accordance with truth." Do you imagine, whoever you are, that when you judge those who do such things and yet do them yourself, you will escape the judgment of God? (Romans 2:1–3).

He will yet fill your mouth with laughter, and your lips with shouts of joy (Job 8:21).

You show me the path of life. In your presence there is fullness of joy; in your right hand are pleasures forevermore (Psalm 16:11). A cheerful heart is a good medicine, but a downcast spirit dries up the bones (Proverbs 17:22). A glad heart makes a cheerful countenance, but by sorrow of heart the spirit is broken (Proverbs 15:13).

Let everyone be quick to listen, slow to speak, slow to anger (James 1:19). Let your word be "Yes, Yes" or "No, No"; anything more than this comes from the evil one (Matthew 5:37).

With all humility and gentleness, with patience, bearing with one another in love, [make] every effort to maintain the unity of the Spirit in the bond of peace (Ephesians 4:2–3).

One generation shall laud your works to another, and shall declare your mighty acts (Psalm 145:4).

Can anything be done about poor communication? Yes. Our communication skills can be improved. You know the old line: "I know that you believe you understand what you think I said, but I'm not sure you realize that what you heard is not what I meant." That doesn't have to be.

Communication is the process of exchanging information, feelings, or attitudes through symbols, sounds, signs, or behavior. So not all communication is verbal: your eyebrows or hands communicate as much as your vocal chords – and sometimes more.

"Communication theory" is built on the idea that all communication involves a sender, a message, one or more channels, and a receiver. The sender "encodes" the message in some form; the receiver "decodes" or interprets the message, and feeds back to the sender some sort of response. But for all this to happen the sender and receiver have to "connect" with some common knowledge and experience. So when a message is "transmitted" it is not necessarily "comprehended."

All meaningful human relationships involve communication, and therefore all involve some conflict when the communication is not understood or is interpreted as a threat. So for communication in a family to be effective, strong personal relationships are essential: that is, there ought to be a commitment to the well-being of the other family members; you should understand their feelings; there ought to be a significant level of trust; and behaviors ought to be fairly predictable.

Here are nine rules for effective communication within a family or community:

1. *Recognize the uniqueness of each person.* They do not inhabit the same "frame of reference" you do. They feel different feelings. They may even understand words or phrases differently. You bring to a marriage the complex communication patterns you experienced with your parents. So always be aware of the possibility of misinterpretation. As a psychologist once said to me, "When married couples say they've never had a disagreement, they are lying, have a poor memory, or one partner has been made a zero in the relationship."

2. *Be committed to moving beyond the superficial to a greater depth of understanding.* There are various levels of communication. The most superficial is the *cliché* level – easy, day-to-day greetings like "Good morning, how did you sleep?" The next level is *reporting* – giving factual information without sharing how you feel. Then there is the *opinion* level. Here you are beginning to take a risk, revealing something of yourself with which another might disagree. In healthy families there is great freedom at this level. Next we have the *feeling* level. In good communication there is congruence between those communicating. We are truly "heard," not only in terms of the words we use, but in terms of the "feeling agenda" behind the words. Finally, the highest level of communication is *oneness* – the rare moments when you feel totally accepted, understood, "at one" with the other. This is "gut-level" communication, where you are unafraid to expose who you really are to another.

A well-put-together person has others with whom they relate at various levels, and they know the most appropriate level with each of those persons. If you don't have anyone at the "oneness" level, find someone, even if you have to pay for the privilege!

3. *Learn to listen.* Good listening is hard work. It involves concentration: your mind must be present, not miles away. And it requires an open mind, not a prejudicial mind-set. If you are making judgments about the communicator or their ideas, you are not able to truly hear them. Avoid emotional interference: if the other's mannerisms or bad grammar bug you, ignore these and still try to listen. Or they may say something that causes a "red flag" to fly in your brain: that will interfere with your hearing too. Remember that you think about four times faster than a person can speak, so you will be summarizing in

your mind what you are hearing, listening between the lines for nuances or interpretations you might otherwise miss.

Feed back words and phrases that indicate you're tracking with the other: "You're saying that ..." "What I hear is ..." "So you feel ..."

4. *Getting through depends on credibility.* Unless others have confidence in you, they will be less inclined to listen to you. So their perceptions of your reliability, honesty, and competence are key factors. And for you to be credible to them, they must perceive that your non-verbal and verbal components agree with each other. People listen carefully to those they trust.

5. *Try not to be defensive.* It's amazing how often married partners will have an irrational argument and then, when they come for counseling, will agree, "It was a stupid little thing that started it all!" Well, if that's the case there's a deeper agenda at work, and you'd better figure out what it is.

For example, if she comes across like an authoritarian mother, the little boy in him will react defensively. If he's preoccupied, she will get angry: maybe her father was like that. If you were criticized a lot as a child, you may tend to be overly critical of your own children.

6. *Negotiate "win–win" conflict resolutions where possible.* You may have to compromise. Here's one way we do it. "Darling, want to go out tonight?" "Well, I've got a lot to do ..." "Well, why not a movie without the dinner this time ... How would that be?" "O.K." Such give-and-take is the essence of a strong relationship.

What if your partner is irresponsible? Don't rescue them. If they're forgetful, don't buy the line "I just forget things!" Arrange together to put a list of birthdays, anniversaries, bills to pay, and so on, in a prominent place.

7. *Realize that males and females, in all cultures, communicate differently.* In Western cultures men do not easily communicate their feelings. So a question like "What's bothering you?" is a tough one for a male. Men tend to talk about facts ("objective reality" is one of my favorite phrases when Jan and I have a different perception about something). Men want to analyze the problem and suggest solutions; women want to empathize. Men have more difficulty than women hearing the "pain agenda" in other people. Men tend to interrupt more than women (and they interrupt women more often than women interrupt men). Women are more active listeners; men more passive. (So

women are more likely to ask "Did you hear me? Are you listening?"). Men need to be in control. They may speak more forcefully or loudly when they feel threatened.

8. *Keep it simple*. The best communicators put interesting or even complicated ideas into simple language. Wisdom and simplicity go together. To communicate clearly, the words and ideas you use should be understood the same way by the hearer. Your aim is to get across your ideas or feelings, not to be impressive. Then, when you have said enough, stop.

However, please note that when some people are asked where they're going, they like to describe the scenery on the way. When I ask my wife, for example, when she thinks she will be ready for us to leave or go to bed or whatever, she lists all the things she has to do in the meantime. Interesting (and I ought to be interested if I love her), but sometimes I only want my question answered!

By the way, men are usually more economical with words. Yes, he had a "good" time; she will fill out many of the details. Men are usually "condensers"; women "amplifiers." There's nothing wrong with either approach, but the amplifier wishes his/her partner would give more details, while the condenser wishes his/her partner would use fewer words. So each has to adapt to the style of the other for the best communication to occur. If your spouse is a condenser, match that style. It works.

9. *Choose your moment to communicate carefully.* "I want to talk, he wants peace and quiet." Two things to avoid here are "nagging" and resentment. He may be quiet for one of two reasons (among others): first, the day has been tension-filled – people, people, people – and he needs solitude; or second, the wife may be intimidating in some way and he withdraws into his shell for protection.

Men tend to close up if they are accused of being insensitive, selfish, unloving, a failure, sports-mad, or sexist. Or if the woman in his life collapses too often into tears! So be quietly direct: "Would you prefer not to talk just now? Is there another way I can put things so I don't come on too strong?" Work on your timing!

10. *Spice your communication with humor.* Couples who laugh together stay together, particularly when each has the kind of self-esteem that doesn't mind a joke at their expense! Research shows that couples who laugh and joke and use pet names for each other have stronger marriages.

Laughter, of course, is contagious: it spreads itself around like an infection. Laughter helps reduce stress, tension, and anxiety. It is therapeutic: people who laugh live longer.

Here are a few examples of common communication hassles in a family:

- "We've been married for 20 years; I shouldn't have to tell him." Well, maybe you haven't been direct enough. Ask for some feedback to make sure he heard you clearly. Don't drop hints, or communicate through a third person. Or maybe you've been too direct: some males don't like being ordered around: have you discovered that? You may need to be more subtle. Or realize that he doesn't want to hear you: for some reason he's determined not to follow through on what you want. You may have to "accept what you cannot change."

- "She really bugs me when she does that!" Communicate your feelings but don't attack your wife personally. Talk about her behavior without putting her down. And own your own feelings; for example, say "I get irritable when such and such happens, and I'm trying to figure out why!" Better still, in a "marriage check-up" time, ask one another what irritates you and listen carefully to the answers.

- "My kids won't do what they're told." Every child needs the security of having to be told only once from when they're very young. If you have to repeat a command, link it with a clear penalty, then apply the penalty firmly if there is still no obedience. Later, children will know the rules and be more willing to participate in conforming to them. As they get older you will negotiate with them the areas of authority, rules, discipline, and work-around-the-house and then invite them, rather than order them, to do this or that. Negotiate household chores and make a list.

Australian clinical psychologist Dr Peter O'Connor (quoted in Glenda Banks, *Your Guide to Successful Family Living*, Blackburn, Vic.: Dove Communications, 1985, pp. 38–40) lists the following warning signals which show we are taking ourselves too seriously:

- *Martyrdom.* The husband sitting on the sofa watching TV holds up his cup wanting a refill. The wife might once have quipped, "What's the matter, broken your ankle?" but now rises wearily with hung head and trudges to the kitchen ...

271

- *One-upping.* One partner has had a bad day, but the other always has had a worse one …
- *Playing out the self-fulfilling prophecy.* He says, "You seem upset." She says, "I'm not." He says, "You look it." She shouts, "I am *not* upset!"
- *Trading off.* This is where one or both partners keeps a list of grievances to slog the other with when tempers flare.
- *Carbon-copying:* "This occurs when we are out of ideas (or the desire) to come up with a reasonable solution to a problem, and instead of throwing up our hands and having a good laugh – or cry – as we might have done before we began to take ourselves so seriously, we retreat behind attitudes we have absorbed from our parents, or others, in times of stress."
- *Scenario.* "Four-year-old sits at the kitchen table refusing to eat his greens. Two-year-old screams to be fed. Mother says 'I can't cope,' and runs from the room. Father either slaps the four-year-old and berates his wife for her inefficiency, or quits the house for the pub – whichever his father would have done. He doesn't laugh and take over."

One study which compared the communication patterns between happily and unhappily married couples found that happily married couples talked more to each other; conveyed the feeling that they understood what was being said to them; had a wider range of subjects they talked about; kept communication channels open no matter what happened; showed more sensitivity to each other's feelings; and used more nonverbal means of communicating. Humans have an immense need to be really listened to, to be taken seriously, to be understood. No one develops into a fully mature human being without feeling understood by at least one person.

Selected Quotations

Love is supposed to conquer all. In such an exalted environment, it seems quite petty to be upset that your husband didn't take the trash out. Or that it takes your wife nearly the time it took Columbus to sail the ocean blue to put on her makeup … Please, listen to me: communicate, communicate, communicate. Deal with your differences immediately. Don't store up grievances. Talk with one another about hurts, problems … If you have to schedule a time each week for a "gripe" session, free from the heat of emotions, do it. If you voice adERion.

your concerns once, and the other spouse doesn't seem to get it, voice them again. Don't ever adopt the attitude "I'll just suppress the things that are bothering me until they go away." They won't. When a person hides a grievance, it will boil and stir, gather other concerns to itself, and come out much the way lava explodes from a volcano.

BILL HYBELS and ROB WILKINS,
Tender Love, Chicago: Moody Press, 1993, p. 103.

If more Americans could be persuaded to carve out of their three or four hours of television viewing each day a period of five minutes at bedtime and use this time to ask their child a simple question – "How did things go today?" – and listen, the result in terms of individual families and society as a whole could, I believe, be highly salutary.

GEORGE GALLUP JR.,
Testimony before the Senate Subcommittee on Family and Human Services,
March 22, 1983. Quoted in James Dobson and Gary L. Bauer, *Children at Risk: Winning the Battle for the Hearts and Minds of Your Children*, Dallas: Word Publishing, 1990, p. 206.

Men follow a distinctive pattern in their communication style. First of all, they mull over the problem. It is put on the back burner to see if the issue will go away on its own and get resolved with as little effort as possible. During this stage of letting the issues simmer, they may feel it is unnecessary to talk. But if mulling does not work, storing the issue deep inside is the next phase. To many men this is the easiest solution of all. But if this does not work, he will talk about it. It could be with a sigh of resignation – or with an explosion. This is a gender distinction, but varies in intensity depending upon cultural conditioning and personality type.

Often men will say ... "I need a little more time to think things through. Somehow she has the idea that wanting time to think is not being open and honest with her. That's ridiculous. I'm not trying to hide anything, I'm just trying to be sure in my own mind before I talk about it" ... Men tend to communicate to resolve. They want the bottom line so they can "fix it." Sometimes you may not know if you want an issue resolved until you have talked about it. Many women want to express themselves because it is their way of interfacing with the world; they enjoy self-expression.

H. NORMAN WRIGHT,
Questions Women Ask in Private, Glendale, Calif.: Regal Books, 1993, pp. 24–25.

It is most often the wife who will recognize the need for deeper communication. We must help our husbands see this need, then think together as to how we can grow deeper in communicating. First we must avoid the tendency to blame our husbands. "He won't talk to me," is a common cry. "Our schedules are too busy." Or, "His work is more important than his family."

Blaming our husbands for a lack of communication in busy marriages with young children is not fair. It's not his fault. It's the season we're in, and it's our problem together. The first step is to recognize the normalcy of the problem and not place blame. We must realize this problem is universal, but we do not have to accept it as something we must live with. God wants us to be growing in our communication, and there are many ways this can happen, even in busy households full of small children.

SUSAN ALEXANDER YATES,
And Then I Had Kids, Milton Keynes: Word (UK), 1992, p. 88.

This week write a love letter to your spouse. Concentrate on one single topic: your mate's good points. What do you appreciate about your husband or wife? Put your thoughts down on paper. Focus only on the positive side of their character – not the negative aspects.

You will be amazed how this simple exercise will change your attitude. Then, as the way you perceive your mate is changed, the problems will begin to dissolve. In fact, many of them will disappear.

Communication is an art. We need to approach it the way we would learn to play the piano or the violin ... Being a good communicator does not come naturally; it is a skill that must be learned and practiced ... True unity develops as husband and wife share their lives by communicating with one another. Communication must, first of all, be intellectual, then emotional and spiritual – finally it will be truly physical.

D. JAMES KENNEDY,
Learning to Live with the People You Love, Springdale, Pa.: Whitaker House, 1987, pp. 32–33.

A common habit of the humourless is to cue in to the worst possible interpretation of a word message sent to him/her. Thus if a husband says to his wife, "Come here my old love," a humourless wife will pick up on the word old, completely ignoring the key word "love." Similarly, if a wife gives her husband a love-pinch on the paunch and calls him "cuddles," a humourless husband will probably react defensively to his own interpretation of her love message, which he reads as criticism of his bulk.

Consequently, when working to restore a sense of humour, it is important to avoid each other's pressure points. Build up each other's self-esteem by laughing at one's self and inviting the other to join you.

Look for role models to copy. Go to funny movies together. Tune in to comedy shows on TV and read out amusing quotes from books, newspapers and magazines to each other. Don't dwell on down trips – your own or other people's.

A medical educator claims, "Laughter can actually relieve muscular tension and reduce hostility and tension in other people.

"Laughter, you see, is the antithesis of anger. We express anger or hostility by threatening gestures which include holding our breath and taking short, deep breaths. Laughter comes out in the expulsion of breath in rapid bursts, so it is impossible to send out hostile signals while laughing."

GLENDA BANKS,
Your Guide to Successful Family Living, Blackburn, Vic.: Dove Communications, 1985, p. 41.

Individual children need individual attention – quality time alone with Mum or Dad. To meet this need, from about eight or nine, plan a weekend away with each child each year. Alternate which parent goes with each child, to foster good communication with both parents.

As far as possible, allow your child to choose where you go and what you do. Budget may demand that you sleep at a relative's house, but don't hang around there. (I love to visit my relatives, but the goal of this trip is to be alone with my daughter. Explaining your goal to relatives should solve any misunderstanding.)

KATHY BENCE,
Turn Off the TV: Let's Have Fun Instead!, London: Marshall Pickering, 1990, p. 9.

There are a number of dos and don'ts that are generally useful with minor squabbles, in keeping the heated-up fight from turning into a serious and hurtful one.

• Reinforce positive behavior and discourage negative behavior seems like a pretty obvious thing to say, but when you realize that negative behavior is sometimes rewarded, as in, "I'll give it to the little lout so he'll shut up," it bears repeating. If a kid feels neglected, we reinforce bad behavior by paying a lot more attention to it than we normally do to the child when behavior is neutral or positive. • Don't use your mouth or your hands before your mind. • Don't jump into the middle of arguments that are heading towards fisticuffs unless you are going to be able to smooth the rippled water. Do be calm and evenhanded so that no one in a conflict feels wronged or that you favor the other. • Whenever possible, physically separate children who are heading toward combat. Be firm, do not match violence with violence. • If you are a part of the problem, remove yourself from the danger zone. • Do not demand justice summarily done, as in "Aren't you going to do something about your daughter? What kind of a mother are you anyway?" or the loaded "Do you know what your son just did?" Similarly, do not bring up problems of discipline with a spouse the minute that person appears on the scene after shopping, working, whatever. The same rule applies at meal-times. • If a fight occurs more than once, look hard at it and figure out the variables … You may find a way of preventing another occurrence. • Be consistent in all of this. Be fair.

JEFFREY and CAROL RUBIN,
When Families Fight, New York: William Morrow & Co., 1989, pp. 262–263.

SSAADD stands for surrender, sarcasm, assumptions, accusations, demands, and demeaning statements. All of these communication errors lead to irrational interactions in the family system. Here are examples of such statements:

SURRENDER: "That's it. I give up. The house is yours. Go to bed when you want to, do what you want to. I resign as a parent."

SARCASM: "Good. Good. Just go and come as you please. We love to wake up in the middle of the night worrying about you. It keeps us alert and reminds us to go to the bathroom."

ASSUMPTIONS: "I'm not naming names, but someone who shall be nameless probably is the one who put the rubber doorstop in the dishwasher. Now we have a nice set of spoons all melted together in one group. This will save us time setting the table. I can't imagine who could have done that, can you?"

ACCUSATIONS: "I know you did it. I saw it. You walked right by and spilled it. You did it. Admit it. You did it. You always are the one who shows no respect for the carpet in this room."

DEMANDS: "Do it. Just do it. This is your father talking now. Get up and go do it. Now. Move!"

DEMEANING STATEMENTS: "Nice going, Mr Kind-and-Gentle. The next time I'm upset with you, I'll just act like little old immature you and punch you like you punched your brother. You are such a child. Really!"

These statements ... show how irrational we can be when we live with a group of people for a long time. They all show the generalizations, magnifications, selectiveness, and absolutism ... [which are at] the central cores of family irrationality.

PAUL E. PEARSALL,
The Power of the Family, Garden City, New York: Doubleday, 1990. p. 104.

A parent without a sense of humour is like a bricklayer without a trowel: the job becomes impossible. What a relief that family life is so funny that it's hard not to laugh.

ANGELA WEBBER and RICHARD GLOVER,
The P-Plate Parent, Sydney, NSW: Allen & Unwin, 1992, p. 5.

Humor is the one saving grace for any family, for any conflict. Comedian George Burns said, "Happiness is having a large, loving, caring, close-knit family in another city." He was joking about the persistent conflicts that are one and the same with a close and loving family. If we are able to realize that our battles in the family stem from our closeness and caring, we can sometimes make time to let humor heal our wounds.

The Muller family told me that they have a rule that never fails them. Whenever an argument or conflict starts, someone in the family times the argument. The Muller family rule is that the family will find something funny – a book, a videotape, an audiotape or record album – to listen to or view together that is equal in length of time to the time spent fighting.

"This hasn't always been easy," said Mr. Muller. "We really have to search for something funny, because sometimes we fight a lot. We have found, though, that we have our favorites that we never seem to get tired of. We love to watch a Bill Cosby tape or listen to one of his albums. They have a lot of family stuff on them, and we can laugh at them a thousand times." Laughter is the first and best of the three ways to shed tears. Cutting onions and crying can't compete with communal laughter. I suggest you get the family together for a group intestinal jog as soon as possible.

PAUL E. PEARSALL,
The Power of the Family, Garden City, New York: Doubleday, 1990, p. 102.

- Learn to listen. Listening is a skill that we can improve with a little effort and the rewards can be substantial.
- Golden rule of listening is looking. In order to hear well we need to see the person, so sit or stand facing the person you are talking to, so that you can pick up all the non-verbal messages. It is surprising how much you miss when you have your back turned.
- Give the other person time to express themselves in their own way.
- A conversation doesn't have to be a grammar lesson. There is nothing more disconcerting than having a train of thought interrupted by "I do wish you'd stop saying 'ain't'."
- The good listener helps the talker to keep focus on the subject, by not distracting with their own anecdotes.
- Give each person time by offering your individual attention or if it's not convenient to talk because you are bathing the baby or getting the dinner, say so, and make a time as soon as possible. Don't be faced with the teenager who says despondently, "Oh, it doesn't matter any more, it wasn't important" (then the moment has been lost).
- Practise talking about the issues of the day over meals. Turn the TV off at meal times.
- Have everyone sit around the table to eat. This is the best setting for developing and improving our communication skills.
- Encourage people to speak one at a time. "You can have your turn in a moment."
- Discourage interruptions. "I can't listen to you all at the same time!"
- Head off too much ridicule or putting down of one person's contribution. The odd joke or sarcasm may be fun, but it can inhibit the shy and inarticulate.
- Try and develop a relaxed atmosphere for meals so that it is not a constant setting for nagging about eating habits or table manners. You may have to give up on "I could never take you lot out to eat anywhere" in favour of "I can never get a word in edgeways."

TERRY COLLING and JANET VICKERS,
Teenagers: A Guide to Understanding Them, Moorebank, NSW: Bantam Books, 1988, p. 24.

A Prayer

Lord,

save me from having endless debates about who is right
as though my very existence depended on my being right.
Rather, give me the security to admit my errors or ignorance —
even, sometimes, to my children.
And if my children find it hard to admit a mistake
even when the evidence is overwhelming,
give me wisdom about figuring out the cause:
somehow the child has not felt safe being wrong.

Lord,

in our family may we find it O.K. to say "sorry,"
especially at the end of the day.
Let us never go to bed without facing up to the pain or hurt
of any conflict.

Teach me that saying "sorry" is not
admitting defeat
or even assuming responsibility
or excusing another's behavior;
rather, it gives the assurance that we are still family;
we still care for one another
deeply.

So may our family life be enriched by hearing sometimes:
"I was wrong."
"I am sorry."
"I love you."
Amen.

A Benediction

May God, who communicated his desire for our friendship in our creation, and
who tells us of his care in every sunrise and every good gift he gives us, and who
came among us in the ultimate communication, Jesus of Nazareth, empower you
to communicate in love to those with whom you live. Amen.

22

How "church" can become "family"

All who believed were together and had all things in common; they would sell their possessions and goods and distribute the proceeds to all, as any had need (Acts 2:44–45).

Now I appeal to you, brothers and sisters, by the name of our Lord Jesus Christ, that all of you be in agreement and that there be no divisions among you, but that you be united in the same mind and the same purpose (1 Corinthians 1:10). For whoever does the will of my Father in heaven is my brother and sister and mother (Matthew 12:50).

There is no longer Greek and Jew, circumcised and uncircumcised, barbarian, Scythian, slave and free; but Christ is all and in all! As God's chosen ones, holy and beloved, clothe yourselves with compassion, kindness, humility, meekness, and patience. Bear with one another and, if anyone has a complaint against another, forgive each other; just as the Lord has forgiven you, so you also must forgive. Above all, clothe yourselves with love, which binds everything together in perfect harmony. And let the peace of Christ rule in your hearts, to which indeed you were called in the one body. And be thankful (Colossians 3:11–15).

But take care and watch yourselves closely, so as neither to forget the things that your eyes have seen nor to let them slip from your mind all the days of your life; make them known to your children and your children's children (Deuteronomy 4:9). Like newborn infants, long for the pure, spiritual milk, so that by it you may grow into salvation (1 Peter 2:2).

Love one another with mutual affection; outdo one another in showing honor (Romans 12:10). So then, putting away falsehood, let all of us speak the truth to our neighbors, for we are members of one another (Ephesians 4:25). Keep on doing the things that you have learned and received and heard and seen in me, and the God of peace will be with you (Philippians 4:9).

When the "chorus boom" invaded our churches a couple of decades ago, one of the most popular was: "We are heirs of the Father. We are joint heirs with the Son. We are children of the kingdom. We are family, we are one."

But our songs sometimes do not match reality. About that time a popular Christian book had this complaint: "Our churches are filled with people who outwardly look contented and at peace but inwardly are crying out for someone to love them ... just as they are – confused, frustrated, often frightened, guilty, and often unable to communicate even within their own families. But the other people in the church look so happy and contented that one seldom has the courage to admit his own deep needs before such a self-sufficient group as the average church meeting appears to be" (Keith Miller, *The Taste of New Wine*, Waco, Tex.: Word Books, 1965, p. 22).

An unnamed "serious man" once reminded John Wesley that "the Bible knows nothing of solitary religion." He was right. God's antidote for loneliness is community, *koinonia*, rich fellowship, experienced in the church.

The key purpose of the church is to continue to do in our world what Jesus did in his. It's as simple as that. But the key difference between Jesus and the church is that Jesus did not need to be redeemed! The church – every church – is a mixture of good and evil. Jesus the head of the church is there, present with his people, who comprise his body. God's Spirit is at work in the church; so is the devil. The church is not yet spiritually sanitized, just forgiven.

Last week an ex–church leader came to talk to me. He is driving his wife and ten-year-old daughter to church these days but not attending himself. Why? He'd been hurt and was disillusioned by the church. But as we talked I think he came to see that though his diagnosis was right his attitude was flawed. He should be there, with his family, meeting God, who still ministers to us in worship as we minister to him. We are to have the same attitude to the church Jesus has: he loves the church, not because it is perfect, but in spite of its imperfections. Jesus always loves like that. So must we.

So the local church ought to be the best resource in our culture to create "community." It is God's family, where we are accepted with all our faults and sins.

When people attach themselves to your church group they ought to quickly feel at home. Your church circles should be semi-circles, opening to include new people. But here's the rub: deep down many church-folk are scared of their "networks" becoming flexible, because their security is tied up with the predictability of those relationships. In church after church I ask the leaders: Is yours a friendly church? To which they mostly answer, "Yes." Then I ask: name the adults who have joined your church through conversion in, say, the last eight years. Many churches have great difficulty naming them. And when I talk to people who tried to "break into" an established fellowship, they say, "They were nice to me the first few Sundays, but I didn't seem to get invited to any of their homes. They didn't give me the 'cold shoulder'. I just knew I wasn't welcome." Why is this? Deep down we are fearful of new people upsetting the chemistry of the group that satisfies our needs. So we preserve the group intact at all costs – even if we don't realize we are excluding others.

Churches are actually clusters of groups: fellowship groups, service groups, mission groups, social groups, and so on. When someone enters, they need to be attached to one or more of these groups within a few weeks, or they will drift between them and out the back door.

Now the most common fallacy I encounter at this point is "We must get so-and-so onto a committee so he or she will feel involved." But many committees stifle creativity and are not the best place to initiate involvement. In any case, in a church that's alive, the first group ought to be a "faith development" group of some sort, where new people's spiritual gifts can be assessed before they are invited to be involved in ministries.

We can't talk about the church as "family" apart from the notion of "covenant." This means that God has redeemed, rescued, his people and invites them to live in obedience to his will. His will is discovered especially in Scripture and is "incarnated" in Jesus and in the redeemed community. So one of the purposes of the church is to nurture godly families. The image of God is to be transmitted not only genetically, but also in the way that parents raise their children. The laws of God are to be taught to children, who hopefully respond by freely choosing to obey God and walk in his ways.

What is the best way for children to be motivated in this direction? Kids' clubs? Sunday School? Junior Church? I remember the well-known American church consultant Lyle Schaller being asked this question. His response: children's programs are good, but they are not the key ingredient in the development of a living faith. Children watching the Big People "lost in wonder, love, and praise" as they worship is by far the best stimulus to a child's godliness. Also, as children see the church modeling life in Christ by rejecting exploit-ative attitudes and practicing love, forgiveness, and self-sacrifice, they will find the church to be very attractive.

This kind of church family/household is an open community where all are welcome. It will resist buying into cultural attitudes which are ungodly or discriminatory, like legalism and moralism, racism, slavery, sexism, or the greedy exploitation of God's earth. In such a church the marginalized (whoever they are in your town) will find a home.

How does the church-as-family relate to the biological (or extended) families within it? If we had to rank priorities in order I believe the list would look like this:

1. God.
2. Spouse.
3. Children.
4. Vocation – "religious" or "secular."
5. Everything else.

When all these relationships are in balance they ought not to be in conflict with each other. Nevertheless, every church ought to be careful to arrange their activities to avoid dividing families too much or expecting various family members to be at meetings too many nights of the week.

"Family nights" are a good idea – one night a week where all church activities shut down. I would encourage families on this night not to answer the phone, to refuse all other invitations, and, if anyone visits, to explain politely that they might come back at another convenient time. Turn the TV off. Plan talking time over the meal and a fun time afterwards. Maybe older children can go to their homework at, say, eight o'clock.

More broadly, every local church should ask: we can't do everything for everyone, but what can we do well? Those ministries will probably work at one or more of three levels: primary (support networks for those in need of help by the church generally), secondary (self-help and issue-centered groups and the creation of support networks) and tertiary (for example, a church-linked professional counseling service). One church I know, for example, operates half-way houses for homeless youths and women; they have self-help groups for single adults and men in search of their masculine soul; and they run a "Barnabas House" counseling service on a pay-as-you-can basis.

Every church should run father/son, mother/daughter events, James Dobson's *Focus on the Family* films, family picnics … the list is endless. But, more importantly, various families should do things together – and include fractured or single-parent families. In other words, children should have opportunities to relate meaningfully to mature Christian adults other than their parents; adults should be able to find meaningful friendships with other like-minded people; and all should reach out to a limited number of marginalized people. Who in your church, for example, helps older single adults, especially widows? Or seniors? Or the unemployed, early retirees, and single mums?

Every church should have "family services" where whole families participate – perhaps a 9.30 a.m. service every Sunday in large churches, once a month in smaller ones. And every church should run a "How to Help Your Friend" course at least every two years, with marriage and parenting seminars from time to time.

As we've said, the church is uniquely placed to do in its world what Jesus did in his – teaching God's truth to everyone, and relating to the "little people" like the mentally ill, the lonely, and children from dysfunctional families. Then we shall truly be God's family in a heartless world.

Selected Quotations

In a way, family relationships *are* the church. If the church is the body of Christ, the human relationships within the congregation and between congregants and others in the community are the circulatory and nervous systems. The way to know God's love is through relationships with others, so family ministry must be central to the mission of the church. If we cannot get that right, we will not be able to perform any of the other missions expected of us. The Good News itself is that God offers to be our parent, and Jesus promises to be our brother if we follow him. When we do, we find ourselves entering a whole new family of brothers and sisters and parents. Even evangelism cannot take place, then, unless persons are embraced in relationships which mirror the family-like love of God through which the Spirit of God can work.

DIANA S. RICHMOND GARLAND and DIANE L. PANCOAST,
The Church's Ministry with Families, Dallas: Word Publishing, 1990, pp. 235–236.

Early in the life of *Family* magazine we ran a survey among the readers to try to find out about their marriages. We asked about stress points, and found to our surprise and dismay that a major cause of stress affecting both husbands and wives was the pressure of church commitments. In a paradoxical way, that made me feel slightly better. It was a relief to discover that I was not the only one who had faced up to divided loyalties between husband and "things that were being done for God."

ANNE TOWNSEND,
Now and Forever: Christian Marriage Today, London: Fount Paperbacks, 1986, p. 14.

There was a woman in my parish who suffered more physically than anyone I've known. As a young woman she had been a haute couture model and a singer with an operatic-quality voice. A degenerative arthritis slowly destroyed her joints, racked her with excruciating pain, and left her crippled …

Though her faith never wavered, more than once she said to me that God had abandoned her. "Where," she asked, "am I to see God's love for me?"

In her last years, she became the center of attention for a group of women in the parish. Most of them were a generation younger, and had gotten to know her through a women's Bible study and other parish activities. Singly or at times together, without any planning or organization, they simply began to visit her at home and in the hospital when she was there. They would run errands, care for some household duties, but mostly just be with her, pray with her, sit with her, talk with her. Slowly in the depth of her suffering, she began to realize that she had not been abandoned by God. True, there were no moments of mystical intimacy, or interventions of dramatic healing. The love of God came to her in a quiet way, through the calm, patient affection of those women. We cannot live the Christian life in isolation. He calls us into *koinonia*.

KENNETH SWANSON,
Uncommon Prayer, New York: Ballantine Books, 1987, pp. 113–114.

Some two thousand years after the birth of that dynamic community of God, a small group of believers was getting ready to start a church in the northwest suburbs of Chicago. They decided to go door-to-door throughout the community with a survey. Their first question was, "Do you actively attend a local church?" If the answer was "Yes," they thanked the respondent for his or her help and went to the next house. If the person said, "No, we don't go to church," they asked him why. The results were astonishing. Some of the most frequent responses:

- Church is irrelevant to my daily life
- Church is lifeless, boring, and predictable
- The pastor preaches down at me, instead of to me
- There's too much talk about money

I was a part of that group of believers, and I was heartbroken by the responses given to that survey. I vowed, before God, never to allow our church to be boring or irrelevant. If the vision of Jesus Christ is true (and it is), then church should be the most dynamic, compassionate, challenging, and relevant place on planet Earth.

BILL HYBELS and ROB WILKINS,
Tender Love, Chicago: Moody Press, 1993, p. 155.

People come to a church longing for, yearning for, hoping for [a] sense of roots, place, belonging, sharing, and caring. People come to

a church in our time with a search for community, not committee …
Their search is far more profound and desperate than that. They are
looking for home, for relationships. They are looking for the
profound depths of community. They are not looking for transitory,
temporary, annual goals, hurriedly sketched on newsprint or butcher
paper at a planning retreat.

KENNON CALLAHAN,
Effective Church Leadership, San Francisco: Harper & Row, 1990, p. 106.

It is an extraordinarily vital and impressive thing – the Christian
fellowship that meets you in the pages of the New Testament. Here
you have Saul of Tarsus, haughty Pharisee, Hebrew of the Hebrews,
who took care that everybody should know it, sharing his deepest
intimacies with poor illiterate slaves from Greek slums, barbarians,
he would have once called them, Scythians, miserable outsiders – yet
now miraculously his brothers … It was an amazing thing, that early
fellowship; and it meant everything to those who shared it … And
that is meant to be normal Christianity. That is the impact your life
and mine might be making on the world around us, if we were really
men and women of the Spirit.

JAMES STEWART,
"The Fellowship of the Spirit," in *The Gates of New Life*,
Edinburgh: T & T Clark, 1956, pp. 92, 101.

The New Testament thinks of the church as Christ's body
(1 Corinthians 12:27); Christians are their Lord's limbs and organs
(1 Corinthians 6:15). It comes to no less than this: as Jesus' body the
church holds within it "the fullness of him who himself receives
the entire fullness of God" (Ephesians 1:23) …

In community Christians encourage and hold one another
accountable before their Lord. They complement one another's gifts,
providing a fuller and more compelling reflection of Christ in the
world … In the period of its inception … it was a sense of community, of identity and vision granted by the story of Christ, that
once changed the world. Who is to say it cannot do so again?

ROBERT E. WEBBER and RODNEY CLAPP,
People of the Truth: The Power of the Worshiping Community in the Modern World,
San Francisco: Harper & Row, 1988, pp. 53, 67.

Discipleship simply means one man asking another man how he is doing, receiving an honest response, and responding to that need from the depths of his heart and soul. It means that when a man's company is laying off people and he is scared he will lose his job, another man will sit with him and listen to his fears. Perhaps the man who listens will be able to share what God showed him during a similar crisis in his life, put his arm around him and ask what he can do to help or pray with him. When men have this kind of committed, supportive relationship with each other, spiritual growth naturally happens. This is discipleship in real life.

Real discipleship provides a path that moves a boy into deep, holy masculinity. In its most basic form, this kind of discipleship begins at birth. It means that older men, whatever their ages might be, care enough to invest themselves in the spiritual, emotional and physical lives of younger men. It means that older men will surround a boy as he becomes a man so that they can help guide and strengthen him through the stages of life and honor and celebrate his deepening status as a man of God.

A man needs to be a disciple spiritually and emotionally in order to discover his feeling life and to be healed from his father-son wound. This discovery usually does not happen to its own. Most men live without feeling much of anything until they reach midlife and cannot keep their emotions inside any longer. Left on their own, they will do almost anything to keep their feelings at bay – go out and get a new car, a new wife or a new job. They will try everything to avoid dealing with what is in their hearts.

EARL R. HENSLIN,
Man to Man, Nashville: Thomas Nelson Publishers, 1993, pp. 192–193.

The call to the church in this era is a call to be present with its people … [and] to assist in the search for behavior patterns that will enhance the lives of all people. The time has come for the church, if it wishes to have any credibility as a relevant institution, to look at the issues of single people, divorcing people, post-married people, and gay and lesbian people from a point of view removed from the patriarchal patterns of the past, and to help these people find a path that leads to a life-affirming holiness.

JOHN SHELBY SPONG,
Living in Sin? A Bishop Rethinks Human Sexuality,
San Francisco: Harper & Row, 1988, pp. 52–53.

"Molly and me, and baby makes three," in the words of an old sentimental pop song. The point, in Rodney Clapp's words, is simply this: "For the Christian, church is First Family. The biological family, though still valuable and esteemed, is Second Family. Husbands, wives, sons, and daughters are brothers and sisters in the church first and most importantly – secondly they are spouses, parents, or siblings to one another." And Clapp goes on to point out that "exactly as family is how the New Testament church behaves." It extends hospitality to a wide range of Christians and others. Its central sacrament draws on the analogy of a family meal. At their best, both "first" and "second" families are a magnet for unbelievers who are drawn to the love that is shared within and beyond their boundaries.

RODNEY CLAPP,
quoted in "Is the Traditional Family Biblical?", *Christianity Today*,
Vol. 32, No. 13, September 16, 1988, pp. 24–28.

A Prayer

Lord, thank you for the church —
the church around the world and in heaven
and the church around the corner.

Thank you that you are present there
even though the church is imperfect.

Thank you that you love the church
even though we must cause you so much pain.

Thank you that as you died and rose again to form a redeemed
community so you are dying and rising still, giving us
new life and new hope.

Lord, help us to do in our world what you did in yours:
to worship the Father in Spirit and in truth,
to work hard for justice and to promote love,
to heal the sicknesses and loneliness and hurts of "little people,"
to befriend women and men, religious people and reprobates,
to preach the gospel truth even when to do so may invite persecution,
to bring down the haughty from their high seats
and to promote the humble and meek,
to care for little children
and to advance a child-like "kingdom of God" in our church,
to pray in solitude and train disciples.

So, Lord, may I love the church as you love the church and
see in it the incredible potential you obviously saw in it
when you entrusted to it alone the preaching of your Word
in the world. Amen.

A Benediction

And may the risen Christ who dwells in his body, the church, and is redeeming
it from all corruption so that it may be presented to his Father faultless and
without blemish, encourage you to align yourself with that redemptive process.
For his glory alone. Amen.

23

As for me
and my house

You shall love the Lord your God with all your heart, and with all your soul, and with all your mind, and with all your strength (Mark 12:30).

> I will utter ... things that we have heard and known,
> that our ancestors have told us.
> We will not hide them from their children;
> we will tell to the coming generation
> the glorious deeds of the Lord, and his might,
> and the wonders that he has done.
> He established a decree in Jacob,
> and appointed a law in Israel,
> which he commanded our ancestors
> to teach to their children;
> that the next generation might know them,
> the children yet unborn,
> and rise up and tell them to their children,
> so that they should set their hope in God,
> and not forget the works of God,
> but keep his commandments. (Psalm 78:3–7)

A new heart I will give you, and a new spirit I will put within you; and I will remove from your body the heart of stone and give you a heart of flesh (Ezekiel 36:26).

He called a child, whom he put among them, and said, "Truly I tell you, unless you change and become like children, you will never enter the kingdom of heaven. Whoever becomes humble like this child is the greatest in the kingdom of heaven. Whoever welcomes one such child in my name welcomes me. If any of you put a stumbling block before one of these little ones who believe in me, it would be better for you if a great millstone were fastened around your neck and you were drowned in the depth of the sea" (Matthew 18:2–6).

Jesus said, "Truly I tell you, there is no one who has left house or brothers or sisters or mother or father or children or fields, for my sake and for the sake of the good news, who will not receive a hundredfold now in this age – houses, brothers and sisters, mothers and children, and fields with persecutions – and in the age to come eternal life" (Mark 10:29–30).

Now therefore revere the Lord, and serve him in sincerity and in faithfulness; put away the gods that your ancestors served beyond the River and in Egypt, and serve the Lord. Now if you are unwilling to serve the Lord, choose this day whom you will serve, whether the gods your ancestors served in the region beyond the River or the gods of the Amorites in whose land you are living; but as for me and my household, we will serve the Lord" (Joshua 24:14–15).

Joshua challenged his contemporaries, "Choose this day whom you will serve." If they chose to follow the gods of this world, Joshua and his family were prepared to put themselves on the line: they would revere the Lord and serve him alone, in sincerity and faithfulness. The same stark choice faces us.

"As for me," Joshua said. Deciding to serve God is always a personal decision because it involves the very heart of our being. Although Joshua's decision was personal, it could not be private. Joshua not only said "as for me" but "as for me *and my household*." Faith in the living God is more than personal and private; it is also a family affair.

I've heard parents say, "Oh, our children can choose whether they follow God or go to church or whatever they want to believe." Do these same parents say, "We'll let our children decide whether or not they want to go to school and learn to read and write"? Let no one be neutral about faith in God. The Bible is clear on this: if we do not teach our children to serve God, we are teaching them to serve other gods.

Some fathers say, "My house without me." Joshua did not leave religion to the wife and kids. Men: have you determined that not only your house but *you yourself* will serve the Lord, and that you will lead your family in that godly enterprise?

Others say, "As for me without my house." Some may have a go-it-alone attitude of "just Jesus and me." Joshua was not so foolish. He made it clear that his family would be serving the Lord too. He would do everything he could to teach his children the ways of God.

Or you could take the coward's way out and say, "As for me and my house, if everybody else agrees." The religious stance taken by your friends and relatives is important. But your integrity should mean you do what God wants you to do, even in spite of others' opposition. The old argument "But everybody's doing it" carried no weight with Joshua. If all others chose to be idolaters, Joshua and his household were going to serve the Lord – no matter what the consequences.

More commonly these days what we hear is, "As for me and my house, we will serve ourselves." That is the ultimate idolatry, selfishness: "Me, my wife, and my son John. Just we three, no more." We actually serve the Lord by serving others. Jesus said in his parable of the great judgment (Matthew 25) that we will one day be asked about this. When he was poor, homeless, hungry, what did we do about it? When I ask some families, "What does your household regularly do for the good of the deprived or marginalized?" some of them have trouble naming anything.

Still others might change our text around: "As for me and my house, the Lord will serve us." We cast our intellectual vote in God's direction, but our heart's vote is still with the world. A true commitment of faith in Jesus Christ involves a belief that God is infinitely superior to anything this world can offer. The clichés "pie in the sky when you die by and by" and "receiving Jesus as your personal Savior" point to the dangers of a privatized, unbiblical religion.

Another variation is this: "As for me and my house, we will *say* that we will serve the Lord." How could an entire generation grow up and not know God and all he had done for Israel? Because their parents didn't tell them. They had said they would serve the Lord, but they had neglected the most strategic part of service: teaching their children about God.

Or they did it in a perfunctory way. Children can see straight through the hypocrisy of religious faith which has words without deeds; preachments without faith, hope, and love. A well-known "child's letter to God" reads: "Dear God, We got a lot of religion in our house, so don't worry about us. Teddy." As parents, our job is far more significant than uttering exhortations about "religion." We want to teach our children to worship God. Yes, not just in church but also in our homes. And not only in the formal "family altar" (if you have one), but by the way we live and move and have our being with one another.

One of the best-known descriptions of worship is that of Archbishop William Temple:

To worship is

to quicken the conscience by the holiness of God;

to feed the mind with the truth of God;

to purge the imagination by the beauty of God;

to open the heart to the love of God; and

to devote the will to the purpose of God.

This kind of worship is not something you do in sacred places at specific times. It's a whole-of-life experience.

Ask anyone who had godly parents, "What are your earliest most cherished memories?" They will tell you something about their parents' authentic communication of God's love. I can remember vividly, when I was a two-year-old, my mother doing her housework in our suburban Sydney home. Sunbeams danced in the room from the warm morning sun. While she worked my mother sang her favorite hymns. It was in the security and loving warmth of those times that I learned "there's a friend for little children above the bright blue sky, a friend who never changes, whose love will never die."

Bedtime for little children (and even for older ones) is a precious time to "touch the Infinite," to remind ourselves of the loving power behind all things, the caring Father-God who forgives the wrong we have done that day and who will be with us as we sleep. For small children, sung lullabies add a soothing finale to the day. They can be old-fashioned, like Isaac Watts' "Cradle hymn":

Hush, my dear, lie still and slumber,

Holy angels guard thy bed.

Heavenly blessings without number,

Gently falling on thy head.

Or they can be more contemporary, as we discovered recently when before turning in we and our two adult daughters found ourselves humming the Vineyard song playing on our stereo:

Faithful One, so unchanging,

Ancient One, you're my rock of peace.

Lord of all, I depend on you;

I call out to you, again and again,

I call out to you, again and again.

You are my rock, in times of trouble.

You lift me up, when I fall down.

All through the storm, your love is the anchor.

My hope is in you alone.

(Words and music by Bryan Doerksen, USA: copyright © Mercy Publishing, 1989.)

It's beautiful – and very reassuring after a pressured day.

Children learn first and best from their families. Just as by the end of their second year they use the language of those with whom they live, so by the end of their childhood their life-language will be that of their parents and others who have most strongly influenced them. Some children may sing, "Jesus loves me, this I know, for the Bible tells me so." Wouldn't it be great if your kids changed it to "Jesus loves me, this I know, for my parents told me so"? No one is called to a more fulfilling vocation than that of bringing up healthy, happy, godly children.

The story is told of a father who was watching TV when he heard the most horrible sound in our suburbs – a screech of brakes, then a sickening "thump!" He rushed outside to find his ten-year-old dying on the road. Neighbors in the next street heard his wailing: "Danny, you can't die! You can't die! I haven't told you that I love you!"

Now – today! – is the time to express your love. Tomorrow the baby won't be rocked, the toddler won't be asking why, the schoolboy won't need help with his homework, the teenager won't bring friends home for chocolate chip cookies and fun, the young adult will have left for her own life. And you will be left with lots of questions that begin with the words "What if?"

Selected Quotations

Someone has said "When a man loves his wife as Christ loved the church, it will not be difficult for that wife to adapt herself to her husband." This does not imply inferiority or superiority – it implies uniqueness.

And it is important not only that we teach our children how to behave, we must teach them what to believe. We must teach them as soon as they are old enough to talk that God loves them ... A little child can grasp deep spiritual truths ... Read them the great Bible stories, explaining to them the truths found there and help them to memorize its tremendous passages. Teach them to fear the Lord in the finest, noblest sense of that grand old word, which is ... reverential trust. It is the fear of the Lord that puts all other fears into proper perspective.

Why have homes? Because God ordained them. The truly Christian home is the nearest thing to heaven we have on this earth. It is a place of refuge and restoration in a turbulent world. And it can help an unbelieving world to understand the love of God. Is yours such a home?

RUTH GRAHAM,
"Why Have Homes?", closing address to the Southern Baptist Convention, 1978,
reprinted in *The Australian Baptist*, August 9, 1978, p. 7.

Parents who want their children to know God must cultivate their own relationship with God. First and foremost this means a life of prayer. No amount of moral instruction, firm discipline, religious instruction, or church-going can make up for the lack of a praying parent. For it is pre-eminently in and through prayer that we pass from the realm of theory into the realm of reality and personal experience.

How can we convince our children that God is important, if we never give him any of our time? How can we pretend to love him, when we scarcely spend a minute with him alone? Our children may dutifully learn their rituals, and chant their mealtime grace, "God is great, God is good, and we thank him for this food." But, down in the heart, where the real attitudes are formed, our prayerless lives have taught another message: "God is great but he can wait; gotta hurry or I'll be late."

Happy the child who happens in upon his parent from time to time to see him on his knees, who sees mother and father rising early, or going aside regularly, to keep times with the Lord. That child has learned a lesson no lecture could impart. He has seen that God matters – he's important enough to take up our time; and he is personal – you don't just obey his rules, you actually communicate with him.

LARRY CHRISTENSON,
The Christian Family, Minneapolis: Bethany House, 1970, p. 159.

I would like to examine a popular misconception that goes something like this: "I want my child to learn to make his own decisions after he is exposed to things. He shouldn't feel he has to believe what I believe. I want him to learn about different religions and philosophies; then when he has grown up he can make his own decision."

This parent is either copping out or is grossly ignorant of the world we live in. A child brought up in this manner is to be pitied. Without continual guidance and clarification in ethical, moral, and spiritual matters, he will become increasingly confused about his world. There are reasonable answers to many of life's conflicts and seeming contradictions. One of the finest gifts parents can give a child is a clear understanding of the world and its confusing problems. Without this stable base of knowledge and understanding, is it any wonder many children cry to their parents, "Why didn't you give me a meaning for all this? What's it all about?"

Another reason this wait-and-choose approach to spirituality is grossly negligent is that more and more organizations and cults are offering destructive, enslaving, and false answers to life's questions.

These people would like nothing better than to find a person who was brought up in a seemingly broad-minded way. He is easy prey for any group offering concrete answers, no matter how false or enslaving.

It is amazing to me how some parents can spend thousands of dollars and go to any length of political manipulation to make sure their child is well prepared educationally. Yet, for the most important preparation of all, for life's spiritual battles and finding real meaning in life, a child is left to fend for himself.

ROSS CAMPBELL,
How to Really Love Your Teenager, Wheaton, Ill.: Victor Books, 1987, pp. 114–115.

Teaching children God's Word is certainly part of the parents' responsibility in training their children. One of the best examples is found in 2 Timothy 3:14,15 (look it up): ever since he was a young child, Timothy had heard the Word of God. Later, when he was called to be a minister of the Gospel, he found this early training to be invaluable.

The Book of Proverbs is a parent's best child training manual. Every husband and wife should sit down and read through Proverbs and make a list of the things this wise man wanted to teach his son. These are the same things God wants you to teach your children.

HOWARD HENDRICKS,
God's Blueprint for Family Living, Lincoln, Nebr.: Back to the Bible, 1980, pp. 24–25.

No teacher can quite match the importance of the rich gifts that parents can give children in spiritual foundations. No subsequent teacher can easily correct central mistakes made by parents. No teachers following parents have a right to such a high level of implicit trust from the child. The earliest teachers sometimes have the longest influence. Their actions and attitudes become the building blocks of all subsequent understanding. There the self receives primary layers of impressions that will continue throughout the entire history of its development. This conception, sometimes attributed to Freud, was familiar to many centuries of Christian wisdom before Freud ...

Leading figures in the Christian tradition have often credited their own parents with unparalleled influence in their spiritual formation. John the Baptist is remembered as one born of pious parents, Elizabeth and Zechariah, who by their hope prepared the way for his calling and ministry. Timothy also was the son of parents remembered for their virtuous life. A special tribute is paid in Scripture to the parents of Susanna, that they were just and that they instructed their daughter well in the Torah. In subsequent Christian history, there are many such cases: Augustine, Chrysostom, Basil, Gregory of Nazianzus, John Wesley, and many others who largely credited their parents either with bringing them by example into the Christian faith or giving them excellent patterns of spiritual discipline.

THOMAS C. OGDEN,
Pastoral Theology: Essentials of Ministry, San Francisco: Harper & Row, 1983, pp. 145–146.

Some of the most important moments in our home are built around prayer. Our two girls pray on their own now when they turn in for the night. But I usually slip into Zachary's room in the evening to pray with him before bedtime just as my father used to do with me. On the wall of our son's room there hangs a beautiful print of a father praying over his son while an angel bars the window from the evil lurking outside. Not all that long ago I probably would have thought the picture was melodramatic, but now as I tuck in my own flesh and blood and ask God to keep him safe, the evils of the world outside seem very real.

GARY BAUER,
Our Journey Home: What Parents Are Doing to Preserve Family Values,
Dallas: Word Publishing, 1992, p. 88.

When our children were young, I lived under the idea that if we didn't have daily devotions with our children – a family altar – somehow we were failing God. The problem was, family devotions worked for other people, but although we tried all kinds of approaches, they never worked for us. Our children sat still for them on the outside but ran away from them on the inside. Yet we kept at them because I felt that a family altar was at the heart of a Christian family. Then I realized that family devotions wasn't the principle but the application of a principle. The principle was that I needed to bring up my children to know and love God. I had mistakenly been giving to our family devotions the same imperative that belonged to the principle behind it. We then came up with a different approach, one that worked for us. Our two children left for school at different times. Each morning before Vicki left, I would pray with her about the day, about what was coming up. A little later, Torrey and one of his friends came into my study, and we'd sit and pray for five minutes about what their day held. That may not sound as satisfying in a sermon as saying we had devotions as a family at the breakfast table every morning, but for us it was an effective way to honour the principle. A preacher must make a clear distinction between the principle and its applications.

HADDON ROBINSON,
in Bill Hybels, Stuart Briscoe and Haddon Robinson, *Mastering Contemporary Preaching*,
Leicester: Inter-Varsity Press (UK), 1991, p. 63.

1. Plan bedtime to suit your child, not your evening …
2. Regulate your child's body functions by putting her to bed at the same time every night, if possible. She will begin to feel ready for bed at this time.
3. Establish and keep a bedtime routine to add feelings of security. Always reading a story and saying prayers will give your child a feeling of order and completion to the day. Then she knows it is time to sleep because all has been done as usual.
4. Choose a book with a bedtime story for each day of the year if you like. Better yet, send her off to sleep with some thought of God by using a daily devotional such as the *Simon and Sarah* series by Scripture Union. Or read a Bible story from a Bible story book written especially for your child's age.
5. Teach your child the Lord's Prayer as soon as possible. (Children's memories are remarkable!) Teach her also "Now I lay me down to sleep" and let her pray in this bedtime routine (teaching her to talk to God for herself even as young as two or three).
6. For a child who is fearful, remind her that you will be nearby all night; but even more importantly, tell her that God watches over us all since he never needs to sleep.
7. Reassure her of your love with hugs and kisses before leaving the room.

This whole process takes only about ten minutes, and can save the child, and you, from hours of crying and fighting going to bed. For children who still resist, get into bed with them and read stories or allow them to look at books for a few minutes before turning out the light.

Then don't respond to continuous calls for water or whatever else they dream up to get you to come back. Tell them lovingly but firmly that you will be nearby but you will not keep coming back.

KATHY BENCE,
Turn Off the TV: Let's Have Fun Instead!, London: Marshall Pickering, 1990, pp. 100–103.

Not only do we pray for the needs of our children, but there are also specific qualities we should ask God to build into children's lives. I have several that I pray for regularly. My list looks something like this:

- Ability to make decisions
- Ability to discern good and evil
- Sense of humour and of caring for others
- Ability to be a good communicator and listener
- Ability to fail and to cope with failure
- To be a person of integrity
- Ability to attempt the impossible
- Ability to forgive others and to ask forgiveness
- To have a positive outlook and a desire for excellence
- Ability to laugh at self and have a positive self-image
- To put Christ first
- To be secure in parents' love and be kind to all

SUSAN ALEXANDER YATES,
And Then I Had Kids, Milton Keyes: Word (UK), 1992, pp. 171–172.

How do parents prepare their teenagers spiritually? Organized religious instruction and activities are extremely important to a developing child or teenager. However, nothing influences a teenager more than his home and what he is exposed to there. Parents need to be actively involved in a teenager's spiritual growth. They cannot afford to leave it to others, even superb church youth workers.

Parents must teach their teenagers spiritual concerns. They must teach them not only spiritual facts, but how to apply them in their everyday life. And this is not easy. It is quite simple to give teenagers basic scriptural facts, such as who different Bible persons were and

301

what they did. But that is not what we are after ultimately. For we want teenagers to understand what meaning biblical characters and principles have for them personally.

ROSS CAMPBELL,
How to Really Love Your Teenager, Wheaton, Ill.: Victor Books, 1987, p. 115.

Scripture and prayer should always take precedence in the family devotional time, but extra "nonreligious" activities can be included regularly or occasionally with exciting results. These extras are especially appealing and effective with children of elementary school age or older ... By adding extra activities we can help our children relate their spiritual views to the world at large. We want our children to identify their biblical training with all areas of life, since the truths of Scripture are not to be isolated from everyday affairs. When we begin a family activity or project ... we try to help our children understand how it relates to the truth of God's word even when the connection might seem to be remote. If we decide to play a rousing game of kickball, for example, we can comment on the healthy bodies God has given us.

If we frequently apply scriptural principles to these activities, our children will see God's pattern of involvement and influence in all their daily experiences.

MARY WHITE,
"Something Extra for Your Family Devotions," in *Discipleship Journal*,
Issue 6, Nov. 1981, pp. 35, 36.

The way in which we decorate our homes can either dull or intensify our awareness of Jesus. The deep truths of God go beyond the limits of human language. A symbol can express the truth more simply and more profoundly than mere words. Christian symbols are spiritual windows through which God's truth can shine. If Jesus is the center of our family life, then why should not the decor of our homes reflect that – tastefully, artistically – but outspokenly? A cross, a lamb, the Alpha and Omega, three intertwined circles, a nativity scene – all relate an aspect of God. Through pictures, wall hangings, plaques, tableaux, we can surround our everyday life with a silent heavenly language – a quiet reminder of Jesus' presence in our midst.

The story is told of a woman whose three sons, to her great disappointment, all took up the life of sea-faring men. She was relating this to a visitor in the home one day, saying that she could not understand why they had all chosen to go to sea. "How long have you had that picture?" The visitor inquired, pointing to a large painting that hung in the dining room. "Since our children were small." "There is your answer," the visitor said. For hanging on the dining-room wall was the painting of a large sailing vessel cutting smartly through the waves, its sails at full billow, the captain standing straddle-legged on the quarter-deck, his spy-glass in hand, scanning the horizon. Morning, noon, and night – with every meal – the boys had taken into their inner consciousness the sense of high adventure portrayed in that picture. Effortlessly, with never a word being spoken, it had planted in them a hankering for the sea.

The surroundings in the home make a tremendous impact on the growing child. We want our children to cultivate an awareness of spiritual realities. With little effort and expense, we can surround them with subtle reminders of those realities, so that they will grow up "looking not to the things that are seen, but to the things that are unseen" (2 Corinthians 4:18). Silently, effortlessly, Jesus will convey himself to the whole family, through the symbols and representations that decorate our homes.

LARRY CHRISTENSON,
The Christian Family, Minneapolis: Bethany House, 1970, pp. 176–177.

When our oldest daughter was not quite three, we told her about a special Christian who lived a long time ago: "His name was Nicholas, and we call him Saint Nicholas because saint means someone who belongs to God, just like we do. In St Nicholas' town there were many poor children. They didn't have enough food, clothes, or toys. St Nicholas used his money to buy food, clothes, and toys for the poor children. He didn't want them to be embarrassed by his gifts, so he gave secretly.

"St Nicholas also told everyone about Jesus and how much God loved them. Many people became Christians because of what St Nicholas said. Then some mean people who hated Jesus put St Nicholas in jail to keep him from telling people about Jesus and from helping people. St Nicholas kept on telling people about Jesus until the mean people finally had him killed.

"Because of how much St Nicholas loved Jesus, and because of the many gifts he gave the poor children of his town, we still remember St Nicholas at Christmas time. All of the gifts he gave, and all of the Christmas presents we give, are to remind us of the very best gift anyone ever gave: when God the Father gave his only Son, Jesus Christ, to us for our salvation.

"Today there are many people who don't know the truth about St Nicholas. They call him 'Santa Claus' and they tell children pretend stories about him living at the North Pole and having elves and reindeer. But we know the truth, and when we see a department store Santa Claus or a picture of Santa Claus in a magazine, we remember the real Santa Claus, St Nicholas, who loved Jesus so much and whose life and death remind us about God's gift of Jesus Christ to us."

By learning this true story, our children are able to enjoy Santa Claus while being reminded of the gospel and the true meaning of Christmas.

GRETCHEN PASSANTINO,
"Santa Claus and the Gospel," in *Discipleship Journal*, Issue 36, Nov. 1986, p. 44.

Christian parents often express concern about the Santa Claus and Easter Bunny myths. We advocate that if the parents are believing, teaching, and living the life of Jesus in the family, the children can enjoy some of the fun of the myths surrounding Easter and Christmas without losing sight of the historical facts which began the celebrations.

We never told our children that a rabbit could lay eggs. They knew quite early from their own observations that chickens are responsible for those, and that bunnies can only beget bunnies. But once we had taught our children the exciting truth of Christ's death and resurrection, and explained to them as clearly as possible the abundant life made available to them by those events, we saw no harm in celebrating with Easter eggs. Eggs are obvious symbols of new life …

Christmas in our home has always centered about the historical birth of the Son of God and the joy of the fact of his living in us. Our little ones grew up in the delight of being a part of a birthday party for Jesus, all gifts being given in his name. We knew and taught we could love and give only because he first loved us. Christmas morning in the Sandford household begins with a rush of excitement to appreciate for a moment the wonder of all the array of gifts under the tree, then settles quickly into a quiet sharing of prayers of thanksgiving and partaking of family communion. Then the packages are opened slowly, one at a time, each one appreciating, thanking, loving and sharing with every other member of the family. Sentence prayers are offered around the dinner table. This is the substance of the celebration, the Spirit of Christ born anew in our family in the midst of the giving and sharing. Family participation in the music and candlelight worship services at church bring into sharp focus the meaning and priorities of Christmas.

JOHN and PAULA SANDFORD,
Restoring the Christian Family, South Plainfield, NJ: Bridge Publishing, 1979, pp. 252–253.

A Prayer

O God, our heavenly Father,
thank you for ordaining that in families we learn of your love,
thank you for the gift of Jesus your Son, who came to earth and lived in a
simple home.

Our Father in heaven, pattern of all parenthood and lover of children, bless
our homes this day.
Reassure parents who find their high calling difficult.
Give to children who feel bereft of love a deep insight into your love for them.
Help young people to "face forward," dedicating their lives
to a strong and world-changing vision.
Bless our churches: may they be communities of faith, hope, and love.

Bless our nation: may our leaders enact policies in line with
your will for our families and our lives.

And when we stand before you, our Maker, Redeemer, and Judge,
May we be unashamed. Amen.

A Benediction

May the Lord send his light and his love to your family. May each member of
your home grow in grace and in the knowledge of a loving God, and devote
themselves to his will by doing good. Through Christ our Lord, to whom be glory
now and forever. Amen.

When Joshua moves to a small cabin on the edge of town, the local people are at first mystified, then confused by his presence. A quiet and simple man, Joshua appears to seek nothing for himself. He supports himself solely by carpentry and woodworking, and charges very little for his services. Yet his work is exquisite and haunting.

What sort of person is Joshua? How can the townspeople explain the strange rumors about him? Some have reported seeing him effortlessly carrying a huge log on his shoulders. Others talk about the dreadfully ill child who recovered after a visit from Joshua.

As Joshua quietly becomes involved in the lives of the people of the town, many find themselves transformed by his wisdom and loving heart. Yet some of his neighbors are disturbed by him, others frightened. Finally, some church leaders confront him...

An unforgettable story of love and faith, *Joshua* has moved and inspired millions of readers around the globe. This special edition of the international bestseller includes a revealing introduction by the author and an attractive new design.

Dove
An imprint of HarperCollins*Publishers*

ISBN 1 86371 552 5

Joshua and the Children

It seems a peaceful enough village, but Joshua was not deceived. Arriving as a stranger he befriends the village's children, working to bring peace to a people torn apart by violence and religious division. Joshua offers the children a way to overcome decades of hatred, but not before himself paying the ultimate price.

ISBN 1 86371 101 5

The Shepherd

David Campbell was a good man, but one strict in doctrine and tied to tradition. On the night of his consecration as a bishop, he has a terrible dream that changes his life. Guided by the mysterious figure of Joshua, Bishop Campbell sets about a remarkable reform of his diocese that will ultimately transform the Church.

ISBN 1 86371 102 3

Joshua in the Holy Land

Joshua, the fascinating woodcarver, returns to where his earthly life began – the Holy Land. Even after two thousand years, it is a land still poisoned by violent disputes. Returning home, Joshua sets about gathering a new band of followers for one last chance at a lasting peace.

ISBN 1 86371 113 9

Joseph F. Girzone retired from administrative work as a priest in 1981 for health reasons, and began an unexpectedly successful writing career. His imagination, vision and heart-felt conviction created a series of novels featuring Joshua, who makes God's love real for those whose lives he touches. Joseph Girzone is also the author of an autobiographical introduction to spirituality, *Never Alone*.

 Dove
An imprint of HarperCollins*Publishers*

Joshua and the City is a powerful and inspiring novel about the importance of compassion and care in the midst of human suffering and need. It affirms the power of love to transform our troubled world.

In this, the fifth of the *Joshua* novels, the enigmatic carpenter comes to a modern metropolis, bringing its people love and new hope. Faced with the real problems of life in a big city – including loneliness, AIDS, poverty, drug abuse, and unemployment – Joshua brings about imaginative and effective solutions.

Through his tireless care of those he meets, Joshua wins new friends – and new enemies. As sinister forces try to undo his good work, Joshua finds he must take his message of justice and healing to the most powerful leaders of the nation.

The Joshua novels are comforting and insightful explorations of what it might be like to have Jesus come into our society today. Joseph Girzone's imagination, vision and heart-felt conviction have created a series of novels that have moved and inspired millions of readers around the globe.

Dove
An imprint of HarperCollins*Publishers*

ISBN 1 86371 405 7

We're OK! Secrets of happy families

Moira Eastman

'It's not such a secret why some families work better than others. Moira reminds us that answers are often staring us in the face.'

Geraldine Doogue,
Life Matters, ABC Radio

In this little book of family, Moira Eastman reveals the secrets that create a unified, loving and happy family. She leads us step-by-step through the secrets of:

- communication
- affection
- love
- fun and humour
- praise
- power sharing
- ritual and support
- time together

and passes on advice, tips and questions to help us incorporate these things into our daily family journey.

Dr Moira Eastman, a leading authority on family well-being, has lectured throughout Australia for government, local councils, church and school groups. In 1991 she was the first recipient of the Western Australian Government Fellowship on family. She has written several books and papers on the family, including *Family: The Vital Factor*.

CollinsDove
An imprint of HarperCollins*Publishers*

ISBN 1 86371 326 3

FOOTPRINTS

by Margaret Fishback Powers

'My precious child,

I love you and will never leave you

never, ever, during your trials and testings.

When you saw only one set of footprints

it was then that I carried you.'

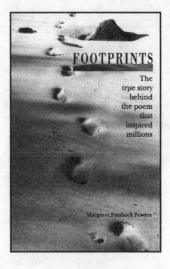

Now the true story behind the all-time favourite religious poem can be told!
'Footprints', a poem that has inspired millions the world over, was composed
by Margaret Fishback, a young woman searching for direction at the
crossroads of her life. The story of the creation of the poem, its subsequent
loss and astonishing rediscovery are intertwined with a life full of challenge,
adversity and joy.

ISBN 1 86371 299 2

 CollinsDove
An imprint of HarperCollins*Publishers*

A HEART *for* CHILDREN

by Margaret Fishback Powers

One hundred years from now
It will not matter
What kind of car I drove,
What kind of house I lived in,
How much I had in my bank,
Nor what my clothes looked like.
One hundred years from now
It will not matter
What kind of school I attended,
What kind of typewriter I used,
How large or small my church,
But the world may be
...a little better because...
I was important in the
life of a child.

In this inspiring new book the author of 'Footprints' captures the joys and challenges of raising children within a nurturing and loving family environment. These reassuring meditations will offer both parents and children emotional renewal and understanding that will profoundly uplift their lives.

 Dove
An imprint of HarperCollins*Publishers*

ISBN 1 86371 607 6